D0935930

# Experimental Determination of Stone Tool Uses

PREHISTORIC ARCHEOLOGY AND ECOLOGY

A Series Edited by Karl W. Butzer
and Leslie G. Freeman

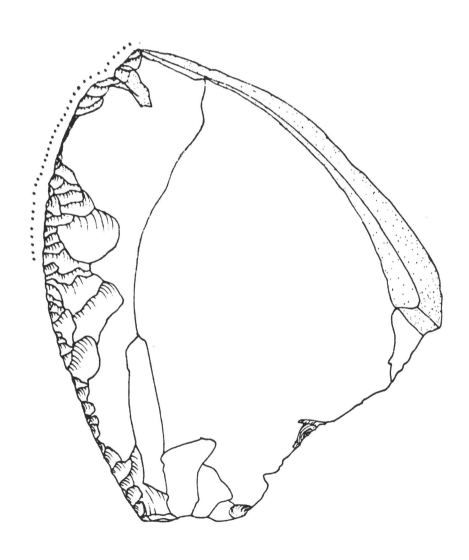

# Experimental Determination of Stone Tool Uses

A Microwear Analysis

Lawrence H. Keeley

The University of Chicago Press
Chicago and London

LAWRENCE H. KEELEY is currently visiting assistant
professor of anthropology at the University of Illinois
at Chicago Circle.

The University of Chicago Press, Chicago 60637
The University of Chicago Press, Ltd., London

Library of Congress Cataloging in Publication Data

Keeley, Lawrence H
    Experimental determination of stone tool uses.

    (Prehistoric archeology and ecology)
    Bibliography:  p.
    Includes index.
    1.  Stone implements.  2.  Stone implements--England.
3.  Paleolithic period--England.  4.  Mechanical wear.
I.  Title.  II.  Series.
GN799.T6K43        930'.1'0285        79-11838
ISBN 0-226-42889-3

To Lesley for everything

CONTENTS

SERIES EDITORS' FOREWORD

For many decades, a major stumbling block to progress in Paleolithic archeology has
been a lack of knowledge on how various kinds of stone tools were used by their makers. It
was to this problem that Lawrence H. Keeley addressed himself in his Ph.D. research at the
University of Oxford. Unlike previous investigators interested in inferring stone tool use
from damage or marks left on the tools, Keeley concentrated on glosses and polishes that
may be discerned and differentiated only under relatively high magnification. On the basis
of laboratory experiments, he found he could readily distinguish the polish left on a stone
tool used to cut meat from that on one used to scrape wood, and so forth. To verify his
findings, he studied tools made and used by Mark Newcomer of the University of London.
Only Newcomer knew in advance how the tools had been used. For the most part, Keeley's
after-the-fact determinations of how the tools were used proved highly accurate, and this
"blind test" constitutes a convincing confirmation of Keeley's argument that his method
can establish how a stone tool functioned.

For the present volume Keeley has revised and updated his methodologically rigorous
studies. Ably summarized here, they will serve as the major reference point for anyone who
wants to pursue the study of ancient stone tool use in the future. More generally, for the
methodology and substantive results it reports, this book should be of considerable interest to all those archeologists whose research puts them in contact with stone artifacts
and the problems posed by their interpretation. We welcome Keeley's book to the Prehistoric
Archeology and Ecology Series and hope that it will stimulate more research as painstaking,
rigorous, and thoughtful as Keeley's.

Karl W. Butzer<br>Leslie G. Freeman

PREFACE

This book is the summary of a course of research on the functions of Paleolithic implements undertaken between 1972 and 1977 at Oxford University. Because it reports on a
particular research project, this book is not several things that the reader might hope,
fear, or expect it to be. It is not a textbook on microwear analysis, nor is it a general
reference book on the functional study of stone implements. However, it does, I think,
provide useful technical and methodological information of value to the would be microwear
analyst and, especially in the case of the photomicrographs reproduced here, it does contain data useful for general reference. With these thoughts in mind, I think it is important to specify what this study does attempt to do and what it does not attempt or succeed
in doing.

When I began my work, I wanted to rectify some of the methodological failings I observed in earlier attempts to study and interpret the wear traces found on ancient stone
implements through comparisons with experimentally produced wear traces. I endeavored to
employ a wide range of techniques and instruments in my work to insure that no distinguishing features of any archeological useful wear traces would be overlooked. With the above
in mind, I hoped to isolate the distinguishing features of the various general categories
of implement use that were relevant to a microwear study of Lower Paleolithic implements
from England. As a test for my experimental conclusions, I wanted to apply my methods to
the study of several British Lower Paleolithic assemblages in hopes of illuminating some of
the ancient activities reflected in them. I did not set out to provide a catalog of experimentally produced wear traces likely to be found on implements made of all conceivable
lithic materials used in all conceivable ways. Instead, I concentrated on replicating
tools and uses known or likely to have been current in the Lower Paleolithic. Because, as
it turned out, the number of implements that were suitable for microwear analysis and retained traces of use was very small in the assemblages I examined, this research does not
purport to be a complete, demonstrably representative study of the functions of Clactonian
and Acheulean implements from Britain. That said, however, I do not feel that one can
lightly dismiss or ignore the results of the analysis. There is absolutely no evidence
that the weathering and slight abrasion that were the criteria for excluding implements
from final consideration occurred more frequently on any particular size, class, or tool
type. In retrospect, I believe that I was perhaps overly fastidious in excluding artifacts
showing very slight traces of weathering and natural abrasion, but I was determined not to
be intimidated by small samples into including dubious examples that might have muddied

the picture or given a false one. There is, of course, no criticism of the method to be found in the fact that the inhabitants of Hoxne used so little of the biface trimming flakes that made up such a sizable portion of that assemblage. In summary then, one can say that my analysis of these Paleolithic assemblages provides useful information which, while it does address some of the important questions concerning the Clactonian and Acheulean in Britain, does not provide conclusive proof of any specific hypotheses.

It is my greatest hope that this book will encourage students to undertake similar work on stone implements of interest to them and to our profession. I also hope that this work will demonstrate to prehistorians that information about the uses of ancient implements does survive and that it will encourage them to pursue alternative methods in seeking additional information about the uses of these implements.

ACKNOWLEDGMENTS

Since autumn of 1972, when I began the research that led to this book, I have received advice, encouragement, and assistance from a number of people. The most patient and steadfast of these have been my wife, Lesley, and Dr. Derek Roe, who supervised my research at Oxford.

I am also indebted to the prehistorians and museum curators who allowed me to carry off to Oxford large portions of the stone tool collections from the Clacton, Hoxne, and Swanscombe sites, chief among them being Dr. R. Singer and John Wymer of the University of Chicago; also the late John Waechter of the University of London; and D. Clarke and G. Davis, of the Colchester and Essex Museum.

The whole staff of the Pitt-Rivers Museum (Oxford) was extremely helpful with all aspects of this work, especially Ray Inskeep (assistant curator), Paul Unsworth (administrative secretary/librarian), and Peter Narracott (photographer).

Those who have offered advice and criticism on aspects of my work and this study are Derek Roe, Ray Inskeep, John Wymer, C. B. M. McBurney, Mark Newcomer, Richard Klein, and Karl Butzer. The proverbial "buck" has never stopped anywhere but in my own hand, and the faults of this work are all attributable to me.

Finally, there can be no denial of my intellectual debt to S. A. Semenov, of the Leningrad Academy of Science. It was his work that showed me where to look.

Some of my research costs were met with grants from the Meyerstein Fund for Archaeological Research of the University of Oxford, and I am grateful for that help. I would also like to gratefully acknowledge the assistance of the UICC Cartographic Laboratory in preparing some of the illustrations used in this book.

### A Note on the Text Figures

On all the drawings of archeological and experimental implements the following conventions were employed.

1. Stippling indicates areas of cortex.
2. Small arrows around the edges of a drawing show the orientation (but not necessarily the direction) of striations and other linear microwear features.
3. The extent of the polish is indicated by a black line a few millimeters away from the implement's edge; the thickness of the line represents the relative intensity of the polish.
4. All drawings (except figs. 20 and 21) are full size.

# 1. TECHNIQUE AND METHODOLOGY IN RECENT MICROWEAR STUDIES

The thirst for information about the functions of ancient stone implements is not just an isolated scholarly fad or the result of natural but theoretically irrelevant curiousity. Prior to the last two decades, the pursuit of such information was irrelevant to the primary concerns of prehistoric archeologists, concerns which centered around working out sequences of archeological "cultures" on local, regional, and occasionally global scales.

In the 1950s, paleolithic archeologists began assigning assemblages to archeological "cultures" not only on the basis of the presence and absence of various "type fossils" but also on the similarities in the varying proportions of tool types. In other words, the criteria for classification of the contents of archeological sites ceased to be the simple presence of one or two types and instead became the whole contents of the assemblage, as summarized by the proportion of types. This led some students to ask whether the higher proportions of certain tool types at some sites and lower proportions at others might be due to the different suites of activities represented by their assemblages. The classic argument proposing this type of hypothesis is that of the Binfords (Binford and Binford 1966) regarding the various facies of the Mousterian, as defined by Bordes. Similar hypotheses have been advanced regarding variants of the Acheulean in Africa (Binford 1972; Clark 1975) and various Middle Pleistocene industries in Europe (Binford 1972).

A crucial test of these "functional" hypotheses would obviously involve the acquisition of detailed data on how stone implements were actually used and on what materials they were used. With the publication in 1964 of an English translation of S. A. Semenov's *Prehistoric Technology*, it seemed that a method did exist for directly inferring tool use from the microscopic traces of wear left on their edges. Since that time, there have been a number of attempts to apply some of Semenov's methods or similar methods to a variety of archeological materials with what must be acknowledged as lukewarm success. The reasons for the lack of progress apparent in these studies are manifold, involving deficiencies in technique and usually a poverty of methodological rigor (see Keeley 1974a).

In an earlier publication, I defined the main goal and general purpose of microwear studies as to reconstruct, as completely as possible, the primary economic activities of prehistoric groups (Keeley 1974a: 323). To attain this goal, microwear studies must (1) attempt to determine, precisely, the functions of individual implements and (2) "obtain as complete a picture as possible of the total uses represented on implements from the archaeological unit . . . under investigation." In order to meet these aims, one must apply the widest possible range of techniques, eventually settling for those most appropriate

1

to the task in hand, and use a methodology based on experimentation. The term *technique* includes all the operations and equipment involved in the initial simple observation of the microwear traces themselves--the details of microscopy, implement preparation, photomicroscopy, and so on. "Methodology" embraces a wider realm which encompasses all the procedures relevant to the interpretation of the microwear traces that have been observed. The following introductory review of the most recent literature on the subject of microwear analysis critically examines both the techniques and methodologies of some prior microwear studies. My own methods and techniques are expounded in detail in chapters 2 and 3.

## Microscopy

Most recent microwear work has been characterized by one of two different technical approaches. By far the most common approach is concerned with the study of wear traces observable with stereomicroscopes at the relatively low magnifications obtainable with such instruments (up to 80X). This approach is epitomized in the work of Tringham et al. (1974) and ardently defended by Odell (1975). The use of low-magnification stereomicroscopy is also characteristic of the work of Ahler (1971), Bordes (1970, 1971, 1973, 1974), Bosinski and Hahn (1973), Brose (1975), Davis (1975), Frison (1968), Gould (1971), Gorman (1971), Hammatt (1970), Hester et al. (1973), Kantman (1970a,b,c, 1971), Keller (1966), Lenoir (1970, 1971), MacDonald and Sanger (1968), White and Thomas (1972), Wilmsen (1968), and many others.

The other approach is characterized by the use of higher magnifications (complementing rather than replacing low-magnification examination), with the emphasis on the observation of polishes and striations. Adherents of this approach are S. A. Semenov and his colleagues (Semenov 1964, 1968, 1970; Korobkova 1969), C. B. M. McBurney (1968), and myself (Keeley 1974a, 1976). Like all such distinctions in human affairs, this division of technical approaches is not absolute. Brose (1975) employed a scanning electron microscope (SEM) in the high-magnification examination of experimental specimens, and Rosenfeld (1971) mentions attempting high-magnification work but without success.

Because of the limited resolution of stereomicroscopes at higher magnifications (>50X) and their poor light-gathering abilities (see chap. 2), their users must restrict their microwear analyses to utilization damage and to the larger types of striation. No such limitations are placed on the analyst who employs an incident-light lab microscope with a good range of magnification, perhaps with a stereomicroscope in support, or who uses the more cumbersome SEM.

A difference in the scale of magnification employed can lead to some sizable difference in results. C. B. M. McBurney (pers. comm.) claims that for an extensive series of flint endscrapers (about 220) from the Epi-Paleolithic levels at the cave of Ali Tappeh (Iran), using high-magnification and metallization (see below), he was able to observe microwear striations on no less than 70% of the implements examined. MacDonald and Sanger (1968) report that in a sample of 300 endscrapers from a fluted-point site in Nova Scotia, they were able to observe "faceting" and striations on the working edges of 1% of the tools (all of these were made of siltstone), with an additional 38% showing a "clear use polish but no additional detail" (they were mostly of chalcedony). From this result, they concluded that harder materials (6 to 7 Mohs) retain poor evidence of tool use; however, since they used neither high-magnification nor metallization, it seems likely that the evidence was present but that they were not able to observe it, especially when one considers the 38% showing polish but no detail. It is more reasonable to conclude from MacDonald and

Sanger's results that harder lithic materials retain traces that differ in extent and possibly in kind from those retained by softer materials, providing both were used in an identical manner.

## Cleaning and Coating

Semenov (1964: 24-26) devotes some space to a discussion of the importance of cleaning
and of counteracting the translucency of most artifactual materials.  The importance of
proper cleaning is particularly crucial when examining experimental implements, the edges
of which often get coated with various organic deposits in the course of their use, deposits
which are unlikely to survive on ancient archeological specimens.  These organic deposits
may obscure the true surviving microwear traces on archeological specimens.  Kantman (1971)
observed various "lustres" and "striations" on some experimental implements which were
probably organic traces and would undoubtedly have been removed by cleaning.  The only
author to mention the cleaning procedures used on experimental (woodworking) implements is
Bordes (1971), who found that the "glosses" and "striations" observable (at low magnification) on working edges prior to cleaning could no longer be seen after cleaning in oxygen-
ated water and dilute nitric acid.

The importance of applying coatings to counteract the translucency of certain types
of stone is a vexed question.  Only Semenov (1964), McBurney (1968) and I (Keeley 1974a)
have favored it.  Brose (1975) and Hayden and Kumminga (1973) coated specimens which were
then examined using a SEM.  Whether vacuum metallization (which is the most commonly used
form of coating) is necessary (see chap. 2) depends on the light-reflecting qualities of
the rock type from which the implements being studied are made and on the lighting arrangements and optics of the microscopes employed.  But the major objection to the use of vacuum
metallization is that it is very time-consuming, and this point has been raised by the pro-
ponents of low-magnification edge-damage analysis (Tringham 1974: 175; Odell 1975: 230).
Another objection, more reasonable, is that metallization can obscure traces of polish
(Odell 1975: 230).  This is because it reduces the contrast in light reflection between the
polished and unpolished surfaces of an edge.

## Experimentation

One of the points of agreement between the two recent critical reviews of microwear
studies (Keeley 1974a; Odell 1975) was that the microwear analysis of archeological specimens could only proceed by means of controlled experimental studies.  Indeed, more recent
microwear work has been informed by experimental studies--that is to say, the fabrication
of replicas of archeological implements and their use on various materials under controlled
conditions, with detailed observation of the results.  In many cases, however, the experiments seem to have been limited to use on only very few materials (Brose 1975; Bordes 1971;
Davis 1975; Ranere 1975; Hayden and Kumminga 1973; Gould et al. 1971), or else the number
of experiments has been very small (Ahler 1971; Keller 1966; Kantman 1971).  When experiments are limited to a few uses on a small number of materials, the possibility that there
may be a convergence of microwear characteristics in wear patterns of diverse origins is
not adequately explored and avoided.  It could, for example, be the case that the scraping
of both bone and wood with high-angled edges will produce identical patterns of utilization
damage, in which case, any conclusions about the distinctiveness of wood- and bone-working
damage based on a comparison of wood-whittling edges with bone-scraping edges would probably
be incorrect.  Even when a variety of uses on a variety of materials is tested

experimentally, if only one or two experiments are completed for each use category, the investigator loses control of the variability of wear patterns produced by a single type of use (for example, whittling) with a single type of edge (for example, low angled) on one material (for example, wood). It seems clear that the experimental background for any microwear study of archeological implements must test a variety of uses on a variety of worked materials and that there should be a substantial number of experiments with each use/material category. Semenov and his coworkers have informally built up such an experimental framework over the last forty years. Only two other formal attempts to construct such a foundation of experimental data have been attempted recently: the work of R. Tringham and her colleagues at Harvard (Tringham et al. 1974), and the work which forms the basis of this study.

## Controlling for Natural and Technological Effects

There are many things that can happen to a stone implement before and after use (if it was used at all) which are capable of producing traces that can, in the absence of adequate controls, be confused with traces of use. Semenov (1964) outlines several natural processes that yield such effects, including natural abrasion through the agencies of wind and water, patination, and weathering changes. Also, soil movements and frost contortions involving archeological deposits can cause scratches and pseudoretouch on stone implements contained in them (Warren 1914; Bordes 1969a). These sources of confusion must be eliminated by (a) experiments which seek to reproduce various forms of natural wear, (b) familiarity with the known forms of natural wear created in archeological deposits, and (c) careful selection, where possible, of archeological samples for examination only from deposits which are little affected by the forces causing natural wear.

There are also, of course, many effects that are the result of human activity, but that are not per se the result of utilization. This includes, most particularly, "technological effects"--that is, traces left by the processes of manufacture that may be confused with traces of use. The clearest examples of such traces would, of course, be found on ground stone tools, but similar effects on a smaller scale may result from various types of platform preparation or even from the simple friction of a hammerstone against an implement as a flake is detached. These traces are more difficult to separate by simple observation from utilization traces than are natural traces, for example, since they are the result of purposeful action and tend to be nonrandomly distributed. Other effects created through human agency, but not as a result of use, can be caused by hafting arrangements or originate in the treatment an implement may receive after it is abandoned on a habitation floor. Implements can be trodden upon, swept about, and treated to all manner of indignities, all of which can be expected to leave traces of various sorts. These "human" effects can to some extent be controlled for by the examination of experimental implements after manufacture but before use and by experiments involving the trampling and abandonment of experimental implements.

The tendency of most microwear reports is to begin with the problem of utilization without any attempt to establish that the traces being observed are, indeed, only the result of utilization. A classic example of how much such an oversight can affect the validity of results is Nance's (1971) interpretation of serrated obsidian projectile points from central California as sawing and whittling implements. He based this interpretation on what he regarded as "wear striations" along the edges; a number of authors (Hester and Heizer 1973; Keeley 1974b; Sheets 1973) have suggested that these striations are actually the result of the "scrubbing" of the edges of these implements to carry out the essential preparation of microplatforms for the removal of the fine pressure flakes with which such projectile points are characteristically finished. The record of control for "technological effects" in other reports is no more impressive than Nance's. Kantman (1970a,b,c) attempted, by the construction of copies, to distinguish between intentional retouches and utilization damage on Mousterian notches, denticulates, and reclettes. But his work was mainly conducted at the macrographic level. Most of the other authors who mention using experimental copies (Sonnenfield 1962; Witthoft 1967; McBurney 1968; Bordes 1970, 1971; Lenoir 1971; Ahler 1971; Hester et al. 1973) appear to have examined them only after they had been experimentally used and not both before and after. The main account of "technological effects" is to be found in Semenov (1964), with a considerable amount of such material also published as a result of what Odell (1975: 229) calls "the Great Stockton Point controversy" (Hester and Heizer 1973; Sheets 1973), but the latter is restricted to the technological effects found on pressure-flaked bifaces. It is not clear, from the published work of the Harvard group exactly what controls for technological effects were incorporated into their experimental program, but it seems likely, judging from their statements (Tringham et al. 1974: 181), that their controls were not extensive (see chap. 3). In the present study, a full account of "natural" and "technological" effects relevant to the Lower Paleolithic will be found in chapter 3.

## The Content and Structure of the Experimental Program

Turning now to the questions of what experiments are necessary for the construction of an adequate experimental framework and what variables are to be recorded, we must bear in mind that the ultimate purpose of any set of use experiments is the interpretation of particular archeological pieces usually from archeological occurrences limited in time and space. A series of experiments designed to investigate the wear traces produced by all possible uses of all possible types of stone tools made of all the rock types from which implements are known ever to have been made would clearly involve the work of several lifetimes and would probably be counterproductive in terms of the usefulness of its results in the interpretation of any particular archeological assemblage, since the latter would contain a limited range of stone tool types, made of a limited number of rock types, and employed in a limited number of ways. My experimental program (see chap. 3) was designed to apply to certain British Lower Paleolithic industries. Those who may in the future consult this study are specifically warned against assuming that my experimental results will serve as sufficient background data for the analysis of other industries from other areas made of rock types very different from English chalk flint. They should, however, provide useful guidance for the planning of specific new sets of experiments. It is, in fact, very important that the experimental framework be relevant (a) to the ecological situation and other general conditions of the site or sites from which the study materials originate, (b) to the likely worked materials (hide, bone, meat, and so on), and (c) to the rock types from which the archeological implements are made. Experiments conducted using implements made of obsidian are unlikely to be much help in interpreting archeological implements made of flint (or chert) which is a harder material and has slightly different fracture and wear-resistant properties. If one is investigating microwear traces on implements from sites where certain types of tropical hardwoods were available (which can be very hard and can contain considerable amounts of silica), then the microwear produced by woodworking experiments conducted on softer temperate hardwood is unlikely to be comparable to any found on the archeological implements. The prospective experimenter should also bear in mind that prehistoric men, their food sources, and their immediate environments were all a good deal grittier than present-day archeological laboratories and their inhabitants, so that some effort, at least, may be necessary to approximate "contemporary" conditions. The traces left on implements used for working the hides of laboratory animals cannot be counted on to produce traces fully comparable to those left by the working of less well-groomed wild or farm animals. Without some close attention to details like these, misleading results could be obtained even from an otherwise admirable series of experiments or comparisons.

One case illustrating the problems that can be created by carelessness about relevance is the attempt by Gould et al. (1971) to identify certain scrapers of the "Quina" variant of the European Mousterian as woodworking tools, on the basis of a careful ethnographic study of Australian aboriginal woodworking. These authors discovered, from a low-magnification microscopic examination of Aboriginal chert and quartzite adzes, which they had observed being used to work Mulga wood, that this use caused "an irregular series of small terminated flakes along the bulbar face of the working edge" (Gould et al. 1971: 166). They further confirmed this by a laboratory experiment using an adze copy (in chert) to work Mulga wood. It might be thought that "small terminated flakes" constitute a rather ambiguous wear trace that could arise from many kinds of use (see Hayden and Kumminga 1973), but, nevertheless, these investigators then went on to apply their results to Mousterian Quina-type scrapers (made of flint). When they found on these Quina scrapers small flake scars similar to those observed on the Australian material, they proposed that these implements might be woodworking tools. This hypothesis was somewhat upset by S. Binford's observation (in Gould et al. 1971) that because of the cold climate of France during much of the Mousterian, hardwoods and trees in general were probably quite scarce. (This observation is now known to be not necessarily true.) The investigators were then left to propose that the Quina scrapers might be bone-working implements. However, when we consider that there is extremely little surviving worked bone from the West European Mousterian, except perhaps in its final stages, while scrapers of the Quina type are relatively common, Gould and his colleagues' results are left dangling. Given, in the first place, the ambiguous nature of the wear traces on which their hypothesis was based, and, in the second place, the looseness of their approach to the local ecological situation and the likely materials worked, the final inconclusiveness of their attempt is not unexpected.

A study of the functions of projectile points from a rock shelter in Missouri by Ahler (1971) illustrates one problem that can arise if the crucial experiments are not done. On the basis of seventeen experiments and a low-magnification study of wear traces on a collection of implements ($N$=114) classified as "projectile points," Ahler (1971: 108) claimed that over 75% of these implements were not used as projectile points but had a variety of other uses because they did not show the kinds of wear traces found on his five experimental projectile points. However, none of his five "projection" experiments actually involved penetration of a large mammal, and, in fact, the points in question only penetrated the local silty soil. Thus, his experiments would appear only to show what type of traces could be expected on projectile points which had missed their target (which is, indeed, relevant information) but to leave unknown the traces to be expected when a projectile point struck its target, presumably a large mammal, like a deer, penetrating its hide, flesh, and possibly its bone. Other uncertainties arise from Ahler's general classification of wear traces ("edge smoothing," "edge rounding," "edge roughening," and so on). The fact that he would not be able to recognize the wear traces characteristic of a projectile

point which had served its true purpose leads one to suspect that it is possible that many
more of Ahler's sample may have been projectile points after all.

## The Conduct of Experiments

When we turn to the actual conduct of experiments and the way in which variables are
recorded, we find that the most explicit statements on this subject have been made in the
publications of the Harvard group (Tringham et al. 1974; Odell 1975), whose experiments, as
already indicated above, were designed mainly to investigate utilization damage patterns,
with little emphasis on striations and polish. A brief critical examination of some of
their experimental methods and procedures may assist the reader in evaluating my own construction of an experimental framework for the microwear analysis of the selected British
Paleolithic assemblages.

The strategy adopted by Tringham et al. (1974) in their experimental program involved
the division of certain aspects of tool use, like the angle of the working edge, the use-
action, the worked material, and so forth, into a number of independent variables whose in-
fluence on the formation of, specifically, edge damage could (in theory) be tested separately. Pursuant to this strategy, they divided the variables describing the angle of the
working edge into two categories: "thin" (20°-35°) and "thick" (45°-65°). The action of
the tool during use was described by a number of "subvariables" like "Direction of the edge
to the worked material" (three categories); "angle of the edge to the worked material" (it
is not clear how many categories were employed, but we are told, "In general the operator
was required to work within a ca. 20° range" [Tringham et al. 1974: 18]; "grip (three categories); and "pressure" (the number of categories is again not clear). The worked materials were divided into seven categories--"skin," "flesh," "bone," "wood," and so on. The
duration of use was recorded by counting the number of "strokes," rather than the elapsed
time. Most of these procedures are the only reasonable ones and, indeed, similar definitions of independent variables have been employed in this study. However, some of the experimental procedures employed by Tringham and her coworkers can produce results which are
unlikely to be comparable to the wear traces found on archeological specimens and which are
irrelevant to the inference of function on ancient implements.

Regarding the recording of variables for use experiments, Odell (1975: 227) asserts
that "*all* the variables must be published" (Odell's italics) and then provides a long list
of the "more salient" of these variables. Surely, in no experiment in any scientific field
does one attempt to record or publish all the possible variables, but only the relevant
ones. The variables recorded should be relevant to the real task of deducing the function
of ancient stone implements.

If, in the experimental situation, one breaks down the more general independent variables of use (like whittling or scraping) into a number of finer and more strictly defined
variables, like the length of stroke, the angle of the edge to the surface of the worked
material, the angle of the edge to the direction of strokes, and so on, then one is driven,
by necessity, to use the implement in an unnatural and artificial manner. If one's variable categories were to have any validity, one would be forced to use a scraper, let us
say, held within 10° of a right angle to the worked material (see Tringham et al. 1974:
181), with its edge *always* at a right angle to the direction of movement, and with a specific stroke length of about 4 cm. The aboriginal user of a similar scraper may have swung
the implement's edge through a range of 60° around a right angle to the worked material,
even during a single stroke, may sometimes have canted the edge to the direction of

movement and may have used strokes varying from 1-40 cm long--he or she was interested in completing some task, not in controlling often irrelevant variables. Even the strategy of measuring the duration of use by counting strokes, rather than simply recording the time elapsed, can increase the artificiality of an experimental use. Unless the experimenter has a confederate whose only task is to count strokes, he will find that he will concentrate on counting and not on using the tool efficiently. If we wish to replicate the wear traces found on prehistoric implements, then our experimental implements must be used in a human, not a mechanical, fashion.

## Quantification of Results

One methodological problem that many microwear analysts have not dealt with very effectively is quantification. While MacDonald and Sanger (1968) have noted the difficulty of quantifying microwear observations, it still seems that some of the information obtained in microwear analysis could be presented in a more rigorous fashion. Semenov and Shchelinskii's (1971) work indicates that even direct metrification of some aspects of microwear observation may be possible if one has the proper equipment. Even without such technical refinements, considerable improvement could be achieved by the simple quantification of qualitative observations. For example, it is possible to record, for both experimental and archeological implements, how often traces occur on both surfaces of the working edge and how often on only one, or the approximate orientation of striations to the working edge (right angle, parallel, low angle, and so on). A good deal can be accomplished in this manner, and a more rigorous formulation of the data is the result. Ahler (1971) pursued such an approach in his recording of the types and locations of wear traces on projectile points.

## Supplementary Information

Another methodological omission quite common in many published microwear studies is the failure to include supplementary independent data that is useful in evaluating the results of the microwear analysis itself. For example, some discussion of the archeological context of the study implements and their *in situ* association with other artifact types or other remains would often be extremely useful and interesting. Even more interesting would be a discussion of the occurrence or absence of certain "functional types" (as defined by microwear analysis) in tool "factors" of the sort derived by Binford and others via factor analysis, or their correlations with other find classes in the manner of McBurney (1968). This use of independent information obviously depends on its availability. When it can be used, not only is this sort of supplementary information useful for purposes of evaluation, but it also allows the investigation of the meaning of the contexts, associations, and factors themselves. I have attempted to provide data of this kind for the British sites with which this work has been concerned and only wish that more of this evidence had been preserved in each case.

## Wear Traces Emphasized

As was noted in the section on technique, microwear analyses can be divided into two groups: (1) those that employ primarily low-magnification stereomicroscopes, and (2) those who employ a wider range of magnifications and microscopes but who rely especially on high-magnification (up to 500X) light microscopes. Correlated with these two technical approaches are two methodological approaches:  (1) concentration primarily on edge damage (that is, the small breakage and chip scars found on implement edges), and (2) concentration on polishes and striations.  The reason the low-magnification specialists rely primarily on edge damage is, of course, because most of the time they are not using sufficient power to observe microwear polishes and striations, let alone to investigate the significance of polish variability.  Odell, for example, claims that polishes and striations lack internal variability and therefore "cannot provide very fine distinctions among the various activities and worked materials" (1975: 231).  This is perhaps true if one restricts oneself to observing them at low magnifications, but, at higher magnifications, with proper lighting, these polishes and striations show internal variability (see chap. 3), which can be related directly to the worked material.  While it is difficult to determine which came first, the stereomicroscope or the concentration on edge damage, there is some suspicion that some analysts have tried to make a virtue out of a necessity.  Whichever is the case, it seems very likely that a good deal of valuable, and even crucial, information will continue to be lost whenever observers restrict themselves to studying and interpreting only one category of wear traces.

## Conclusions

From the preceding discussions of technique and methodology, several preliminary conclusions may be drawn regarding the conduct of any microwear study.

1.  A wide range of magnifications and lighting arrangements should be employed to insure that the maximum amount of information can be extracted from both experimental and ancient wear traces.

2.  The interpretation of microwear traces should proceed through the use of an experimental framework against which any hypothesis about utilization, relative to a particular area and time, can be properly tested.

3.  There should be a good number and range of experiments conducted in at least some of the use/material experimental categories, so that the variability of traces produced by a single type of worked material is understood.

4.  The framework of experiments should be relevant to the actual situation of the site or sites under study and to any other local or temporal factors.

5.  The experiments should be conducted in a "natural" setting to insure that the wear patterns produced will be comparable with those found on prehistoric implements.

6.  All forms of utilization damage and microwear should be investigated to increase the precision and reliability of microwear interpretations.

7.  There should be serious attempts to quantify the microwear data obtained.

8.  As much supplementary data as possible of the sort useful for the independent checking or assessment of microwear interpretations should be provided.

If these conclusions are treated as recommendations for the proper conduct of microwear studies, microwear analysis organized along such lines should become an invaluable tool for the investigation of ancient economies and of any archeological question which involves the functions of stone implements.

## 2. IMPLEMENT PREPARATION, MICROSCOPY, AND PHOTOMICROGRAPHY

In view of the serious obstacles to useful microwear analysis that can arise when too little attention is devoted to the techniques of microscopic examination, I have experimented with a number of techniques and procedures in order to discover those which would be the most efficient and productive both in general and with regard to the particular applications that are the subject of this study.

### Cleaning

The cleaning of implements is a particularly important and often neglected process in the preparation of pieces for microwear analysis. Extraneous material is often deposited on an implement surface while the implement is buried in the archeological deposit or during the handling of it after recovery by the archeologist and the microwear analyst. Such material obscures existing wear traces and may even be liable to misinterpretation as an effect of use. Semenov (1964) provides some information about cleaning that is very useful and gives some good advice about the removal of the "sweat and fatty excretions of the hand" (Semenov 1964: 24) which are a constant nuisance to the microwear analyst. However, it would be useful to elaborate on the cleaning methods briefly mentioned by Semenov and to outline some that he did not mention.

During cleaning, it is best to monitor the proceedings by occasionally microscopically examining a piece (a sample piece if cleaning is done in batches) to determine the success of the techniques thus far applied, as some pieces require more cleaning than others. In some cases, notably when dealing with artifacts recovered from dry caves, where the conditions of preservation are right, organic material which may assist in determining an implement's function may survive on implement edges (Wylie 1975). In such a situation, special care in cleaning and handling is required. This type of preservation is unlikely for Paleolithic implements from sites such as Clacton, Hoxne, and Swanscombe, with which the present studies are concerned: never in the course of the examination of these implements prior to cleaning was anything seen on the implement edges which could have been surviving organic debris.

Perhaps the best way to present the cleaning process employed in this study is to list a series of steps, encompassing the full range of procedures used. Not every piece, either archeological or experimental, needed to be subjected to every step, but most did go through most steps.

1. The implement is examined, first with the naked eye and then if necessary, under

10

the microscope, to determine the existence of any deposits on the implement's surface.

2. The implement is wiped with white spirit or methylated spirits to remove finger grease and then washed in hot water and detergent (proprietary grit-free ammonia-based household cleaners are particularly useful). If the implement is free of soil deposits, this washing may be accompanied by a gentle rubbing with the fingers. If there is any deposit still adhering, then the piece should be left to soak in the solution for a few minutes.

3. The next step involves the immersion of the piece in warm HCl (10% solution) and NaOH (20% to 30% solution). The HCl removes any lime deposits and most other mineral deposits. The NaOH removes most extraneous organic deposits. Obviously, experimental pieces will not require the removal of mineral deposits, and the archeological specimens used in this study did not require the removal of extraneous organic deposits, but both archeological and experimental implements were treated with both solutions, in order to maintain strict comparability between the two classes of implements. Care must be taken not to leave an implement in the NaOH solution for too long a time, as this can cause a light, white patination on the piece (20 to 30 minutes is safe if the solution is cooling).

4. Immersion in an ultrasonic cleaning tank (in a detergent solution and clear water successively) may be necessary to remove small particles of sand, silt, dust, and clay still adhering to implement surfaces. If the piece is to be placed in the ultrasonic tank in a glass beaker, particular care must be taken in the positioning of the piece in the beaker. Those parts of the implement in contact with the glass will, through their vibrations, pick up a smooth, glossy deposit of glass (see fig. 128F) that, while it could not be mistaken for a microwear polish, might obscure the real traces of use.

5. Finally, it has often been the case with the archeological specimens (especially from Hoxne) that they display a shallow mineral deposit that withstands all the above cleaning procedures, and can obscure or, when confined to the edge, be confused with the real traces of use. One component of this deposit is evidently iron oxide, since, when the deposit is thick enough, it is colored orange or red. When it is thin, colorless, and confined just to the edge (a rare occurrence), it can be deceptive, as it reflects more light than, and is smoother than, the normal flint microtopography and, because it is soft, shows many striations. However, it can be identified by its appearance under polarized incident-light, since it often shows irridescent effects, unlike a true microwear polish. Also, because it is softer than either flint or a microwear polish, it will show a change in the direction of its striations when wiped with a soft cloth or lens tissue. If its presence is detected or suspected, it can be removed by prolonged immersion in hot HCl. In most cases, pouring hot HCl (on a prewarmed implement) and leaving it to cool for several hours is sufficient. But in exceptional cases, prolonged, repeated immersions over several days may be necessary. It is important not to subject the implement to too much heat, too suddenly, lest thermal cracks appear in the specimen.

After the initial cleaning, the piece may need to be recleaned at intervals to remove deposits left by handling during examination and, particularly, by the plasticine used to affix the implement to a circular glass plate for positioning under the microscope.

## Counteracting Translucency

Semenov (1964: 24-25) recommends the use of ink and chemical colorizers, as well as dusting with powders and vacuum metallization, to counteract the translucency of flint and limit the reflection of light from a flint implement to the microsurface (that is, the interface between the flint and the air). The problem is that much of the light directed onto a flint microsurface is absorbed into the flint body, so that only a portion of the available light is actually reflected back to be gathered up by the microscope's objective lens; the image of the flint microsurface (which is what the microwear analyst is interested in observing), then, is dim. Increasing the amount of light may not solve this problem, as light reflected from various interfaces in the interior of the flint (at the boundaries of loosely packed crystal "grains," fossil or other small inclusions) can "flood-out" the image created by light reflected from the microsurface. The use of inks and chemical colorizers is unsatisfactory because they tend to cover up and obscure the very microsurface one is trying to observe. Vacuum metallization is the most useful technique for increasing the reflection from the microsurface. This technique involves spraying (by heat vaporization) a very thin (a few molecules thick) film of metal (gold, silver, or aluminum) onto the surface of an implement in a high vacuum chamber. Early in this study, several implements, experimental and archeological, were coated with a thin aluminum film in a vacuum metallizer. It was found that even metallization can obscure important features of the microtopography. For example, the contrast between a microwear polish and the surrounding, unaffected surfaces may be lessened, although striations generally show us more clearly on a metallized surface. Fortunately, because the flint from which the experimental and Paleolithic implements examined in this study were made was fine grained and dense (English chalk flint), and because the microscope employed possessed adequate light-concentrating capabilities, it was never necessary for me to employ vacuum metallization. Metallization can be necessary, however, when one is dealing with coarse-grained rock types or with well-patinated flint.

## Microscopy

Two microscopes were used in this study: a stereomicroscope (WILD M5) and a lab microscope (WILD M20) with an incident-light attachment. The stereomicroscope was found to be of limited usefulness for several reasons. Its normal range of magnification was from 4X to 50X, but this could be extended, by use of stronger oculars and lens attachments, to 200X. However, the deterioration of the image at the higher magnifications was so profound as to render the microscope useless for purposes of microwear analysis beyond 50X. The light intensity with the stereomicroscope, unlike with the incident-light microscope, *decreases* as the magnification increases, which means that observation and, especially, photography is difficult above 25X. And another apparent disadvantage (noted by other stereomicroscope users as well: C. Bonsall, pers. comm.; G. Lau, pers. comm.) is that, despite the good depth of field in focus, photographs are very difficult to obtain at any magnification. There are some advantages to the stereomicroscope, however, such as the three-dimensional image, the ease with which stereophotomicrographs can be taken, the good depth of field (except in photography), and the long working distance. The working distance is important when observing pieces with considerable variation in topography. For example, with a short working distance, it may be difficult to observe features at the bottom of a hollow because the objective lens apparatus will not fit between the adjacent high points. But all the disadvantages of the stereomicroscope add up to one general disadvantage which outweighs its advantages--the higher magnification necessary for the close examination (and even observation) of the polishes and striations that is one of the principal interests of the microwear analyst cannot be obtained without such a serious degradation of the image that proper observation and examination of the microtopography is impossible.

The binocular incident-light lab microscope was found to be vastly superior to the stereomicroscope for microwear analysis. Its disadvantages are its close working distance, its two-dimensional image, and the difficulty of taking stereophotographs. But its working distance, in the majority of cases, was completely adequate. The two-dimensional aspect of the image is not a serious limitation since, by the use of the fine-focus adjustment, the investigator soon develops an easy appreciation of the three-dimensional character of the microtopography. And stereophotomicrographs could be taken through the M20 microscope, although it took some adjustment of the prints under the stereoviewer to obtain a three-dimensional image. The incident-light microscope's advantages are of particular importance for microwear analysis--the light intensity *increases* as magnification increases, which means that the image at 400X is better than the image at 40X, so that high-magnification work is easy and productive. The abundance of light makes photography relatively simple, as well. In addition, the WILD M20, with its various attachments, has a considerable flexibility of lighting arrangements--light-field or dark-field illumination, various filtering arrangements, and two polarizing filters, one with an analyzer. In light-field illumination, the light is focused on to the observed surface by the objective: light strikes the subject at an angle of 90° to the focal plane (fig. 1a). In dark-field illumination, light is directed on to the observed surface from all around, striking it at an angle of 45° to the focal plane (fig. 1b). With dark-field illumination, those surfaces in the microtopography which are parallel to the focal plane reflect very little light, while sloping

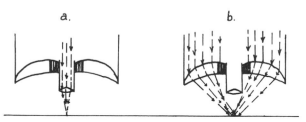

Figure 1. Lighting arrangements on the WILD M20 microscope. (a) Light field illumination; (b) dark field illumination.

surfaces at various angles to the focal plane reflect more light. Dark-field illumination is most useful at lower magnifications (24X to 60X) for observing edge damage and other gross features, but not very useful at higher magnifications (100X+), since polished surfaces do not reflect any light when arranged at right angles to the optical axis of the microscope. The various filters are particularly useful in photography but can be helpful in any circumstance. The red filter increases contrast, and the blue filter increases definition and resolution. In certain circumstances, it is necessary to reduce the light intensity, and the polarizing filters are very useful for this purpose. For example, sometimes considerable reflection from features (usually fossil inclusions) just below the flint surface will interfere with the observation of the microsurface itself. By the use of the polarizing filters and by increasing the brightness of the lamp, this interference can be reduced. Also, under crossed polarizers, certain types of extraneous deposits on the implements are distinguishable from true surface features. All of these capabilities of the incident-light microscope greatly enhance its utility and broaden the range of detectable microwear features.

Semenov claims that "in practice only diagonally reflected light can be used in studying tools and other archaeological material . . ." (1964: 23). This is not true. Normal 90° incident-light illumination shows all the features of interest to the microwear analyst and, if "shadowing" effects are required (and have not been produced coincidentally by the microtopography), they can be obtained by tipping the area being examined out of the perpendicular, or, less satisfactorily, by switching to dark-field illumination. Since, in most cases, the microtopography of implement edges consists of complex surfaces and not planes, incident lighting produces enough variations in light reflection to make the microtopography clear. Besides, all types of microwear features are the result of changes in surface texture, as well as simply of topography, and incident-light is admirably suited to distinguish these textural differences.

Some experimentation with the scanning electron microscope (SEM) was undertaken early in the study but was not pursued beyond that stage. The problem with using the SEMs available at Oxford is that their stage areas are too small (15 mm diameter) to hold most implements, which means that implements must either be broken up, clearly not a possibility with archeological specimens, or else the time-consuming and expensive process of making carbon replicas of the surface, which does not always provide reliable results, must be undertaken. Because of these drawbacks and the fact that no immediate benefits of very high magnifications were apparent, more extensive use of the SEM was not pursued. However, when SEMs of more flexible design are available, it would be worth experimenting further with them in microwear analysis (Brothwell 1969).

## Photomicrography

All the photomicrographs provided to document this study were taken with a camera attachment which fits both the M5 and M20 microscopes. Most photomicrographs were taken on 35 mm roll film, but some polaroid shots were taken as well. The 35 mm roll films found most satisfactory for this work were Ilford FP4, Kodak Plus-X, and Kodak Panatomic-X. Ilford FP4 was the film primarily employed, as it seemed to offer the best compromise between ideals of speed, fineness of grain, resolution, expense, and availability. Kodak Panatomic-X, for example, is finer grained but, under the light conditions in this study, it required exposure times of over a second; when filters were used, the exposure times could be as long as 5-10 seconds. When exposure times are as long as this, even the slightest vibrations transmitted to the microscope can result in blurred negatives.

Some stereophotographs were taken particularly with the M5 stereomicroscope. The taking of stereophotographs through the M20 microscope, unfortunately, involved complicated and crude repositioning of the specimen being photographed.

# 3.  THE EXPERIMENTAL PROGRAM AND ITS RESULTS

## General Principles and Aims

Since the aim of these experiments was to provide a background for the microwear
analysis of selected English Lower Paleolithic industries, certain principles were adhered
to that would insure that the wear patterns observed on the experimental pieces would be
most likely to replicate wear patterns produced in antiquity.

1.  The experiments were conducted with a restricted range of materials.  The flint
used for the implements was English chalk flint.  The implements were used on material
either known or likely to have been worked in Lower Paleolithic times--such as wood,
bone, meat, hide--and they were employed in a manner likely to have been current.  For
example, very few experiments were conducted using burins to work bone and antler, as
this technique does not appear to have become common until the Upper Paleolithic;
again, the woodworking experiments were conducted with modern examples of woods known
to be present from the evidence of pollen diagrams from the Hoxnian Interglacial.

2.  As many of the experiments as was possible were conducted outdoors, on the ground,
in case the amount of grit introduced between the implement edge and the worked material should be artificially reduced by experimenting indoors on clean floors or
countertops.  Many of the experiments were done with dirty hands, since the ancient
users of these tools were unlikely to wash their hands once a week, let alone several
times a day.

3.  In each experiment, the work being done was purposeful, rather than mechanical.
Other experimenters have sometimes conducted their experiments in a mechanical fashion, with the implement held at a constant angle, in a constant grip, and moved
against the worked material in a repetitive manner.  This method does not replicate
aboriginal conditions.  The Paleolithic users of tools were concerned, perhaps crudely, with efficiency and undoubtedly used their tools in an efficient and varying manner.  The microwear traces, but particularly the edge-damage patterns, which arise
from mechanical experiments are likely to give a false and deceptively tidy picture
of use alterations to edges.  Therefore, all the experiments conducted in this study
accomplished some simple task, like pointing a spear, splitting open a long bone to
get at the marrow, scraping the flesh off a fresh hide, and so on, to insure comparability with Paleolithic implements.

4. A large number of experiments were conducted using each type of material, so that the "characteristic" microwear features observed could be statistically verified and to insure that random effects were not interpreted as diagnostic of either a worked material or a method of use.

5. A careful study, by experimentation where possible, was made of the traces left on flint artifacts by various natural processes and by the processes of their manufacture, so that these traces would not be confused with actual traces of use on archeological implements.

## Raw Material

The flint implements used in most of these experiments were made using several types of English chalk flint. I obtained most of the flakes from nodules of East Anglia flint, principally Brandon flint. However, some of the flint came in the form of beach cobbles, from Pleistocene gravel deposits in Sussex, and some nodules from a chalk quarry at Kensworth in Bedfordshire. The Brandon flint, like most East Anglian flint, is black and relatively homogeneous in structure. Some of it is mottled gray and black, the gray areas generally being coarser in texture. The Sussex and Bedfordshire flint was generally dark gray, mainly homogeneous in structure, and often showed quantities of fossil inclusions. A few experiments were done using tools made of a milky gray Danish flint. Under the microscope, all of these flints appeared quite similar in structure (excepting, of course, some of the larger fossil inclusions) and were indistinguishable in terms of their receptivity to microwear traces. In the experiments, the type of flint involved had no effect on the formation or appearance of any of the microwear features.

## Production of Flakes

The flake blanks for use in the utilization experiments were all produced by direct percussion with a quartzite hammerstone. Some of the struck flakes, particularly the large ones, were caught in the hand, but most were allowed to fall free of the core and drop approximately a foot or so to the ground. The majority of the flakes that were to be used in the experiments were set aside immediately after they were struck. A few were selected, for control purposes, from the accumulated flaking debris after the core had been exhausted and were examined microscopically for traces that might be confused with true microwear. A few of these control flakes were used in the experiments after they had been examined microscopically and had been found to be free of any potentially confusing microscopic traces.

Some of these flakes were retouched on their working edges before use. Most retouch was done with light blows against the flake edge with a small pebble. Other hard-hammer methods used included pressure against an anvil stone, and "Clacton notching" (a single blow with a moderate-sized hammerstone directed up to 2 cm from the edge). Some pieces were retouched by the so called "bar-hammer" technique, using an antler hammer. All these retouched pieces were, of course, examined microscopically after retouch and before use to control for technological effects. There was some retouch on approximately 60% of the experimentally used implements but, except in the cases just mentioned, this retouch did not affect the working edge, as its purpose was merely to blunt sharp edges and cusps that would injure or discomfort the hand during use. Retouch of this kind ("accommodation retouch") is, of course, a very frequent feature of Lower Paleolithic implements. Such blunting, or accomodation retouch, which was usually heavy and involved crushing, was also examined to add to information about technological effects.

## Independent Variables Recorded

On each experimental piece, data was recorded relating (a) the size of the piece, (b) how it was used, and (c) what it was used on. The following paragraphs define the terms used.

### Size (see fig. 2)

$L$, length:  the maximum dimension of a flake measured at right angles to the striking platform (not as in Wilmsen 1968, the maximum distance from the point of percussion). $B$, breadth:  the greatest dimension perpendicular to $L$.

$Th$, thickness:  the maximum depth of the flake measured perpendicular to the general plane of percussion.

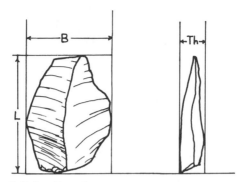

Figure 2.  Measurement of flake dimensions.

### Material Worked

$HW$, hardwood:  fresh and seasoned birch, sycamore/maple (*Acer pseudoplatinus*), and oak wood.

$SW$, softwood:  fresh and seasoned yew, pine, and spruce wood.

$B$, bone:  fresh or cooked pig and beef bones.

$DH/L$, dry hide/leather:  dried or tanned pig, beef, or hare hide.

$GH$, greased hide:  dried or tanned pig, beef, or hare hide rubbed with grease or fat.

$FH$, fresh hide:  fresh hare or pig hide.

$M$, meat:  fresh or cooked flesh of pig, beef, hare, and various types of fish and fowl.

$V$, vegetable materials:  the various nonwoody portions of edible or otherwise useful plants.

$DA$, dried antler:  the dry antler (not fresh) of red deer.

$SA$, softened antler:  the water-soaked antler of caribou.

### Activities

*Whittling.*  Shaving off material with the working edge of the implement held at roughly a right angle to the direction of use; one aspect of the edge is held at a low angle to the worked surface; edge angle is usually acute (fig. 3a).

*Planing.*  Shaving off material with the working edge held at roughly a right angle to the direction of use; the ventral or bulbar aspect is held at a low angle to the worked surface;

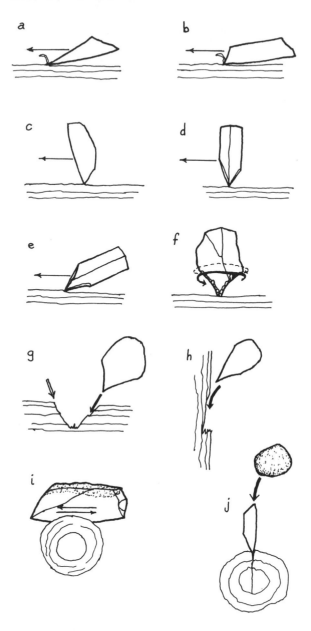

Figure 3. Method of use. (a) whittling; (b) planing; (c) scraping; (d) graving, high
angle of attack; (e) graving, low angle of attack; (f) boring; (g) chopping; (h) adzing;
(i) sawing, or cutting; (j) wedging

*Sawing.*  Insertion of an edge using bidirectional strokes, with the working edge held parallel to the direction of use; one or both aspects of the edge are held at approximately
a right angle to the worked surface.  The term "sawing" is used when the worked material
is hard, like wood, bone, and antler.  Most sawing edges were not intentionally denticulated (fig. 3i).

*Cutting/Slicing.*   Insertion of an edge using bidirectional (cutting) or unidirectional (slicing) strokes with the working edge parallel to the direction of use; one or both aspects of the edge are held at approximately a right angle to the worked surface.  The terms "cutting" and "slicing" are used when the worked material is soft, like meat, hide, and vegetable material; much less pressure is implied than in the sawing of a harder material.

*Chopping.*   Repeated insertion of an edge by blows, with the bisection of the angle formed by the two edge aspects striking at a high angle 60°-90° to the worked surface; blows are essentially heavy, with a slow recovery time (fig. 3g).

*Adzing.*   Repeated insertion, by blows, of an edge with one aspect of the edge at a low angle to the worked surface; blows are lighter than chopping and quickly repeated (fig. 3h).

*Scraping.*   Scraping with edge held at very high angle to worked surface; edge held at approximately a right angle to direction of use; the leading aspect of the edge is pulled rather than pushed (fig. 3c).

*Boring.*   Insertion with a semirotary, two-way action; implement is held at right angle to worked surface (use is similar to that of a modern awl).

*Wedging.*   Insertion by indirect percussion of an edge held at roughly right angles to the worked surface; the end of the flake roughly opposite to the working edge is struck with a hard or soft hammer (fig. 3j).

## Edge Angle

This is defined as the angle between the general planes of the two edge aspects (fig. 4a).  In most cases, this is equivalent to Wilmsen's (1968) "edge angle" and the "spine angle" of Tringham et al. (1974) and can be measured with a goniometer.  But when this type of measurement would not adequately describe the sharpness or thinness of the edge, such as when the surface between the edge and a dorsal ridge is markedly convex near the edge (fig. 4b), then the angle at the edge is measured by comparison with a polar coordinate grid. Sometimes, the angle of a working edge varies considerably along its length and it is necessary to derive an average.  This may be done by taking angle measurements at appropriate intervals along the used portion of the edge (say, every 5 mm) and averaging the obtained values.

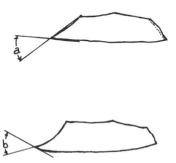

Figure 4.  Measurement of edge angles.

## Edge Outline Shape

This is the general shape of the portion of the edge showing microwear traces.  Classifying edges by shape is tricky business, since flint edges, especially in the Lower Paleolithic, are seldom elegantly and regularly retouched into a desired and formalized shape.  As well, utilization damage can alter the shape of an edge and confuse classification. For example, how is an edge to be classed if use damage has created a small concavity in an otherwise straight or convex edge? Some of these difficulties are overcome if one classifies only that portion of the edge showing the microwear and/or utilization damage (where it can be delineated), but it should be noted that all the classifications are liable to retain a degree of approximation. The classifications used are:  concave, convex, straight, cusp (a sharp projection from an edge), and complex (a residual category for any edges which cannot be placed into any of the preceding classes).

## Retouch

It was recorded whether the edge was retouched or unretouched and, if retouched, which type of retouch was used--hard-hammer, soft-hammer, or pressure against a hammerstone. This information is, of course, definite in the case of experimental pieces and estimated for the archeological ones.

## Kinematics

Under this heading, a simple description was given of the method of use. Usually a small sketch showing the orientation of the piece in relation to the worked material (also called "the angle of attack") and the type of grip employed. The number of strokes and/or the time in use was also recorded.

## Dependent Variables Recorded

After each experimental piece was used (and on all archeological specimens) data was recorded which described:  (a) the type of wear traces found, (b) their placement on the implement, and, (c) the direction of linear microwear features in relation to certain morphological axes.

## Placement of Wear Traces

*Edge area.* This is the portion of the usable edge that shows the microwear traces. On most regular flakes, the edge can be divided into two lateral and a distal end edge. When the flake's bulbar (or ventral) surface is face down and the platform is nearest the observer (fig. 5), the lateral edges are designated the right lateral and the left lateral edge. They keep these designations regardless of which way they are observed. The platform has two edges, the dorsal platform edge and the bulbar platform edge (fig. 5). Of course, dorsal ridges can be used and may show microwear traces as well.

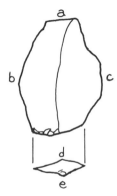

Figure 5. Edge and platform edge areas. (a) distal end edge; (b) left lateral edge; (c) right lateral edge; (d) dorsal platform edge; (e) bulbar platform edge.

*Edge aspect.* Every edge has two aspects. On flakes, these may be called bulbar and dorsal (fig. 6). On implements that lack a positive mechanical fracture surface (for example, a retouched and used thermally fractured piece), or on bifacially worked implements which show a markedly plano-convex cross-section, the edge aspect which is on the flattest surface (the equivalent of the bulbar aspect on mechanical flake edges) is called the ventral aspect, and the opposite aspect is still called the dorsal. On bifacial implements with a relatively symmetrical (usually lenticular) cross-section, the aspects are simply numbered Aspect 1 and Aspect 2. On experimental whittling/planing, grating, and adzing edges, the aspects were retitled the contact, or leading, aspect and the opposite aspect. The contact, or leading, aspect is that aspect of the working edge which is in greater contact with the worked matter and/or leads during use movement (fig. 6). The aspect which has less contact with the worked material and/or follows during use movement is called the opposite aspect (fig. 6).

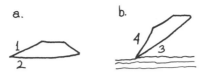

Figure 6, a and b. (1) dorsal aspect; (2) bulbar aspect; (3) contact or leading aspect; (4) opposite aspect.

*Burin bits.* Dihedral burin bits (working edges) have special features, which require special terms to describe the placement of microwear traces. The bit edge is the edge formed by the intersection of the two burin facets (fig. 7). This edge has two aspects which can be described as a leading bit aspect and an opposite bit aspect. The wear traces can also occur on the facets of the bit formed by the dorsal and bulbar surfaces of the flakes; these are called the dorsal facet and the ventral facet. Wear can occur on any of the four facet ridges formed by the intersection of the burin facets and the dorsal and ventral facets (see fig. 7).

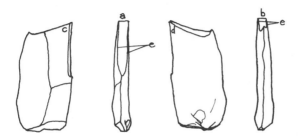

Figure 7. Burin bit edge areas. (a) bit edge, seen from one aspect; (b) bit edge, seen from opposite aspect; (c) dorsal facet; (d) bulbar facet; (e) facet ridges.

## Direction of Linear Microwear Features

Some kinds of microwear traces, such as striations, show a "preferred" direction which is important in interpreting the functions of the tool. This preferred direction needs to be expressed by reference to some baseline, and the various angles involved are defined as follows:

*Angle to the working edge.* This is a simple measurement on a relatively straight edge, but not on convex or concave edges. On the latter, the angle of the linear features (striations, abrasion tracks, and so on) is measured from the chord of the outward-curving or inward-curving semicircle described by the edge (fig. 8a). The chord is drawn from the points where concavity or convexity ends or recurves. On a complex edge (concave-convex, and so on), the angles are better measured to the flake axis.

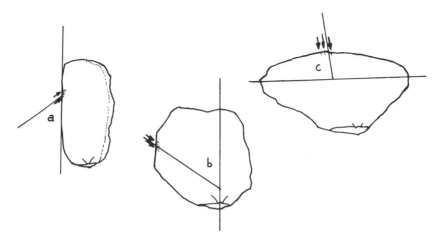

Figure 8.   Gauging the direction of linear wear traces.   (a) angle to the working edge; (b) angle to the flake axis; (c) angle to the long axis of the piece.

*Angle to the flake axis.* The direction of these linear features may be reckoned from the flake axis, which is the line passing through the point of percussion and at right angles to the plane of the platform (fig. 8b).

*Angle to the long axis.* On implements without a striking platform, or on bifaces, the long axis of the piece becomes the reference line. The long axis is the line that connects the two most distant points of the edge (fig. 8c).

*Angle to the bit axis.* Striations and the like on borers and some burins may need to be recorded in relation to the bit axis. The bit axis is the central axis of the bit projection, or, on burins, the line which bisects the angle formed by the two burin facets or the burin facet and a snap or retouched facet (fig. 9a).

*Angle to the bit edge.* On burins, the line of the bit edge provides a further reference axis for the recording of the direction of linear microwear features (fig. 9b).

It should be noted that none of the angles defined above are meant to be used for statistical purposes--they are simply descriptive conventions.

## Polish

The actual appearance of a microwear polish can be described in terms of its brightness or dullness (that is, how much light it reflects) and its roughness or smoothness, as well as the presence or absence of certain topographical features, like pits, undulations,

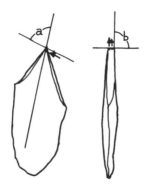

Figure 9.  Gauging the direction of linear wear traces on burins.  (a) angle to the bit axis;  (b) angle to the bit edge.

and so forth.  Since the appearance of the microwear polishes proved to be highly corre-lated with the material worked, it became convenient to refer to them simply as "wood" polish, "bone" polish, and so on.  The characteristics of these polishes are fully de-scribed in later sections.

## Striations and Abrasion Tracks

Striations may be subdivided according to their width and depth.  The classification used in this study does not use length to provide further divisions, as the independent variables affecting this characteristic seem to be legion, whereas, the width and depth of striations seem to be related more directly to the material worked, the size of hard par-ticles that come in contact with the edge during use (most of which are provided by the utilization damage spalls from the working edge, the size of which are also roughly related to the material worked and the method of use).  The width of striations can be easily meas-ured using the calibrated graticule in the microscope eyepiece, but their depth must be es-timated by the observer from the shadows formed in the striation troughs when the lighting is from a slightly oblique angle.  The striations are classified as follows:

Narrow deep:  deep striations with a width of no more than 2 microns (see pl. 37).
Narrow shallow:  shallow striations, which only affect the microelevations of the microtopography, having a width of no more than 2 microns.  Such striations were not found on any implements, experimental or archeological, so this classification is hypothetical at present.
Broad deep:  deep striations with a width of greater than 2 microns.
Broad shallow:  shallow striations with a width of greater than 2 microns (pl. 20).

Abrasion tracks result, like striations, from contact, under pressure, between the flint of the tool and materials as hard as, or harder than, itself.  Abrasion tracks, un-like striations, are usually quite broad ( 10 microns); often show multiple, parallel-running, deep tracks; are usually short; and sometimes have the appearance of being gouged out of the flint surface.  Such tracks, when found in association with microwear polish and other wear traces, can provide information, as can the striations, about the direction in which the implement was moving during use.  But abrasion tracks can be caused by a vari-ety of other processes:  for example, they occur when implements are rolled in water with sand or gravel, moved in deposits by soil processes, or struck with a hammerstone.

Empirically, considering both the experimental pieces and the archeological specimens, there seems to be no basis for a meaningful subdivision of abrasion tracks into various types.

## Edge Damage

Since often edge-damage patterns are mixtures of several types of sizes of scars, in this study the edge damage has been coded in order to separate and specify the particular scar types and to record the character of the mixture. The smallest unit of analysis, then, is the individual damage scar. The scars were classified according to their general appearance, depth, and size and were recorded simply as being present on the working edge. This is similar to the scar-classification criteria suggested by Odell (1975: 232). But recording the presence or absence, obviously, only poorly reflects the "patterning" of the scars. However, it is difficult to suggest any way of recording this patterning or even of describing it.

The types of damage scar are classified as follows:

Large deep scalar (*LD*): Deep, scale-shaped scars, with a maximum dimension parallel to the working edge (that is, maximum width) greater than 2 mm (fig. 10a). As with striations, the "depth" of damage scars is not measured but is assessed visually. These scars and, more often, the smaller kinds of deep scalar scars are the principal components of those edge-damage patterns generally referred to as "fine retouch" (Movius et al. 1968) or, more graphically, as "nibbling" retouch.

Small deep scaler (*SD*): Deep, scale-shaped scars with a maximum width of not more than 2 mm and not less than 0.5 mm (fig. 10b).

Microscopic deep scalar (*MicroD*): Deep, scale-shaped scars with a maximum width of less than 0.5 mm.

Large shallow scalar (*LS*): Shallow scalar scars with a maximum width greater than 2 mm (fig. 10c). This type and the small shallow scalar type have a truly "scalar"

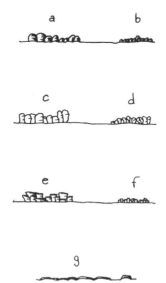

Figure 10. Edge damage types. (a) large deep scalar, *LD*; (b) small deep scaler, *SD*; (c) large shallow scalar, *LS*; (d) small shallow scalar, *SS*; (e) large stepped, *L Step*; (f) small stepped, *S Step*; half-moon breakages, ½Moon.

appearance (that is, they actually look like fish scales) and often show "feathering" at the distal ends of the scars.

Small shallow scalar (*SS*):  Shallow scalar scars with a maximum width of not more than 2 mm (fig. 10d).  No smaller category of shallow scalar scar was found to be necessary, as such scars are so rare (for whatever reason is hard to determine) on used edges as to be practically nonexistent.

Large stepped (*L Step*):  Generally shallow, abruptly terminated flake scars with a maximum width greater than 2 mm (fig. 10e).

Small stepped (*S Step*):  Shallow, abruptly terminated scars with a maximum width of not more than 2 mm and not less than 0.5 mm (fig. 10f).

Microscopic stepped (*MicroStep*):  Shallow, abruptly terminated scars with a maximum width less than 0.5 mm.

Half-Moon Breakages (*½Moon*):  Crescent-shaped breakages (fig. 10g), ranging in width from 1 to 10 mm on a used edge (*½Moons* larger than 10 mm are usually the result of processes other than use).  These are caused, as the experimental work has shown, when low-angled edges are tightly held in the material being worked and the edge is moved laterally.  They show neither a point of percussion nor any of the other features typical of conchoidal mechanical fracture, like percussion "rings" or stress fissures.

## Technological Effects

Technological effects are the traces, both macro- and microscopic, left on an artifact by the processes of its manufacture.  These traces can happen during the removal of a flake from the core, when a flake strikes the ground, or, especially, when an implement is being retouched.  They are important in the present context because they can resemble "true" microwear and need to be distinguished from it.

Information about these effects was gathered by the microscopic examination, at various stages of their manufacture, of the flakes I made for the utilization experiments.  A number of experimental pieces were retouched, but not subsequently used, in order that they could serve as reference pieces illustrating the visible effects of various methods of retouch (for example, hard-hammer, soft-hammer, pressure against a stone, and so on).

When a flake is being struck off from a core, the point and area of percussion receives a certain amount of abrasion and crushing from the hammerstone, but because of its placement on the flake (that is, on the striking platform at the point of percussion), this creates no problems for the microwear analyst.  However, if the flake is restricted or held as it flies off the core, which can occur, for example, if one holds one's fingers across the face of the core, or holds it against one's thigh, it will pivot part of its edge against the core with enough force to cause a series of small, retouchlike scars (pl. 9). Mark Newcomer (1976) calls this type of edge damage "spontaneous retouch," and he has studied it in some detail.  Spontaneous retouch is more likely to occur during the removal of blades, where one places the fingers along the controlling ridge on the core face to diffuse and carry the force of the blow and thereby to increase the length and regularity of the blade.  This same use of the hand (and the thigh) to control the shape and dimensions of flakes is useful, however, in any kind of flintknapping.  Sometimes, spontaneous retouch may be accompanied by a thin band of abrasion on the edge of a flake or blade, which could be mistaken for a "microwear polish" when examined at low magnifications.  At magnifications of 100X to 200X, it is clear that this "polish" is actually abrasion.  The placement and the morphology of the spontaneous retouch scars can often mimic utilization

damage (see figs. 11, 12) and when they are accompanied by abrasion, they can prove a serious difficulty in studies based only on low magnification.

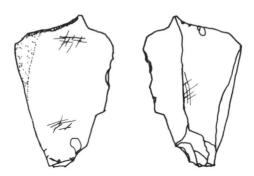

Figure 11.  Exp 22.

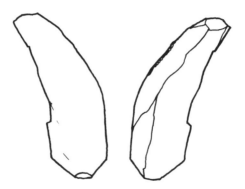

Figure 12.  Exp 121.

After a struck flake is free of the core and comes into sudden contact with the
ground, if it is not caught, more edge damage can occur, particularly if there is an accumulation of flaking debris on the spot where the flake lands.  Most of the time, this
results in a few, isolated, randomly distributed damage scars on the edge and a few isolated and randomly distributed abrasion tracks, which should present no problem for the
microwear analyst.  But, occasionally, this type of damage can occur as a series of flake
scars of types commonly resulting from utilization.  Plate 5 shows part of such a damage
pattern on experiment 108, consisting of a series of ½Moon breakages, *SS*, and *MicroStep*
scars.  While there are no associated microscopic effects, like abrasion, if one were relying solely or primarily on edge damage, one might be tempted to interpret this implement
as a saw.

Hard-hammer retouch creates a number of potentially confusing traces.  When an edge is
struck with a hammerstone, not only is the intended retouch flake removed, but a whole
series of smaller flakes and chips are removed as well.  Often a single large retouch flake
will be removed, let us say 10 mm in length, but a whole series of microflakes with no
dimension greater than 2-3 mm will come off at the same time.  Often these smaller flakes
leave delicate scalar and stepped scars that are very similar to utilization damage.

Experiment 108 shows such a result most clearly (pl. 6, fig. 56): a broad, Clacton notch was created on the left lateral edge by a single blow with a small, quartzite hammerstone (weight 140 g); around the center of the resultant notch, at the point of percussion, a series of *SS* scars, the longest about 2.3 mm long, was created, accompanied by some *Micro-Step* scars (pl. 6). Thus, with a single blow, this piece was comprehensively retouched (the removal of the notch spall left sharp edges on either side of the point of percussion) and "utilized." Compare experiment 108 (fig. 13) with an implement from the Clacton Gravel, CL 982 (fig. 14). A microscopic examination, at high magnifications, found no microwear traces at all on CL 982, yet the unwary would no doubt classify it as a utilized notch because of the delicate *LS* and *SS* edge damage at the center of the concavity, which, in fact, corresponds very closely with the damage found on experiment 108. Where hard-hammer retouch scars are closely packed on an edge, as in the case of many kinds of scrapers, the small, pseudoutilization damage scars will cover the retouched edge almost continuously. The problem of sorting out true utilization damage scars from the small, pseudoutilization retouch scars on a used, retouched edge is virtually impossible to solve.

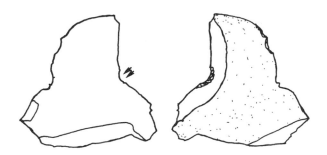

Figure 13.  Exp 38.

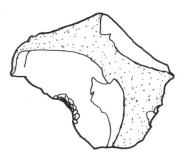

Figure 14.  CL 982.

Tringham et al. (1974: 181) claim that a distinction can be "made on the basis of size and . . . patterning of scars." These criteria are certainly useful for distinguishing a retouched edge from an unretouched used edge, but the real problem is to distinguish an unused retouched edge from a used retouched edge. The size distinction cannot be applied in such a situation because the small flake scars might be either utilization damage or the small components of the retouch. As for "patterning," Tringham et al. claim (1974: 181) that retouch is more "regular" than utilization damage, but this only applies to the larger, intentional scars of the retouch, not to the small, unintentional retouch scars which are as irregular in distribution and morphology as any utilization damage.

The microscopic traces left by hard-hammer retouch consist of hammerstone scratches and "smears" (pls. 7, 8), abrasive beveling of the edge (pl. 8), and "gouging." While these traces share a similar origin and appearance with some forms of microwear, such as abrasion tracks and broad, deep striations, they can usually be distinguished from these and are not similar (under high magnification) to any of the microwear polishes:  hard-hammer traces are usually more severe than any similar traces left, for example, when bits of flint become embedded in some worked material during use, and are concentrated at the very edge, while striations tend to be more invasive.  The hard-hammer scratches are broader and show multiple tracks in the abrasion (pl. 7).  If the traces are of the hammer-stone "smear" variety, they will appear as broad, very flat, bright areas, not unlike the polish left when a flint surface is rubbed against glass (cf. pls. 8, 10).  Therefore, this smearing, rather than scratching, probably occurs when the siliceous minerals in the hammerstone are softer than flint.  Beveling (pl. 8) is also usually very flat and smooth, unlike any type of microwear.  Whatever problems hard-hammer retouch causes for the interpreter of edge damage, it presents very few for the microwear analyst.

Soft-hammer retouch causes the same edge-damage problems as hard-hammer retouch, perhaps even more, since the small pseudoutilization scars are more delicate than those produced by the hammerstone.  My own experiments, which involved the soft-hammer retouch of flakes using an antler baton, produced very few microscopic traces on the finished edge. Such traces as there were consisted of sporadic tiny patches of bright abrasion on the un-retouched aspect at the point of percussion of the larger retouch flakes.  The examination of implements retouched with antler hammers by a more skilled lithic technologist (P. Jones) showed no traces of this kind, which would suggest that such traces are likely to be rare on archeological specimens, as their makers were at least as skilled at soft-hammer retouch as Mr. Jones.

Because my experiments were designed with a Lower Paleolithic application in mind, no experiments in the area of pressure retouch were conducted, except the use of pressure a-gainst a hammerstone to blunt or shape an edge. While the retouch scars created by such pressure were quite similar to certain types of utilization damage (such as that produced by scraping bone or antler), the microscopic traces were quite similar to hard-hammer effects (which, in effect, is what they are).  Edge beveling by abrasion was quite common in this situation.

In conclusion, we may say that technological effects, examined with due care, demonstrate many appreciable differences with true microwear, but it must be admitted that the distinctions between technological and utilization edge damage are more difficult to isolate and in some cases no appreciable differences seem to exist.

## Traces Resulting from Natural Processes

When examining implements from archeological contexts, one wishes to be sure that the microscopic traces observed are truly the result of ancient human use and not the result of some natural process.  Semenov (1964) details most of the processes that affect archeological specimens and gives a discussion of the traces they leave.  He lists patination, water abrasion, wind abrasion, and natural gloss (which is a type of patination), but he does not mention *in situ* soil movements, which seems an important omission, made also by most other workers in the field.  A summary of the effects left by the various natural processes follows.

## Patination

The patination of flint is an effect which can seriously interfere with microwear analysis, as some of the processes involved in the formation of flint patina can erode the implement's microsurface, thereby destroying any but the grossest traces of use or altering the light-reflection qualities of the flint so that the microsurface and the microwear cannot be observed with light microscopes.

A few (three) of the writer's experimental implements were artificially patinated after they had been used and microscopically examined for traces of use. This was achieved by prolonged immersion in a warm, 30% solution of NaOH. The following account of patination effects is based on the results of these experiments, on the relevant remarks of Semenov (1964), and on the detailed experimental work of Rottländer (1975).

Rottländer's (1975, 1976) work has shown that what archeologists tend to see as a single phenomenon, that is, patination, is really several separate phenomena having diverse causes. Some of the causes of these diverse patinations are alkaline environments, sunlight (UV radiation) and, in acid environments, certain chemicals released by plants. When white patination, which can be caused by all the above agents, is severe, the microsurface of the flint becomes pitted and very granular, which destroys any traces of use. However, as Semenov (1964: 11) says, "a shallow patina hardly changes the micro-relief of the surface of the flint and so does not affect the traces of use on the tool." Since microwear polishes reduce the amount of surface area vulnerable to chemical action by smoothing the microtopography, the polished areas are less affected by chemical attack than unaltered areas on the same implement. On some archeological implements which have been subject to glossy patination, areas of microwear polish may appear pedestaled above the surrounding unworn microsurface which has been "weathered" by the patination.

Sometimes the white patination is restricted to the edges and dorsal ridges, and it can be accompanied by a "polish," the origin of which is unknown. It does appear different from true microwear, but these differences are hard to describe; plate 11 shows some of this polish on an implement from Clacton. This "patination polish" is smooth and featureless--in fact, very similar to the polish left by glass rubbing (pl. 10) and is, of course, restricted to the white patinated areas of the edge. Therefore if one encounters a "polish" which is coexistent with white patination and which occurs on all angular surfaces of the implement, it can be excluded from consideration as microwear. Once one is familiar with true microwear polishes, effects like this present very little difficulty in interpretation.

In summary, the effects of patination are not likely to be confused with microwear, but it is more likely that severe patination will render implements unusable for microwear analysis.

## Abrasion by Water-borne Sediments

I acquired information about the effects of abrasion by water-borne sediments mainly by examining a series of implements from each of the Lower Paleolithic sites of Clacton, Hoxne, and Swanscombe, the physical condition of which ranged from the very obviously "rolled" to very fresh. These series were examined to get a clearer picture of the abrasion effects which were common and characteristic of the particular sedimentary environments of the respective sites. Otherwise, a program of experiments would have been necessary involving the time-consuming testing of abrasion in sediments of various particle sizes and size mixtures. Besides, the techniques available for imitating water abrasion, such as agitating implements, water, and sediment in a plastic container (Tringham et al.

1974: 191), or in a tumbling mill (Shackley 1974), do not really replicate the steady flow of water and sediment along a streambed or the lapping of silt-laden water on a shoreline.

"Water" abrasion is generally quite easy to recognize, even with the naked eye, especially when it is severe, but when implements have been abraded only fairly briefly and by fine sediments, only microscopic examination can readily distinguish it. The heavier abrasions usually cover extensive areas of the implement (if not the whole surface), but especially affect the edges and the ridges (pl. 12). The striations on these abraded surfaces are numerous and usually randomly oriented, although sometimes a predominant direction can be discerned.

Myra Shackley has provided an easy method, based on experimental evidence, of assessing the degree of abrasion by measuring the width of the abraded dorsal ridges. However, a few of the features she notes as indicating the early stages of "water" abrasion can also be seen on freshly struck flints. She claims that the initial stages of the abrasion of the ridges "are marked by the appearance of stress cracks . . . which develop a 'braided' appearance" (1974: 501). The stress cracks she mentions are a typical micro- and macroscopic feature of percussion-fractured flint. Indeed, any kind of friction will bring out these features where they were before latent, as utilization will also bring them out on the working edges of experimental implements. But they are commonly present on the ridges of freshly flaked implements, sometimes even showing a braided appearance, especially on high-angled ridges (>140°).

It would seem that some of the other features Shackley mentions, such as abrasion and percussion craters on the ridges, can also be found on implements subjected to *in situ* soil movements, and she did not make a comparative study of such pieces. But on pieces which show signs of having been subjected to *in situ* soil movements, percussion craters on the ridges are rare and are sporadically distributed on the pieces that do show them. Water abrasion can nevertheless be fairly easily distinguished using the information and methods proposed by Shackley.

## Abrasion by Wind-borne Sediments

Without a wind tunnel, or sandblaster, experiments investigating abrasion by wind-borne sediments are impossible. Except for those affected by the phenomenon of "desert polish," wind-abraded artifacts are likely to be difficult to distinguish from implements abraded by water-borne silt. Whitney and Dietrich (1973) suggest that some types of "desert polish" are more likely to have been caused by fine silt particles suspended in the wind than by saltating sand grains. This means that conditions favorable for the formation of this type of abrasion may have occurred on sparsely vegetated areas adjacent to Pleistocene rivers, on exposed lake margins, or on loess plains, and it is therefore possible that some of the implements from the archeological sites investigated in this study which were rejected because they were regarded as slightly water-abraded, were, in fact, subject to wind abrasion. But the microwear analyst is more concerned with excluding both water and wind abrasion effects from his study than in deciding which agency was responsible, however important the distinction might be from other archeological or geological points of view. So far as we are concerned here, the pieces in question had been abraded to an extent that rendered them useless for microwear analysis.

## Soil Movement Effects

The natural effects that are likely to create the most serious problems for the functional analyst are those created by *in situ* soil movements (using "soil" in the loose

sense, meaning simply the sediment containing archeological implements).  The more severe
of such movements are solifluction and crytobation, which leave recognizable stratigraphic
effects.  The problem for the functional analyst, however, comes from the slight edge damage and localized abrasions created by minor soil movements that leave no such gross stratigraphic features.  These minor movements might be the result of freeze-thaw action, minor
distortion, or even simply settling under the pressure of overlying sediments.  An archeological layer under the pressure of overlying deposits is subject to compression and
stresses that can result in minor, imperceptible distortions.  These distortions would
bring the implements contained in the subject layer into pressure contact with each other
or with other resistant particles in the deposit, and abrasion and edge damage would certainly result.

There are some difficulties involved in modeling such movements in the laboratory.  As
inquiries at Oxford established, with various types of equipment one can reproduce movement
or pressure (that is, compression), but not both simultaneously.  Cahen and Moeyersons
(1977), in a paper dealing with the vertical dispersion of artifacts, demonstrate that non-
deformable objects (artifacts) in unconsolidated sediments move at different rates relative
to their containing sediments under compression.  Their experiments were conducted on pris-
matic wooden blocks in monaxial shearing apparatus and, therefore, no observations of the
type of traces left by vertical compression on flint artifacts could be made.  For the purposes of this study, the investigation of soil movement effects has had to proceed by argu-
ing from the traces found on implements known to have been subjected to *in situ* soil movements.

Amazingly enough, few recent Paleolithic archeologists have paid much attention to
this problem, even those particularly interested in the study of wear traces.  At the beginning of this century, the long and virulent debate over "eoliths" finally abated when most
archeologists accepted that natural processes, particularly soil movements under pressure,
could produce flake scars that very closely resemble human workmanship.  This history appears to have been forgotten by any number of archeologists and functional analysts, who
are not at all surprised to find that the bones in an archeological deposit have been
crushed and distorted by soil pressure and movement, but will nevertheless see every edge-
damage pattern on the flint implements from the same level as being the result of either
use or retouch.  The exceptions are few.

Bordes (1961) recognizes that some layers in cave sites contain implements with natural "retouches."  These implements were from layers that show signs of disturbance (often
represented by rounded calcareous elements).  Bordes (1961: 46) says, "Ces actions
naturelles arrivent parfois à simuler des petits grattoirs à retouche abrupte, des
encoches, des denticulés, des becs burinants alternes."  If such disturbances, even in the
shelter of caves, could produce flake scars large enough to be mistaken for retouch, then
surely less severe disturbances could produce scars likely to be taken for utilization edge
damage.  Anyone relying heavily on edge damage for functional information is likely to run
into serious difficulties if due consideration is not given to this source of error.

There are, of course, both macro- and microscopic traces that indicate soil-movement
damage.  If the movement has been severe, the edge damage will consist of roughly alternating edge-damage scars, the ridges will show crushing and "percussion craters" (see
Shackley 1974), and often a number of small, incipient cones of percussion will be distributed about the thicker portion of the piece (these cones are sometimes also seen on
water-rolled pieces).

One sure clue to soil movement is the presence of "white scratches" clearly visible to the naked eye on the surfaces of the implement. These were discovered by the author during an earlier study of edge damage on the collections from the Caddington (Beds.) Paleolithic floors. When examining a sample of implements from the "contorted drift," which were abraded and extensively damaged, I observed that they were covered with curious white scratches. In fact, Worthington Smith, the discoverer of the Caddington sites, noted that the first implement he found *in situ* at Caddington, which came from the "contorted drift," was "faintly white-pencilled" (1894: 93), which is as apt a description of these marks as any. The bottoms of these scratches usually show crushing as well as scratch tracks. There will often be a "halo" of white patination around the scratch on pieces without any other white patina (pl. 13), which is a clue that the scratching took place after the initial glossy "patination" (which can forestall white patination, see Röttlander 1975: 109). The scratch opens a new microsurface to chemical action, which allows the agents of white patination to diffuse into the surrounding flint from the crushed area of the scratch. This is a clear indication that these scratches are postdepositional. The depth and breadth of these scratches indicate that pressures greater than can be developed by unaided human strength were involved in their formation. Plate 12 shows a broad white scratch that consists of a progressive series of incipient cones, accompanied by abrasion. Scratches as wide or as deep as these white scratches were never developed in the course of any utilization experiment; nor could they be reproduced by intentionally scratching the surface of one flint with another, using an unaided hand, even with the weight of the body behind it. All the distinctive features of these scratches point to a soil-movement origin.

These scratches are most commonly found on the bulbar surfaces of flakes, especially on the bulb of percussion (see R. A. Smith 1931: pl. 2). This is presumably because the smooth, bulbar face presents the least resistance to movement, whereas the dorsal surface, with its ridges, would be gripped by the sediment and would resist movement. It is also worth noting that these scratches were found on certain implements from Clacton, for example CL 1222 (fig. 15) *under* lime encrustations, again pointing to an *in situ* origin. Dick Stapert found similar scratches (1976a: figs. 10, 11) on pseudoartifacts from Holland, which he independently deduced were caused by soil movements.

It seemed to me, when examining the collection of implements taken by W. G. Smith from the Caddington floors (not the "contorted drift"), that there was an association between edge damage and the white scratches. This association was investigated by statistical means using $t$-tests and Pearson's $r$. It was found that the pieces with white scratches had significantly larger percentages of their edges damaged than the implements without the scratches. A correlation coefficient was calculated, using only white-scratched pieces, between the percentage of the total edge that had been damaged and the number of visible white scratches. This turned out to be highly significant ($r=0.678$, $df=160$, $P<.005$). This result certainly indicates a common cause for both the edge damage and the white scratches (since we cannot argue that the scratches cause the edge damage, or vice versa). It seems likely that the white-scratched pieces came both from the contorted drift and also from those portions of the floors which had been warped and distorted by soil movement, while the unscratched pieces were from the undisturbed portions (see fig. 16).

There was a suspicion that even the Caddington implements without white scratches had been affected by soil movements, a suspicion which was heightened by the fact that over 70 percent of all observable (at less than 20X magnification) edge damage at Caddington occurred on edge angles of less than 50°, and these are the edges that would be most

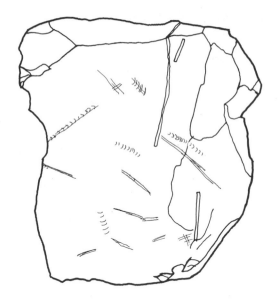

Figure 15.  CL 1222.

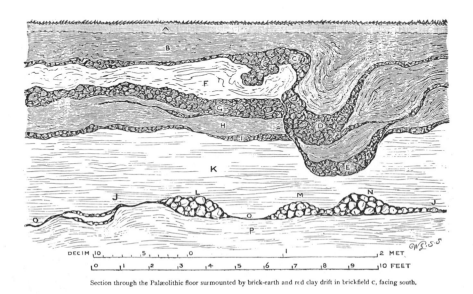

Section through the Palæolithic floor surmounted by brick-earth and red clay drift in brickfield c, facing south.

Figure 16.  Caddington section by W. G. Smith (Smith 1894: fig. 46).  Fresh conjoinable implements were found in layers G and H; J--J is an undisturbed floor.

vulnerable. The damage usually consisted of abrupt nibbling "retouches" (mostly *SD* scars), some implements recalling Bordes's "petits grattoirs à retouche abrupte." The doubts that arose from the Caddington study, coupled with the subsequent investigation of implements from Clacton, Hoxne, and Swanscombe, have led once again to the conclusion that overreliance on edge damage, as opposed to true microwear, is likely to lead to some serious mistakes.

There is another type of scratch or striation that is likely to be the result of soil movement. The striations are broad (up to 60 microns wide), deep (probably as deep as 50 microns), and have a U-shaped cross-section (pl. 14). Unlike abrasion or wear striations, the bottom of the trough is not bright and smooth, but is usually about as rough and grainy as the unaffected flint surface. These are found, like the white scratches, primarily on the bulbar surfaces of flakes and particularly on the bulbs of percussion themselves. The edge damage on pieces showing these scratches seems to be of natural origin, often consisting of random *LD* scars alternating on most of the flake edge. Striations of this kind are probably just soil-movement scratches that have not been attacked by the agents of white patination.

Soil movements cause other identifiable microscopic effects besides scratches and edge damage. The most common are abrasion tracks on the ridges. This abrasion is generally similar in appearance to hammerstone scratching and is usually found on the highest points of the dorsal surface. This almost certainly arises from movement against pebbles or other implements. Another effect which is also found on dorsal ridges is a dull, rough polish or abrasion, not dissimilar to that illustrated by Shackley (1974: fig. 6). It does not closely resemble any of the true microwear polishes and is usually accompanied by percussion craters. The main clue to its being natural is the fact that it may sometimes cover all of the ridges on a hand ax, let us say, something no microwear polish could do. It may be water-abrasion, but since the "polish" is often restricted to just the ridges and does not affect the hollows of the flake scars in between, it is more probably the result of soil movement. Again, its cause is irrelevant, so long as the microwear analyst does not confuse it with true microwear.

Finally, there is the question of the traces left by men and animals trampling implements into the soil. To reproduce such effects, I left four flake implements in loamy soil, in an area where they were stepped on almost every day over a long period. The implements settled into the soil and disappeared, presumably by worm action, after a few weeks. Two of the implements were recovered after six months, and the other two after a year. There were no real differences between the traces found on all four, except on one of the pieces which lay on top of one of the others. It had a short run of *SD* damage scars along one edge, accompanied by a few short abrasion tracks on the aspect opposite the damage, which is exactly similar to the traces left by pressure retouch against a hammerstone. The piece that was below it (fig. 11) showed some ½*Moon* breakages on its thinner edge and a run of *SS* scars on its distal edge. It had some abrasion tracks on its dorsal ridge, which was the part in contact with the overlying flake. The other flakes had only rare *MicroD* scars distributed in a random fashion around their edges. All four flakes had some curious areas of very shallow striations (pls. 16, 17) located, in each case, in the central portions of the dorsal and bulbar surfaces, away from the edges. The appearance of this light "abrasion," whatever its cause, is so unlike true microwear that it is unlikely to create any problems, especially since it was never seen to occur on the edges.

Most natural processes, then, leave traces which are unlikely to cause much confusion for the microwear analyst, once he is familiar with them and with true microwear features, and provided he studies them at high enough magnifications. However, it seems clear that reliance on low magnifications and on edge damage alone will often not allow the analyst to distinguish between damage caused by natural processes and that resulting from human use. Such a reliance will lead to faulty interpretations for edges that have not been used and, hence, to an overestimation of the number of used implements. Indeed, this is probably what happened in an earlier low-magnification study of implements from Hoxne (see chap. 7).

Dick Stapert of Groningen (mentioned above) was working independently on natural traces on flint implements while I was doing my work. He has published his results in a paper (Stapert 1976b), well illustrated by photomicrographs, and his conclusions parallel mine. Although somewhat pessimistic on some points concerning potential confusions between natural traces and microwear, this paper is highly recommended to everyone interested in the subject.

## Woodworking Traces

### General Effects

In almost all of the woodworking experiments (that is to say, in 54 out of 59), a distinctive polish was formed on the working edges, which had a consistent appearance regardless of whether the wood was a hard- or softwood species, fresh or seasoned, and regardless of the manner of use. This polish can be distinguished from the polishes formed from working other materials. It is very bright (that is, it reflects a considerable quantity of light) and is very smooth in texture (pls. 18-27). The polish surface, once it becomes visible, is very rarely a flat plane but is commonly gently curved or domed on the high points of the microtopography. These domes gradually enlarge, as work progresses, and link up. This implies that some material is being deposited on the flint microsurface, whatever other alterations may be taking place (that is, additive polish). When the polish is intense, after prolonged use, it will show gentle undulations on its surface (see pl. 18), with the lines of the "troughs" and "crests" running in the general direction of use. Because the polish develops on the elevations of the microtopography first, until the affected area is substantially covered by polish, the gross appearance of the polished area will be affected by the original texture of the flint surface. If the texture of the flint surface is coarse, as in plate 19, the polish, in its early stages of development, will be distributed in a reticular pattern, whereas on a fine-grained flint surface, as in plate 18, the polish will develop more evenly over the affected area. However distributed, the bright, smooth character of the wood polish remains constant.

Striations were not a particularly common occurrence on the woodworking implements, being present on only 29 of the 59 experimental edges. However, it seems that one type of striation occurs solely on woodworking implements. It is broad (approximately 15 microns) and shallow, unlike the narrower and deeper striae that occur on hide-, bone-, and meat-working edges (cf. pl. 20 with pls. 37, 47). Often, the woodworking striations will comprise nothing more than tracks formed by the shaving off of the elevations in the microtopography. Not all striations on woodworking implements were of this type, but it was never found on implements used on other materials. Brian Hayden (pers. comm.) has also observed that such striae occur exclusively on woodworking edges.

The utilization damage (as opposed to the polish and striations) produced in the course of these experiments showed no consistent variation that could be related to the working of wood. Some form of edge damage could be discerned on 50 of the 59 pieces, but

none of the scar types was found to occur only, or even primarily, on woodworking implements. Nor was there any typical or definitive combination of scar types. The type of
utilization damage scars produced was determined more by the method of use or activity conducted, and by the edge angle, than by the material worked.

## Variations Related to Wood Type

As stated above, the particular type of wood worked made no difference as far as the
development and nature of wood polish was concerned. But there were some differences of
degree in the microwear and edge-damage pattern that are associated with variations in the
more general nature of the wood worked. Thus, dense woods and seasoned wood of most species cause less polish when worked than unseasoned wood and less dense species. Hayden
and Kumminga (1973: 6) have also noted this phenomenon in their woodworking experiments.
This is because the seasoned or dense wood is more resistant, and the implement edge does
not cut as deeply into the material, so that the area subject to polish-producing friction
is more restricted. The experiments showed that seasoned wood is much harder to work with
than freshly cut wood, and it seems likely that in the Paleolithic, unseasoned wood was
worked for most purposes.

It seems also that scraping or whittling the bark off of a piece of wood creates more
striations than the working of the wood proper. This may be explained by the greater abundance of dust and other environmental grit particles in the bark, as opposed to the wood.

One experiment which involved the "charring-and-scraping" method of working wood (exp.
160) demonstrated that, despite the alterations induced in the wood by charring, the microwear polish produced was typical wood polish.

## Variations with Method of Use

*Whittling and Planing* (see table 1). As one might expect, the polish develops mainly on
the aspect of the working edge which is in contact with the wood. The polish will round
the edge and, on low-angled edges, after prolonged use, will develop very weakly on the
opposite edge aspect. The striations also are formed mainly on the edge aspect that is in
contact with the wood. The indications of direction observable in the microwear--furrows,
striations, and so on--will indicate a direction of use between 45° and 90° to the working
edge.

None of the edge-damage type shows any particular association with whittling or planing (see table 1), but small, ½Moon breakages are common on thin or low-angled edges.
Isolated *LS* and *SS* scars can occur on the contact aspect, but not commonly. It is clear
from these experiments that utilization damage does not occur only on the aspect opposite
the one in contact with the worked material, as Kantman (1971) and Tringham et al. (1974:
189) claim.

The characteristics of microwear on wood-whittling knives and planes are: wood polish
predominantly on one aspect of the working edge; indications of direction of use running
at angles between 45° and 90° to the edge; ½Moon scars on thin edges and sometimes isolated
*SS* scars on the same aspect of the edge which shows the polish.

*Sawing* (see table 2).

With sawing, the polish forms on both edge aspects, as do the striations. Striations
and areas of flint-on-flint abrasion are very common. The reasons for this are not difficult to discover. All but one of these experiments used unretouched edges, and ½Moon
breakages were quite common. The spalls from these breakages often become embedded in

*Table 1*
*Whittling/Planing Wood*

A. Edge Aspect and Wear Trace Occurrence

| | Polish | Striae | LD | SD | MicroD | LS | SS | L Step | S Step | Micro-Step | ½Moon |
|---|---|---|---|---|---|---|---|---|---|---|---|
| Leading or Contact Aspect | 20 | 9 | 1 | 1 | 1 | 2 | 4 | | | 1 | |
| Both Aspects | | | | | | | 2 | | | | 6 |
| Opposite Aspect | | | | 3 | 1 | 1 | | | 3 | 2 | |

N=20

B. Edge Angle and Wear Trace Occurrence

| | Polish | Striae | LD | SD | MicroD | LS | SS | L Step | S Step | Micro-Step | ½Moon | N |
|---|---|---|---|---|---|---|---|---|---|---|---|---|
| <35° | 3 | 2 | | 1 | | 1 | | | | | 2 | 3 |
| 35° - 49° | 7 | 4 | | 2 | 1 | 1 | 1 | | 1 | 2 | 3 | 7 |
| 50° - 64° | 7 | 2 | 1 | 1 | 1 | 2 | 4 | | 2 | 1 | 1 | 7 |
| 65° - 79° | 1 | 1 | | | | | | | | | | 1 |
| 80° - 95° | 2 | | | | | | | | | | | 2 |
| Totals | 20 | 9 | 1 | 4 | 2 | 3 | 6 | | 3 | 3 | 6 | 20 |

*Table 2*
*Sawing Wood*

A. Edge Aspect and Wear Trace Occurrence

| | Polish | Striae | LD | SD | MicroD | LS | SS | L Step | S Step | Micro-Step | ½Moon |
|---|---|---|---|---|---|---|---|---|---|---|---|
| Dorsal Aspect (only) | | | 1 | 2 | | 1 | | 1 | 1 | | |
| Both Aspects | 7 | 5 | | | | | | | | | 6 |
| Bulbar Aspect (only) | | | | 1 | | 1 | 2 | | 1 | | |

N=7

B. Edge Angle and Wear Trace Occurrence

| | Polish | Striae | LD | SD | MicroD | LS | SS | L Step | S Step | Micro-Step | ½Moon | N |
|---|---|---|---|---|---|---|---|---|---|---|---|---|
| <35° | 6 | 5 | 1 | 3 | | 1 | 1 | 1 | | | 5 | 6 |
| 35° - 49° | | | | | | | | | | | | |
| 50° - 64° | 1 | | | | | 1 | 1 | | 1 | | 1 | 1 |
| 65° - 79° | | | | | | | | | | | | |
| 80° - 95° | | | | | | | | | | | | |
| Totals | 7 | 5 | 1 | 3 | | 2 | 2 | 1 | 1 | | 6 | 7 |

the side or bottom of the cut and scratch the flint as it moves past (see pl. 28).  It is interesting to note that these ½Moon breakages improve the efficiency of the tool, rather than detract from it.  The resulting striations and abrasion tracks run roughly parallel to the working edge.

In conclusion, the distinguishing features of microwear on wood saws are:  wood polish on both edge aspects; striations and other indications of direction running roughly parallel to the working edge; ½Moon breakages on low-angled or thin edges; edge damage occurring on both aspects of the working edge.

*Scraping* (see table 3).  Depending on the angle at which the implement is held relative to the wood surface during use, the polish will be found primarily on the aspect in contact (that is, the leading aspect during movement), the opposite aspect, or, most commonly, both.  When the polish appears on the opposite aspect, it is confined to the ridges between the utilization damage scars or the retouch scars (if any) and the very edge of that aspect.  If the implement's leading aspect is held at close to 90° to the wood surface during use, then the polish is formed mainly on the opposite aspect; if it is canted at an angle of less than approximately 60°, then the polish will form primarily on the leading or contact aspect (see fig. 6).  There are occasions when the polish will not develop because the friction-affected area is constantly being carried away by utilization damage.  This only occurs if the edge used is thin, and, therefore, more subject to utilization damage, and only used a short time.  These thin edges, as the experiments make clear, are not very efficient tools for scraping, so it is unlikely that our ancestors would have used them very commonly.  Striations, while less common, follow the same pattern as the polish and are oriented at right angles to the edge.

The utilization damage is created primarily on the opposite aspect.  Table 3 shows that *SD* scars are a common occurrence, but this is more an effect of the thin edge angles used than this particular use.  On steep angles, the damage scars become shallower and often stepped.

The common features of microwear on wood scrapers, then, are: wood polish usually on both aspects of the working edge; striations and indications of direction disposed at roughly right angles to the edge; utilization damage occurring primarily on one aspect; *SD* damage scars on the opposite aspect of thin working edges.

*Chopping and Adzing* (see table 4).  The experiments showed that when one is chopping wood with a hand-held stone implement, it is most efficacious to strike the wood surface at a slight angle, thus bringing one edge aspect into greater contact with the wood.  In chopping, one alternates aspects, while in adzing, the same aspect is in contact with every blow (see fig. 3g).  This is why the wood polish occurs primarily on one aspect of the edge of adzes.  The wood polish which does form is usually very weakly developed, probably because the friction created during chopping is not as great as that created by other methods of use, like whittling or grating.

The striations which do occur often are found at some distance from the edge, unlike other methods of use, where the striations occur at the edge or leading from the edge.  They are oriented between 75° - 90° to the edge.

The significant feature of the edge damage is that the large scar types (*LD*, *LS*, *L Step*) are the most common.  Again, we find a few instances of ½Moon scars (on thin, unretouched edges) because the edge can become embedded in the wood and, when it is freed or moved, ½Moon breakages occur.

*Table 3*
*Scraping Wood*

A. Edge Aspect and Wear Trace Occurrence

| | Polish | Striae | LD | SD | MicroD | LS | SS | L Step | S Step | Micro-Step | ½Moon |
|---|---|---|---|---|---|---|---|---|---|---|---|
| Leading or Contact Aspect | 2 | 1 | | | | 1 | 1 | | | | |
| Both Aspects | 8 | 3 | | | | 1 | 2 | | | | |
| Opposite Aspect | 2 | 1 | 1 | 9 | | 1 | 1 | 1 | 2 | 2 | 2 |

N=14

B. Edge Angle and Wear Trace Occurrence

| | Polish | Striae | LD | SD | MicroD | LS | SS | L Step | S Step | Micro-Step | ½Moon | N |
|---|---|---|---|---|---|---|---|---|---|---|---|---|
| <35° | 4 | 2 | 1 | 5 | | 2 | 1 | 1 | | | 2 | 5 |
| 35° - 49° | 2 | 1 | | 3 | | 1 | 1 | 1 | | | | 3 |
| 50° - 64° | 2 | 1 | | 1 | | 1 | 1 | | | | | 2 |
| 65° - 79° | 1 | | | | | 1 | | | 1 | 1 | | 1 |
| 80° - 95° | 3 | 1 | | | | | | | | 1 | | 3 |
| Totals | 12 | 5 | 1 | 9 | | 3 | 4 | 2 | 2 | 2 | 2 | 14 |

*Table 4*
*Chopping/Adzing Wood*

A. Edge Aspect and Wear Trace Occurrence

| | Polish | Striae | LD | SD | MicroD | LS | SS | L Step | S Step | Micro-Step | ½Moon |
|---|---|---|---|---|---|---|---|---|---|---|---|
| Leading or Contact Aspect | 5 | | 1 | 1 | | 1 | 1 | 1 | 1 | | |
| Both Aspects | 2 | 2 | | | | | | | 1 | | 3 |
| Opposite Aspect | | | 1 | 1 | | 2 | 1 | 1 | 1 | | |

N=8

B. Edge Angle and Wear Trace Occurrence

| | Polish | Striae | LD | SD | MicroD | LS | SS | L Step | S Step | Micro-Step | ½Moon | N |
|---|---|---|---|---|---|---|---|---|---|---|---|---|
| <35° | | | | | | | | | | | | |
| 35° - 49° | 2 | 1 | 2 | 1 | | 2 | 1 | 1 | | | 3 | 3 |
| 50° - 64° | 2 | | | 1 | | 1 | | 1 | 2 | | | 2 |
| 65° - 79° | 2 | 2 | | | | | | | 1 | | | 2 |
| 80° - 95° | 1 | | | | | | 1 | | | | | 1 |
| Totals | 7 | 3 | 2 | 2 | | 3 | 2 | 2 | 3 | | 3 | 8 |

The characteristics of microwear on wood choppers and adzes are: a faint wood polish on both edge aspects of choppers, but on predominantly one aspect of adzes; striations oriented at roughly right angles to the edge and sometimes found several millimeters from the working edge; when utilization damage is present, it is commonly of the larger types, with ½Moon breakages common on thinner edges.

*Wedging* (see table 5). When considering the damage inflicted on flint pieces used as wedges, one must observe not only the edge which has been in contact with the wood (or bone, and so on), but also the part of the implement which takes the battering. All wedges, whether driven with a hammerstone or a soft-hammer, will show a battered edge where the driving blows fell. If the hammered section is flat (like a platform), the damage scars will occur on either edge of the platform, with numerous incipient cones on the surface itself. If the hammered area is an edge, the damage flakes will be larger and more invasive. Often these flake scars will be primarily on one aspect, usually the flatter or "ventral" aspect; figure 17 shows how this occurs. The aspect which has a high point closest to the hammered edge (for example, a dorsal ridge, in the case of a flake) will sustain the least damage. It will, in fact, serve as a platform for the removal of the flat flakes on the ventral surface. As hammering continues, the removal of flakes from the ventral surface steepens the angle until flakes begin to be removed from the dorsal surface. Usually the resultant hammering damage is distributed asymmetrically, forming a classic *outil écaillé* edge (see fig. 12). If a hard-hammer is used for driving, the edge is subject to crushing, whereas this crushing is absent on pieces driven in with a soft-hammer.

On the working edge, the wood polish forms very slowly. It usually occurs on the inner lips of the utilization damage scars and on the ridges between utilization scars. This polish forms on both aspects, if it forms at all. These patches of polish are usually accompanied by short striations running at right angles to the edge, either in the polish or close to it.

*Table 5*
*Wedging Wood*

A. Edge Aspect and Wear Trace Occurrence

| | Polish | Striae | LD | SD | MicroD | LS | SS | L Step | S Step | Micro-Step | ½Moon |
|---|---|---|---|---|---|---|---|---|---|---|---|
| Dorsal Aspect (only) | | | | 1 | | | 1 | | | | |
| Both Aspects | 2 | 2 | | | | 1 | | 1 | | | 3 |
| Bulbar Aspect (only) | | 1 | | | | 1 | 1 | | 1 | | |

N=3

B. Edge Angle and Wear Trace Occurrence (Contact Edge)

| | Polish | Striae | LD | SD | MicroD | LS | SS | L Step | S Step | Micro-Step | ½Moon | N |
|---|---|---|---|---|---|---|---|---|---|---|---|---|
| <35° | 1 | 2 | | 1 | | 1 | 1 | 1 | 1 | | 2 | 2 |
| 35° - 49° | 1 | 1 | | | | 1 | 1 | | | | 1 | 1 |
| 50° - 64° | | | | | | | | | | | | |
| 65° - 79° | | | | | | | | | | | | |
| 80° - 95° | | | | | | | | | | | | |
| Totals | 2 | 3 | | 1 | | 2 | 2 | 1 | 1 | | 3 | 3 |

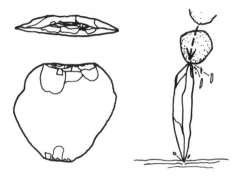

Figure 17.  Utilization damage on wedges and its formation.

The nature and quantity of edge damage on the working edge depends, as always, on the edge angle, but ½Moon scars are common, and on the ventral or bulbar surface, large, shallow flakes can be taken off.  If the implement is deeply embedded in the wood, long "fluting" flakes can be removed, with their point of origin on the working edge.  Ranere (1975: 191) noted this feature in his experiments wedging wood with chalcedony implements.  Generally the damage scars are shallow, with a tendency to terminate in a "step."

The characteristics of microwear on wood wedges, then, are: wood polish occurring on high points on both aspects of the working edge; striations running at right or high angles to the working edge; shallow scalar and stepped utilization damage of various sizes, origi- nating on the working edge; opposite the working edge, an area of battering signaled either by a multitude of flake scars or a number of incipient cones of percussion if the hammered area is a platform rather than an edge, or both.

*Boring* (see table 6).  The wood polish tends to form on both aspects but is more developed on the ridges and high points of the dorsal aspect and the lateral edges.  Striations are rare, but the polished areas usually show directional features at right angles to the axis of the implement.

*Table 6*
*Boring Wood*

Edge Aspect and Wear Trace Occurrence

|  | Polish | Striae | LD | SD | MicroD | LS | SS | L Step | S Step | Micro-Step | ½Moon |
|---|---|---|---|---|---|---|---|---|---|---|---|
| Dorsal Aspect (only) | 1 | 1 | | | | | | | | | |
| Both Aspects | 2 | | | | | | | | | 1 | |
| Bulbar Aspect (only) | | | | | | | 3 | | | 2 | |
| | | | | | | | | | | | N=4 |

The utilization damage type found usually comprises *SS* and *MicroStep* scars.  The small, shallow scars occur on the bulbar aspect.  The *MicroStep* scars are found on the bulbar as- pect as well, but this is because the dorsal aspects of the bit edges are retouched, which means that the utilization damage scars cannot be distinguished from the retouch scars.

When the movement during use is primarily unidirectional, that is, the working pressure is applied only when the implement is rotated in one direction, then stepped damage will occur on only one lateral edge of the bulbar aspect and one lateral edge of the dorsal (if the utilization damage can be isolated) (fig. 18).

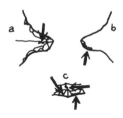

Figure 18.  Utilization damage formation on unidirectional borers.  (a) dorsal view; (b) bulbar view; (c) end-on view.

The characteristics of microwear on wood borers are: wood polish on high points on both aspects of the bit; the indications of direction running at right angles to the bit axis; small, shallow scars on the bulbar surface of the bit and *MicroStep* scars on the lateral edges of the bit.

*Graving*.  Three experiments were conducted using burin bits to grave wood.  It was found, in the course of these experiments, that it was best to begin a groove by pushing the implements so that their bit axes were at a low angle to the surface of the worked material (fig. 3e).  Once the groove was begun, the implements were shifted to an upright position and moved with their bit axes held at approximately a right angle to the surface of the wood (fig. 3d).  After use, wood polish was found on all the bit edges of all three implements.  The polish was usually best developed on the contact or leading bit aspect of the bit edge.  There were no striations found on any of the three implements.  A few *MicroStep* scars were found on the opposite bit aspect of the bit edge on two of the pieces.

## Variations with Edge Angles

Both wood polish and striations form independently of the particular edge-angle employed.  They are affected by the edge angle only insofar as if the edge angle is less suitable for a particular task (a high angle for sawing, for example), then less work will be done, less friction generated, and less polish and fewer striations will develop.

Which type of utilization damage scars are formed by any particular use will be especially dependent on the edge angle.  A glance through tables 1-6 will show that certain types of damage, like ½*Moon* breakages and *SD* scars, are most likely to be formed on low-angled edges, whereas *S Step* and *MicroStep* are more likely to occur on steeper-angled edges.  It is also apparent that edge damage of any type is rare, whatever the use, if the edge angle is greater than 64°.

## Bone-Working Traces

### General Effects

The working of bone also produces a polish which may be distinguished from the microwear polishes formed while working other materials.  This bone polish forms much more slowly than wood polish, so that even after relatively lengthy use, it is seldom very extensively developed. However, bone polish was present on the majority of the experimental implements (32 out of 34) I used to work bone. This bone polish (after cleaning and chemical baths) appears bright, in sharp contrast to the unaltered surfaces of the flint. Its most distinctive feature is the presence of innumerable tiny pits in the polish surface (see pls. 29, 34). It does not have the smooth surface of wood polish and some antler polishes or sickle gloss. At magnifications of 100X and less, it will have a slightly grainy appearance, which is resolved into a micropitted texture at higher magnifications. These pits have diameters slightly smaller than one micron. The polish, while forming first on the high points of the microtopography, does not spread as the working continues, as it does in the case of woodworking. Instead, the polish on the high points becomes more intense and more distinctive. For this reason, bone polish is seldom very extensive but is localized at a few points along the working edge.

One curious phenomenon, which was noted in the study of bone-working implements, may shed some light on the formation of bone polish and particularly on the cause of its distinctive pitting. Early in the experimental study, I failed to wash some of the implements used on bone in warm HCl. In those circumstances, bone polish appeared to have an irregular but smooth appearance and a pronounced greasy luster. These same pieces were recleaned using the full cleaning procedure, including HCl, some months later and reexamined. Comparisons with earlier photomicrographs showed that the greasiness of the luster was diminished, especially where the polish was most intense, and the micropitting had appeared (Cf. pls. 29, 31.) This led to a series of experiments in which the piece was examined and photographed after an initial cleaning employing all the procedures outlined in chapter 2 except the warm HCl bath. These implements were then immersed in hot HCl and reexamined (see pls. 32, 33). The results confirmed that the pitting appeared after the HCl and that the greasiness of the polish became much less pronounced. And, too, the area apparently covered by the polish in the pre-HCl examinations was substantially reduced after the application of HCl. It is quite clear that some material, which must be of an inorganic nature, since it survives the warm NaOH bath, is deposited on the working edges and is included in the microwear polish. This material is destroyed by HCl, and its removal leaves the characteristic pitted bone polish. The obvious candidate is bone apatite, which is destroyed by HCl. Apatite is present in bone in the form of very minute needlelike crystals with a hexagonal cross-section which run alongside the organic collagen fibers in fresh bone. This mineral may be spread on the working surface of the flint, and broken apatite crystals may be incorporated in the polish. When HCl is applied, the apatite dissolves, leaving only the altered flint surface and, possibly, small pits where the broken sections of apatite crystals had been.

Striations were more common on bone-working than on woodworking implements. Striations and/or abrasion tracks were present on 24 of the 34 experimental edges, and they were usually of the deep, narrow type. Since the working of bone tends to produce more extensive edge damage than the working of wood in activities like sawing, flint-on-flint abrasion is more common. This fact may produce some difficulties when attempting to distinguish wood sawing, let us say, from bone sawing, since large areas of flint-on-flint abrasion are usually very bright and, therefore, superficially similar to wood polish. Since bone polish forms so slowly and seldom covers much area, the abrasion tracks are likely to be the most striking microwear feature. But these abrasion tracks are deeply scored, with multiple parallel tracks, and lack the gentle undulations of wood polish; also, they are linear features and do not cover areas along the edge, in contradistinction to wood polish.

While the utilization damage which occurred on bone-working implements was generally more intense and included generally larger damage scar types, it was not possible to isolate any scar type of scar pattern which could be correlated with bone-working per se. Some recognizable form of utilization damage did occur on 32 of the 34 experimental edges.

## Variations Related to the Type of Bone Worked

Typical bone polish was formed, regardless of whether the bone worked was from pig, sheep, or cow. It appears, though, that the greasy luster of the bone polish is more pronounced on edges which were used for working cooked bone. The cooked bones I worked with were roasted pork bones and were saturated with grease, which would have served as a lubricant and might, therefore, have caused a smoother polish surface to be produced. The working of cooked, as opposed to fresh, bone had not affected the micropitting of the polish surface. The working of dried bone resulted in no polish formation and extensive, severe utilization damage. This experiment merely demonstrated that the working of dry bone, using only flint implements, is not a practical proposition, though fresh, uncooked bone can be worked easily enough. However, it seems that the working of bone that is several months old but that has not been allowed to weather or dry will produce a rough but unpitted polish (see pl. 64). One can argue, nevertheless, that bone in this condition is unlikely to have been worked in the earlier stages of the Paleolithic.

## Variations with Method of Use

*Whittling and Planing.* Only one experiment was conducted which involved the working of bone by planing. The edge angle employed was 45° and the edge was straight. Bone polish was produced on the edge aspect in contact during use (in this case, the bulbar aspect) and a number of short striations and abrasion tracks running roughly at right angles to the edge. The utilization damage was similar to that on analogous edges used for whittling and planing wood. The utilization damage on the dorsal aspect (the aspect not in contact during use) consisted of *SD* and *MicroStep* scars, while the damage on the bulbar aspect consisted of a few isolated *SS* and *S Step* scars. Planing bone, which is a much more resistant material than wood, was demonstrated by this experiment to be such a clumsy and inefficient method of shaping or reducing it, and other methods proved so much more productive (especially scraping), that no further planing experiments were conducted.

*Sawing* (see table 7). As with wood sawing, the polish (in this case, typical bone polish) forms on both aspects of the working edge, as do the striations and abrasion tracks where they occur.

The utilization damage patterns show some contrasts with those on edges used for wood saws. The most striking is the comparative rarity of ½Moon breakages. This may be a function of the edge angles employed, since most of the wood saws had edge angles of less than 35°, while most bone saws possessed edge angles in the range of 35° to 49° (see tables 2B, 7B). And it is clear that ½Moon breakages occur more commonly on very acute edge angles (see table 7B). One difference between the utilization damage patterns of wood and bone saws, not related to the difference in edge angles employed, is the greater frequency of occurrence of the larger scar types (*LD* and *LS*) and a greater frequency of edge damage overall. Since the higher edge angles employed in the bone-sawing experiments are more resistant to damage, this difference must be the result of the greater resistance offered

*Table 7*
*Sawing Bone*

A. Edge Aspect and Wear Trace Occurrence

|  | Polish | Striae | LD | SD | MicroD | LS | SS | L Step | S Step | Micro-Step | ½Moon |
|---|---|---|---|---|---|---|---|---|---|---|---|
| Dorsal Aspect (only) |  | 1 |  |  |  | 3 | 3 |  | 3 | 2 |  |
| Both Aspects | 9 | 6 | 4 | 2 |  |  | 1 |  |  |  | 2 |
| Bulbar Aspect (only) |  | 1 |  | 2 | 2 |  |  |  | 2 | 2 |  |

N=9

B. Edge Angle and Wear Trace Occurrence

|  | Polish | Striae | LD | SD | MicroD | LS | SS | L Step | S Step | Micro-Step | ½Moon | N |
|---|---|---|---|---|---|---|---|---|---|---|---|---|
| <35 | 1 | 1 | 1 |  |  | 1 |  |  | 1 | 1 |  | 1 |
| 35° - 49° | 5 | 3 | 2 | 4 |  | 2 | 2 |  | 2 | 1 | 2 | 5 |
| 50° - 64° | 3 | 3 | 2 |  |  | 2 | 2 |  | 2 | 2 |  | 3 |
| 65° - 79° |  |  |  |  |  |  |  |  |  |  |  |  |
| 80° - 95° |  |  |  |  |  |  |  |  |  |  |  |  |
| Totals | 9 | 7 | 5 | 4 |  | 5 | 4 |  | 5 | 4 | 2 | 9 |

to a working edge by bone. *MicroStep* damage occurs on bone saws but not on wood saws, but this may also be a function of the difference in edge angles.

The distinguishing features of microwear on bone saws are: bone polish on both aspects; striations, abrasion tracks, and other indications of direction running roughly parallel to the working edge; edge damage on both aspects of the working edge; edge damage on both aspects of the working edge; occasional areas of microstepping usually confined to one edge.

*Scraping* (see table 8). Unlike the wood scrapers, the polish on bone scrapers occurs primarily on the leading, or contact, aspect of the working edge and very seldom on both aspects. However, striations and utilization damage occur on the opposite aspect more commonly on bone scrapers. The confinement of the polish to the leading, or contact, aspect is best explained by the tendency for bone polish to stay localized on microtopographic elevations in substantial contact with the worked material.

As with wood scrapers, the utilization damage occurs most commonly on the opposite aspect of the working edge but, as noted above, damage can occur on the contact aspect as well. The frequency with which certain types of edge damage are found shows some differences from wood scraping. *LS*, *L Step*, *S Step* are much more common on bone scrapers. This cannot be attributed to differences in edge angles since, except for more acute-edged (<35°) wood scrapers, their respective edge-angle distributions are quite similar (see tables 3B, 8B), and the differences occur principally on the higher edge angles (greater than 35°).

The striations which occur on bone scrapers are usually of the deep, narrow type and are generally very short. Short abrasion tracks are also quite common. They are generally oriented at right angles to the edge.

The characteristic features of microwear on bone scrapers, then, are: bone polish on on the leading, or contact, aspect of the working edge; striations and other indications of direction disposed at right angles to the edge; relatively intense utilization damage on the opposite or both aspects of the working edge; frequent occurrences of *LS*, *S Step*, and *MicroStep* damage scars.

*Chopping and Adzing* (see table 9). The chopping of bone turned out to be very difficult even with a heavy flint chopper. Only three bone-chopping experiments were performed. One of these involved chopping dried bone, which caused extensive damage to the edge, while very little damage was done to the bone. Chopping dried bone produced neither polish nor striations.

*Table 8*

*Scraping Bone*

A. Edge Aspect and Wear Trace Occurrence

| | Polish | Striae | LD | SD | MicroD | LS | SS | L Step | S Step | Micro-Step | ½Moon |
|---|---|---|---|---|---|---|---|---|---|---|---|
| Leading or Contact Aspect | 10 | 5 | | | | 1 | 1 | | | 1 | |
| Both Aspects | 1 | 1 | | | | 2 | 1 | | 2 | 2 | |
| Opposite Aspect | | 2 | 2 | 2 | | 2 | 2 | 4 | 3 | 3 | |

N=11

B. Edge Angle and Wear Trace Occurrence

| | Polish | Striae | LD | SD | MicroD | LS | SS | L Step | S Step | Micro-Step | ½Moon | N |
|---|---|---|---|---|---|---|---|---|---|---|---|---|
| <35° | 1 | 1 | | 1 | | | | | | | | 1 |
| 35° - 49° | 4 | 3 | 1 | 1 | | 3 | 2 | 1 | 2 | 3 | | 4 |
| 50° - 64° | 2 | | 1 | 1 | | 1 | 2 | 1 | 1 | | | 2 |
| 65° - 79° | 2 | 2 | | | | 1 | | 1 | 1 | 2 | | 2 |
| 80° - 95° | 2 | 2 | | | | | | 1 | 1 | 1 | | 2 |
| Totals | 11 | 8 | 2 | 3 | | 5 | 4 | 4 | 5 | 6 | | 11 |

The other two bone choppers were used on cooked and fresh bone, respectively. The cooked-bone chopper had an edge angle of approximately 45° and was used in such a manner that the edge contacted the bone surface at approximately a right angle. The result was patches of bone polish and striae on the bulbar aspect and a few striae and a faint polish on the dorsal aspect. The utilization damage consisted of continuous *LD*, *LS*, and *S Step* damage on the bulbar aspect, with a few areas of *LS*, *SS*, and *S Step* damage on the dorsal aspect. The fresh-bone chopper had an edge angle of 68° and was used in exactly the same manner as the cooked-bone chopper. On this steeper-angled edge, the polish formed on both aspects on a few scattered high points. The edge consisted of *Step* scars on the dorsal aspect and *MicroStep* scars on the ventral aspect. No striae were found.

The chopping of bone itself, as opposed to the use of choppers for breaking joints and for other heavy butchering tasks, is likely to have been a relatively uncommon activity in the Paleolithic. If it is necessary to crack and crush a bone, any heavy stone will serve, and a prepared edge is unnecessary. If one wishes to split a bone, the use of wedges provides the most efficient means. If bone choppers are present in an archeological

*Table 9*
*Chopping Bone*

A.  Edge Aspect and Wear Trace Occurrence

|  | Polish | Striae | LD | SD | MicroD | LS | SS | L Step | S Step | Micro-Step | ½Moon |
|---|---|---|---|---|---|---|---|---|---|---|---|
| Dorsal Aspect (only) |  |  |  |  |  | 1 |  |  | 1 |  |  |
| Both Aspects | 2 | 1 | 1 | 1 | 1 |  |  | 1 | 2 |  |  |
| Bulbar Aspect (only) |  | 1 |  |  |  |  |  |  |  | 1 |  |

N=3

B.  Edge Angle and Wear Trace Occurrence

|  | Polish | Striae | LD | SD | MicroD | LS | SS | L Step | S Step | Micro-Step | ½Moon | N |
|---|---|---|---|---|---|---|---|---|---|---|---|---|
| <35° |  |  |  |  |  |  |  |  |  |  |  |  |
| 35° - 49° | 1 | 1 |  |  |  | 1 | 1 |  | 1 |  |  | 1 |
| 50° - 64° |  |  |  |  |  |  |  |  |  |  |  |  |
| 65° - 79° | 1 |  | 1 | 1 |  |  |  | 1 | 2 | 1 |  | 2 |
| 80° - 95° |  |  |  |  |  |  |  |  |  |  |  |  |
| Totals | 2 | 1 | 1 | 1 |  | 1 | 1 | 1 | 3 | 1 |  | 3 |

collection, however, the microwear traces on them should be characterized by: bone polish on both aspects of the working edge; striations running roughly at right angles to the working edge; on low-angled edges, probable dominance of the large, edge-damage types.

*Wedging* (see table 10).  The kinds of severe damage that is inflicted on wedges by hammering has been discussed above in the section on wood wedges.

Bone polish generally forms on both aspects of the working edge.  Striations and abrasion tracks are quite common but are seldom found at any distance from the edge, unlike the striations on wood wedges.  These striations are not always oriented at right angles to the edge but can be found at even low angles to the edge.  This is probably because the wedge in a bone crack is less tightly gripped than in a wood crack and, thus, has a greater tendency to skew away from the perpendicular with slightly misdirected blows.

The utilization damage found on bone wedges is generally similar to that found on wood wedges.  It tends to be more intensive and more likely to be dominated by larger damage scars.  ½Moon breakages are common, as are LS scars.  The long, "fluting" flakes that can be found on wood wedges are not to be seen on bone wedges; this is presumably because the bone wedge is seldom inserted as deeply into the worked material as the former.

The characteristics of microwear on bone wedges are: bone polish on both aspects of the working edge; ½Moon breakages, LS, and stepped scars on both edge aspects; striations running at various angles but tending toward right angles to the edge; an area of battering opposite the working edge, as described for wood wedges.

*Boring* (see table 11).  Two bone-boring experiments were performed.  On one of these, neither bone polish nor striations were formed.  This is probably accounted for by the fact that considerable utilization damage was inflicted on the bit, which would have carried away any polish or striations that may have formed.  This utilization damage consisted

*Table 10*

*Wedging Bone*

A.  Edge Aspect and Wear Trace Occurrence

| | Polish | Striae | LD | SD | MicroD | LS | SS | L Step | S Step | Micro-Step | ½Moon |
|---|---|---|---|---|---|---|---|---|---|---|---|
| Dorsal Aspect (only) | 1 | | | | | | 1 | 2 | | 1 | |
| Both Aspects | 5 | 3 | 1 | | 1 | | 1 | 1 | | | 5 |
| Bulbar Aspect (only) | | 1 | | 1 | 2 | | | | | | |

N=6

B.  Edge Angle and Wear Trace Occurrence

| | Polish | Striae | LD | SD | MicroD | LS | SS | L Step | S Step | Micro-Step | ½Moon | N |
|---|---|---|---|---|---|---|---|---|---|---|---|---|
| <35 | 1 | | | | | | | | | | 1 | 1 |
| 35° - 49° | 4 | 3 | 1 | 1 | 3 | | 2 | 3 | | | 3 | 4 |
| 50° - 64° | 1 | 1 | | | | | | | | 1 | 1 | 1 |
| 65° - 79° | | | | | | | | | | | | |
| 80° - 95° | | | | | | | | | | | | |
| Totals | 6 | 4 | 1 | 1 | 3 | | 2 | 3 | | 1 | 5 | 6 |

*Table 11*

*Boring Bone*

Edge Aspect and Wear Trace Occurrence

| | Polish | Striae | LD | SD | MicroD | LS | SS | L Step | S Step | Micro-Step | ½Moon |
|---|---|---|---|---|---|---|---|---|---|---|---|
| Dorsal Aspect (only) | | | | | | | | | 1 | | |
| Both Aspects | 1 | 1 | | | | | | | | | |
| Bulbar Aspect (only) | | | | | | | 2 | | | 2 | |

N=2

of *SS* and *MicroStep* scars on the bulbar surface of the bit and a few *S Step* scars that could only be distinguished from the retouch scars because of a pre-use microscopic examination; it is doubtful whether such scars could be distinguished from the retouch on archeological specimens.  On the other borer, bone polish formed on isolated high points on the bit.  Since the bit of this implement was trihedral, the polish was found principally on the three ridges.  A few striations and abrasion tracks oriented at right angles to the bit axis were found as well.  No utilization damage could be isolated on the retouched portions of the bit, but on an unretouched portion on the bulbar aspect, one *SS* scar could be observed.  By comparing table 11 with table 6, we can see that the total wear pattern of the bone borers is quite similar to that of wood borers, excepting, of course, the fact that the polish on the bone borers is bone polish.

The distinctive features of microwear on bone borers appear from this rather limited amount of experiment to be: bone polish (if it forms) on the high points of the bit; indications of direction running at right angles to the bit axis; *SS* and *MicroStep* scars on the bit edges.

*Graving.* Four experiments in bone graving were carried out as part of the present experimental program, even though there is very little evidence (in the form of engraved bones) of such an activity from the Lower Paleolithic. Two of the bits employed were formed by burin scars and, therefore, were "chisel-ended," and the other two bits were simply sharp-edged cusps. All four of the implements showed typical bone polish on their bits after use, as well as striations running at high angles to their bit axes. On the burin bits, the polish and striations were most developed on the bit edges, while on the cusp bits, the microwear was best developed on the dorsal and ventral aspects of the cusp. On the burin bits, the utilization damage, which consisted of *SD* and *MicroStep* scars, occurred primarily on the opposite bit aspect. On the cusp bits, the utilization damage, again *SD* and *Micro-Step* scars, occurred on both the dorsal and bulbar aspects of the cusp edge.

## Variations with Edge Angle

As with woodworking, the angle of the edge does not affect the appearance of the microwear polish, nor does it affect the appearance of striations.

Reference to tables 1 to 6 indicates that, despite some difference in the proportions of the utilization-damage scar types occurring on bone- and woodworking edges, certain types are again more likely to be found on certain edge angles. *SD* scars are more likely to occur on lower-angled edges, while *LD*, *LS*, and *SS* scars occur on moderate edge angles. Although *Step* scars of all sizes are more common on bone-working tools, as in the case of woodworking, these scars are proportionately more common on high-angled edges.

## Hide-Working Traces

### General Effects

The working of hide of various kinds does not produce a single type of polish. The polishes caused by hide working range from the relatively bright, greasy polish that is the result of working fresh, wet hide to the dull, pitted, matt polish which results when working leather or dry hide. These differences are mainly attributable to the differential presence of various natural or applied lubricants.

The working of wet, fresh hide results in a slow-forming greasy polish which, as one might expect, is very similar to meat polish. This polish, while bright, lacks the smoothness of wood polish, and, while rough and "bumpy," lacks the deep micropitting of bone polish (pls. 36, 41). As the hide becomes drier (over a period of days) after the initial fleshing and scraping, it contains fewer lubricants. The polish produced by the working of this drier hide is more intense, and the matt texture of its surface is more pronounced. Only when the hide is fully dry or tanned does the microwear polish produced become dull, with an intensely matt texture (pl. 37).

One interesting feature of the dry-hide/leather polish is the occasional presence of small, circular pits associated with it. These are not simply depressions in the microtopography that have been unaffected by the polish, as they are invariably regular in outline, and, indeed, they often occur on elevations in the microtopography. These pits are usually around 5 microns in diameter but can be smaller. Their depth is hard to estimate, but, judging from their appearance in slightly oblique light, they are roughly hemispherical in shape. There are no clues which would conclusively establish their cause, but one cannot help but notice their resemblance, albeit on a very small scale, to "potlid" fractures found on flint that has been subject to "thermal" stress. Purdy (1975: 136) claims that "Potlids always occurred during the heating process, never during the cooling process . . . ." The frictional heat developed during the working of dry hide in the near absence of lubricants may be intense enough and develop rapidly enough to cause microscopic potlid fractures, the spalls of which are plucked out by the friction of the hide (when they may cause striations). These "micropotlids," if that is what they are, have not been found associated with any other type of polish.

A polish with an appearance which is generally similar to dry-hide/leather polish, but also shows some features of the fresh-hide polishes, is formed when fat or grease have been rubbed into a dry hide before working. It is often duller than dry-hide polish, and it forms almost as quickly. But it lacks the coarse and intensely matt texture of dry-hide polish and has a slightly greasy luster (Plate 38). In general, it is more similar to the dry-hide than the fresh-hide polishes.

Two microwear features link all the hide polishes: (1) relatively severe attrition (that is, removal of flint material from the edge by a means other than breakage) of the edge, which results in a markedly rounded edge; (2) diffuse, shallow linear features running in the direction of use. The attrition of the edge is more severe in those situations where the level of lubricants is low, even when the edge has been used for slicing rather than scraping (see pl. 39). The linear features, which hardly deserve the title "striation," can be seen clearly running parallel to the edge in plate 39, and less clearly to the right of the sharp, narrow striae in plate 37, running at right angles to the edge. As plate 37 indicates, these features occur independently of true striations. The hide polishes, in general, tend to reach into the flake scars along the edge and to round and smooth their sharp boundaries (well illustrated by pls. 39, 40). Hide polish of some type occurred on all but two of the sixteen experimental edges, and the exceptions were an implement used for de-hairing a hide, where the contact between the hide and the edge was very limited, and a piercer, the tip of which kept breaking away.

The striations which occurred on hide-working edges were basically of two types: (1) narrow, deep striations of varying lengths and sizes which appeared sharp and well-defined (pl. 37), and (2) relatively broad, shallow striations which were ill-defined and sometimes difficult to observe, except with slightly oblique lighting. These latter occurred most commonly on the rounded edges themselves, rather than on the aspects on either side of the edge. They may be related in some way to the diffuse linear features mentioned above. Neither the narrow nor the broad striations occurred on every experimental hide-working edge.

There is not much to say about the utilization damage caused by hide-working, except to note that it is usually very minute. *MicroD* and *MicroStep* scars are the predominant types found. Of course, on retouched aspects of working edges, these minute damage scars cannot be distinguished from the small components of the retouch scar pattern.

## Variations Related to Hide Type

The variations in the appearance of hide polish which are induced by varying degrees of hide dryness have already been discussed above. It only remains to be said that no consistent variation in the polishes could be associated with use on the hides of particular animals.

## Variations with Method of Use

There are not many ways in which one can use flint edges on hide, compared with other materials. Chopping and wedging, for example, are not likely hide-working activities. And fleshing and de-hairing are not equivalent to whittling or planing. The primary hide-working activity is, of course, scraping, but piercing (or, more accurately, boring) and fleshing are other activities which may be accomplished with flint tools.

*Scraping* (see table 12). Depending on the angle of attack at which the implement is held during use, the polish will be more extensive on one aspect of the edge than the other. If the implement, with a steeply retouched edge, is held at a right angle to the worked surface, then the microwear traces will occur mainly on the unretouched (usually bulbar) edge aspect.

The striations and other linear microwear features will be oriented at approximately right angles to the edge. As use continues and the edge becomes rounded, striations (like the polish itself) will curve around the edge.

*Table 12*
*Scraping Hide*

A. Edge Aspect and Wear Trace Occurrence

| | Polish | Striae | LD | SD | MicroD | LS | SS | L Step | S Step | Micro-Step | ½Moon |
|---|---|---|---|---|---|---|---|---|---|---|---|
| Leading or Contact Aspect | 1 | | | 1 | | | | | | 1 | |
| Both Aspects | 10 | 6 | | | | | | | | 2 | |
| Opposite Aspect | | | | | 3 | | 1 | | | 3 | |

N=11

B. Edge Angle and Wear Trace Occurrence

| | Polish | Striae | LD | SD | MicroD | LS | SS | L Step | S Step | Micro-Step | ½Moon | N |
|---|---|---|---|---|---|---|---|---|---|---|---|---|
| <35° | | | | | | | | | | | | |
| 35° - 49° | 3 | 1 | | 1 | 3 | | | | | 2 | | 3 |
| 50° - 64° | 1 | | | | | | | | | 1 | | 1 |
| 65° - 79° | 4 | 3 | | | | | | | | 2 | | 4 |
| 80° - 95° | 3 | 2 | | | | | 1 | | | 1 | | 3 |
| Totals | 11 | 6 | | 1 | 3 | | 1 | | | 6 | | 11 |

The utilization damage consists, as we noted for all hide-working edges, primarily of *MicroD* and *MicroStep* scars, which are usually considerably eroded by the attrition associated with hide polish. They occur on both aspects of the working edge but tend to be more numerous on the aspect opposite the direction of movement. Needless to say, these scars are easiest to pick out on unretouched surfaces or aspects. On retouched aspects, they cannot be distinguished from the smallest scar elements of the retouch pattern.

*Fleshing*. Fleshing is the removal of flesh and fat from the inner surface of the hide with a sharp edge, by a combination of slicing and shaving motions (as opposed to the "grating" motion of hide scraping). One experiment was conducted involving this activity. The polish left by fleshing was, as one might expect, very similar to meat polish. It was bright and rough, with a pronounced greasy luster. The linear features characteristic of hide polish were present and ran parallel with the edge (see pl. 42). The polish had formed on both aspects of the edge but only within 200 microns of the edge. It would be very difficult to distinguish, on archeological specimens, a meat knife from a fleshing knife. The only aid in making such a distinction would perhaps be the greater extent of the polish on both aspects of the edge of a well-used meat knife.

There were no striations associated with the polish, only the diffuse linear features mentioned above.

The utilization damage consisted of scattered *MicroStep* scars on both edge aspects.

*Slicing.* One experimental implement was used for slicing leather. Even though the leather was held against a flat wooden surface, no wood polish was formed, only a typical dry-hide polish on both edge aspects (pl. 39).

The striations and other indications of direction ran parallel to the edge. The diffuse linear features were particularly pronounced, especially at the very edge.

The microwear pattern extended to about 1 mm from the edge.

The utilization damage was made up of eroded *MicroDeep* and *MicroStep* scars on both aspects, with a single *LS* scar on the dorsal aspect.

*Piercing (Boring).* Although one might not immediately think that making small-diameter holes in hide involves boring, the movement of the tool during the piercing of a hide is exactly the same as that of a wood or bone borer. A flint point sharp enough and thin enough to pierce the hide without any drilling motions, using just a straight push, is usually so brittle that it breaks very quickly. A flint point strengthened by fine retouch is less liable to breakage, but usually must be inserted with a drilling motion. Bone, antler, and even yew wood awls are much more suitable for the straight-push method of insertion.

Two experiments using flint implements for piercing dry hide were conducted. The first (exp. 37) was an attempt to use an unretouched trihedral bit for piercing using the straight-push method, but the tip broke off on successive tries and quickly rendered the implement unusable. No microwear was found on the tip that remained, nor could any fragments of the former tip large enough to be examined under the microscope be found. The second (exp. 19) involved the use of a retouched bit. Initially, the straight-push method was tried with this bit as well and proved very inefficient. But where a drilling method of insertion was adopted, the work progressed very quickly. The description of wear that follows is for this second experimental piece.

Although the material worked was leather, the polish was more similar to the greased-hide polishes than the dry-hide polishes, being brighter, with a slightly greasy luster. Why this should be is not clear. The polish was found on all the high portions of the bit. On the unretouched (bulbar) aspect of the bit, the polish was lightly developed over the whole surface, becoming more intense near the edges and the tip. On the retouched (dorsal) aspect, the polish was most intense on the ridges between the flake scars, but it could also be clearly seen, in a lightly developed state, in the scars themselves.

The polish could be seen as far as 7 mm from the tip, even though the leather was only 2 mm thick, maximum, and the tip of the bit only extended a millimeter or so out of the opposite side of the hide at the deepest penetration. The unaccounted-for 3-4 mm of polish was explained by the fact that the hide (which was not backed, but held in the left hand) depresses away from the bit and engulfs it to the depth of a few millimeters, thus bringing the proximal portions of the bit in contact with the hide.

There were only two striations--one on the bulbar and one on the dorsal aspect of the bit. Both were at high angles to the bit axis and were very narrow and short. The characteristic linear features of hide polishes were only sparsely represented, but some did occur on the lateral edge near the tip. These ran at approximately right angles to the bit axis.

No utilization damage was found on the bulbar aspect of the bit, and none could be isolated on the retouched dorsal aspect.

*De-hairing.* A single de-hairing experiment was conducted on a hare hide that had been left in damp condition for a week to loosen the hair. The implement was used with a two-handed grip, draw-knife fashion. Since the implement quite efficiently removed the hair (which was, however, not uniformly loosened), the period of use was very short. No microwear or utilization damage could be discerned on the edge after use.

## Variations with Edge Angles

If we refer to table 12, we can see that, for hide scraping, the angle of the edge does not affect the type of utilization damage present. *MicroStep* and *MicroD* are practically the only type of damage scars present. In experiments 17 (slicing) and 100 (fleshing), the damage also consists primarily of *MicroStep* scars.

The edge angle does not affect the appearance of the microwear polish or the striations.

## Meat-Cutting and Butchery Traces

## General Effects

The slicing of meat and the cutting activities associated with the butchering of animals (that is, cutting through joints, cutting tendons, but not chopping or sawing bone) leave a microwear polish which is similar to fresh-hide polish but is distinguishable from the polishes left by wood, bone, dry hide, and antler. This meat polish varies in brightness but, in most of the experiments described here, was relatively dull. Unlike the other microwear polishes, it showed little contrast with the unaltered areas of the flint (see pls. 43-48) in terms of brightness. Because of this low contrast, it does not show up on photographs very clearly. While meat polish cannot be very easily distinguished from the raw flint surface in terms of its relative brightness, it can be distinguished by its different surface texture and by its pronounced greasy luster. What little brightness meat polish does show may be accounted for by this greasy luster (best seen in pl. 46). This luster seems to be the result of a smoothing of the microtopography on a very small scale. The normally grainy texture of a raw flint surface is replaced by a slightly matt texture, which seems to preserve the very minute elevations and depressions of the raw surface (the linear distance between the top of one of these "elevations" to the bottom of an adjacent "depression" is near the limits of resolution of the microscope at 200X (approximately 700 nm), but the slight smoothing joins them into a semicontinuous surface. Flint is composed of very minute crystalline scales or platelets which are, in turn, built into the larger scales which give flint its grainy appearance to the naked eye and at magnifications of up to 200X. The slopes of the microtopography, therefore, are stepped or "terraced" at a very microscopic level. It may be that a soft, yielding material like meat affects the whole surface of the raw flint microtopography--unlike the other polishes, which tend to affect only the elevated portions of the microtopography--and, while it does not produce enough friction to remove or alter the larger platey structures, it may affect the exposed edges of the smaller "terraces" on their slopes. There is, however, no way to verify, with the equipment available, that this is what is taking place, and the foregoing suggestion is simply a model which helps to describe the appearance of meat polish.

Except when an implement has been used for cutting close to joints, very few striations are created. The striations which do occur are usually very minute. They are narrow (<1.5 microns); deep, relative to their width; and usually short (<20 microns). They are very difficult to distinguish even at 200X and can only be properly examined at 400-500X. In pl. 47, several of these striations may be seen running at low angles to the implement edge. Brose, in a series of experiments investigating microwear traces left by various butchering activities, found similar small striations visible "at 300X magnifications with a scanning electron microscope" (1975: 87).

The utilization damage on meat-cutting or butchering edges, when it occurs, usually consists of scattered *MicroStep* and *MicroD* scars which tend to occur primarily on the dorsal aspects.

## Variations with Worked Material

There were no significant variations in microwear traces that could be attributed to variation in the type of meat worked (beef, pork, and so on). It is my personal impression that the meat polish developed more quickly when the meat being cut was raw rather than cooked. If true, this is probably because cooking breaks down the meat structure, thus lowering its frictional resistance to the flint edge, and releases lubricating fats which further slows the formation of the polish.

If one conducts one's butchering on the uncovered ground, striations are much more common, but they are still of the minute type described in the preceding section.

However, if one uses an implement edge to cut through a joint, or if it comes into frequent contact with bone or cartilage during use, considerably larger utilization-damage scars result. They will still be classifiable primarily as *MicroD* scars, with a few *SS* scars. However, extrapolation from the rather delicate joint-breaking experiments I carried out to the situation where one is breaking the really robust joints of large mammals, one might expect the utilization damage pattern to include even larger scar types. Along with this increase in frequency and severity of utilization damage, striations and abrasion tracks of a different character also occur. These striations are deep and broad (3-5 microns wide): one such striation may be seen running parallel to the edge in the center of plate 48. They are undoubtedly the result of the small flint chips, which are the spalls from the utilization-damage scars, being held against the moving edge by the less yielding bone and cartilage.

## Variations with Method of Use

There are not many ways one can vary the method of use when butchering or cutting up meat. It is possible to conceive some variations, like slicing (cutting with a sawing motion), cutting with a straight movement at right angles to the edge, or chopping (which is similar to the preceding); but, in practice, it makes little sense to adhere strictly to any of these kinematic patterns. When cutting meat and butchering, one usually slices most of the time, cuts occasionally and chops at gristle, ligaments, and tendons when exasperation sets in. Any set of experiments which separated out these various actions would yield results that would compare poorly with the wear patterns found on archeological implements, whose users were primarily concerned with getting the job done.

Therefore, the descriptions of microwear traces in the two preceding sections provide a catalog of what can be seen on most butchering knives. The polish is usually found on both aspects, although the striations are not usually distributed so symmetrically (see table 13A). On meat and butchering knives, most of the striations run at low angles (that is, nearly parallel) to the edge, but some, or several, striations run at higher angles, or even right angles, to the edge. The important difference between these knives and any saw is that the striations on a saw are usually parallel with each other and the edge.

## Variations with Edge Angle

Table 13B does not show any particular associations between utilization damage and edge angle. It might seem that striations are much more common at angles of 50° - 64°, but this is a false association, as some of the implements in this range were used to cut meat near the bone, and the work was done outdoors, which results in more striations. No variations in the microwear polish were correlated with variations in the edge angle.

*Table 13*
*Cutting Meat and Butchery*

A. Edge Aspect and Wear Trace Occurrence

|  | Polish | Striae | LD | SD | MicroD | LS | SS | L Step | S Step | Micro-Step | ½Moon |
|---|---|---|---|---|---|---|---|---|---|---|---|
| Dorsal Aspect (only) |  | 3 |  |  | 3 |  |  |  |  | 4 |  |
| Both Aspects | 9 | 2 |  |  | 3 |  |  |  |  |  |  |
| Bulbar Aspect (only) | 1 | 1 |  |  |  | 1 |  |  |  |  |  |

N=11

B. Edge Angle and Wear Trace Occurrence

|  | Polish | Striae | LD | SD | MicroD | LS | SS | L Step | S Step | Micro-Step | ½Moon | N |
|---|---|---|---|---|---|---|---|---|---|---|---|---|
| <35° |  | 1 |  |  | 1 |  |  |  |  | 1 |  | 1 |
| 35° - 49° | 3 | 1 |  |  | 2 |  |  |  |  | 1 |  | 3 |
| 50° - 64° | 7 | 4 |  |  | 3 |  |  |  |  | 2 |  | 7 |
| 65° - 79° |  |  |  |  |  |  |  |  |  |  |  |  |
| 80° - 95° |  |  |  |  |  |  |  |  |  |  |  |  |
| Totals | 10 | 6 |  |  | 6 |  |  |  |  | 4 |  | 11 |

## Antler-Working Traces

Even though the experimental program was constructed in order to serve as background for the microwear analysis of British Lower Paleolithic implements, a period during which worked antler, however crude, is so rare in Britain as to be practically nonexistent, some antler-working experiments were undertaken. It was hoped a few experiments would give a reasonably clear idea of the kind of traces to be found on antler-working implements. Unfortunately, their microwear polishes, particularly, show a diversity that is more complicated than those polishes that result from the working of the other materials already discussed.

## General Effects

The working of antler produces two distinctive types of polish under different conditions. The commoner type is very bright and smooth. This variety of polish is produced by the scraping, planing, or graving of antler. The other type of polish is bright, but rough and pitted, and is produced by the sawing of antler.

The smooth antler polish can be virtually indistinguishable from wood polish, particularly in the early stages of formation (see, for example, pl. 49 and compare with pls. 22, 23). However, when this smooth polish is well developed, its surface displays small, diffuse depressions which give the polish an evenly pockmarked appearance, rather like that of a melting snowbank. This "melted snow" microtopography is *not* the same as the gentle undulations characteristic of wood polish. Plates 50 and 51 show this feature very clearly. It is also present, in less severe form, in plates 52 and 49, but has not photographed very well.

The rough antler polish is quite unlike the smooth polish and is more similar to bone polish but seems to lack its characteristic micropitting (pl. 53). The general similarities with bone polish are strong nevertheless--compare plate 53 with plate 34. While the antler polish compares in roughness with dry-hide polish, it lacks its matt finish. Rough antler polish is unlikely, however, to be confused with dry-hide polish, since this variety of antler polish only appears on saws, which have a somewhat characteristic utilization-damage pattern and a more extensive area of polish quite different from the corresponding damage and polish on implements used for slicing hides. Sawing is not a likely method of processing dry hide.

Striations of any kind are not common on antler-working implements. Even on antler saws, abrasion tracks are rare. The striations that do appear are usually narrow, not particularly deep, and short (an example can be seen in the lower left corner of pl. 53).

There are no particular scar types or utilization-damage patterns that can be associated exclusively with antler working, although stepped scars of various sizes are quite common, regardless of the method of use of the implements on which they are found.

## Variation with Antler Type

The only type of antler that was available to me for use in these experiments came from an Alaskan caribou; therefore, it is very difficult to say whether antler from other species, like roe deer, red deer, or elk (moose), would leave different wear patterns from those described here. Future experimental work could determine this. If an analogy can be made between antler microwear variation and the variation (or lack of it) shown in the microwear produced by processing similar broad categories of material (for example, hide, wood, bone, and so on), then it seems unlikely that the particular species of antler would have any significant effect on the microwear pattern produced.

My first antler-working experiments involved attempts to scrape, saw, and plane hard, dry antler. These proved remarkably unproductive. Dry antler is so hard and resistant th that the working edges of these tools were quickly dulled by severe, extensive utilization damage, while the amount of material removed from, and the amount of work accomplished on, the antler was negligible. Tringham et al. (1974: 191) also found antler-working particularly destructive of flint working edges, and their experiments were also conducted with dry antler (Tringham, pers. comm.). However, if antler is soaked in water for a day, it becomes quite easy to work, and the working edges of the tools, accordingly, retain their efficiency for a much longer period of time. Since the working of dry antler seems a singularly pointless undertaking, only experiments that were conducted on soaked antler have been reported on in this study.

## Variations with Method of Use

*Whittling/Planing* (see table 14). Since all four of these experiments were conducted using high-angled edges (table 14B), planing is a better description of the activity involved than whittling.

The antler polish, which was of the smooth type, was found predominantly on the aspect which was in contact with the worked material (on these implements, the bulbar aspect). The one exception was an obliquely angled edge (100°) which showed polish on both aspects of the working edge.

Striations and abrasion tracks were not common. But the polishes had a directional cast, by virtue of their distribution around elevations in the microtopography. There was, however, some difficulty in telling that the direction of use had been at right angles to the edge. This makes it likely that antler planes might be confused with antler scrapers when analyzing archeological specimens.

*Table 14*
*Whittling/Planing Antler*

A. Edge Aspect and Wear Trace Occurrence

| | Polish | Striae | LD | SD | MicroD | LS | SS | L Step | S Step | Micro-Step | ½Moon |
|---|---|---|---|---|---|---|---|---|---|---|---|
| Leading or Contact Aspect | 3 | 1 | | | | | | | | | |
| Both Aspects | 1 | | | | | | | | | 1 | |
| Opposite Aspect | | | | | 1 | | | | 2 | 2 | N=4 |

B. Edge Angle and Wear Trace Occurrence

| | Polish | Striae | LD | SD | MicroD | LS | SS | L Step | S Step | Micro-Step | ½Moon | N |
|---|---|---|---|---|---|---|---|---|---|---|---|---|
| <35° | | | | | | | | | | | | |
| 35° - 49° | | | | | | | | | | | | |
| 50° - 64° | | | | | | | | | | | | |
| 65° - 79° | 2 | | | | 1 | | | | 1 | 2 | | 2 |
| 80° - 95° | 2 | 1 | | | | | | | 1 | 1 | | 2 |
| Totals | 4 | 1 | | | 1 | | | | 2 | 3 | | 4 |

The utilization damage, which consisted mainly of *S Step* and *MicroStep* scars, was found primarily on the aspect of the edge opposite the one in contact with the worked material. The predominance of stepped scars may be simply the result of using steeply angled edges, rather than being peculiar to antler planing.

The characteristic features of antler planes, then, are: a smooth antler polish situated primarily on one aspect of the working edge; few indications of the direction of use; utilization damage occurring predominantly on the aspect opposite that displaying the microwear polish.

*Sawing* (see table 15). The antler polish on both these implements was of the rough type. It was distributed symmetrically on both aspects of the working edge. The striations, which ran parallel to the edge, were also found on both aspects.

The utilization damage, like that on wood and bone saws, was diverse but asymmetrically distributed, so that seldom did a scar type occur on both aspects of the edge. ½*Moon* scars were present on both implements.

The characteristics of antler saws seem to be: rough antler polish on both aspects of the working edge; striations running parallel to the working edge; a utilization damage pattern consisting of ½*Moon* scars plus various other scar types.

*Table 15*
*Sawing Antler*

A. Edge Aspect and Wear Trace Occurrence

| | Polish | Striae | LD | SD | MicroD | LS | SS | L Step | S Step | Micro-Step | ½Moon | |
|---|---|---|---|---|---|---|---|---|---|---|---|---|
| Dorsal Aspect (only) | | | 1 | 1 | | | 1 | | | | | |
| Both Aspects | 2 | 2 | | | 1 | | | | | | 2 | |
| Bulbar Aspect (only) | | | | | | | 1 | | | 1 | | N=2 |

B. Edge Angle and Wear Trace Occurrence

| | Polish | Striae | LD | SD | MicroD | LS | SS | L Step | S Step | Micro-Step | ½Moon | N |
|---|---|---|---|---|---|---|---|---|---|---|---|---|
| <35° | | | | | | | | | | | | |
| 35° - 49° | 2 | 2 | 1 | 1 | | | 2 | | | 1 | 2 | 2 |
| 50° - 64° | | | | | | | | | | | | |
| 65° - 79° | | | | | | | | | | | | |
| 80° - 95° | | | | | | | | | | | | |
| Totals | 2 | 2 | 1 | 1 | | | 2 | | | 1 | 2 | 2 |

*Scraping* (see table 16). The antler polish on both these implements was of the smooth type and, in both instances, was found on both aspects of the working edge. The polished area on the contact aspect was slightly larger than that on the opposite aspect.

The striations (present on only one of the two experimental pieces) and other directional indications ran at right angles to the edge.

The utilization damage was dominated by stepped scars of all sizes on the thinner edge (edge angle 39°). These stepped scars occurred primarily on the contact aspect, which is quite different from the distributions on wood and bone scrapers, which display most of their utilization damage on their opposite aspects.

The characteristics of antler scrapers seem to be: smooth antler polish on both aspects of the working edge; striations and directional indications running at right angles to the edge; various sizes of stepped scars primarily occurring on the contact aspect.

*Graving.* Two implements, retouched by simple burin blows, were used for graving antler. The resultant antler polish, of the smooth type, formed on both aspects of the burin bit edge, as well as on all four of the ridges formed by the intersection of the two burin facets and the dorsal and bulbar faces of the implement. In neither case did the polish extend more than 3 or 4 mm from the bit edge along these ridges. On both these implements, the right lateral edge led during the use movement, and, as a consequence, the polish was heaviest on the ridges of the burin facet that runs down the right lateral edge.

The striations and abrasion tracks were found running at a high angle to the bit axis on the dorsal and bulbar facets of the burin bit and at right angles to the bit edge on both aspects of that edge.

The small edge-damage scars which were created by the retouch blows around the points of percussion of the burin facets made it impossible to distinguish whatever utilization damage scars may have been caused by use. The general impression received from the before- and after-use microscopic examinations was that there was a general increase in the number of *MicroStep* scars on the aspect of the bit edge opposite the direction of use.

*Table 16*
*Scraping Antler*

A. Edge Aspect and Wear Trace Occurrence

|  | Polish | Striae | LD | SD | MicroD | LS | SS | L Step | S Step | Micro-Step | ½Moon |
|---|---|---|---|---|---|---|---|---|---|---|---|
| Leading or Contact Aspect |  | 1 |  |  |  |  |  | 1 | 1 | 1 |  |
| Both Aspects | 2 |  |  |  |  |  |  |  |  | 1 |  |
| Opposite Aspect |  |  |  |  |  | 1 | 1 |  |  |  |  |
|  |  |  |  |  |  |  |  |  |  |  | N=2 |

B. Edge Angle and Wear Trace Occurrence

|  | Polish | Striae | LD | SD | MicroD | LS | SS | L Step | S Step | Micro-Step | ½Moon | N |
|---|---|---|---|---|---|---|---|---|---|---|---|---|
| <35° |  |  |  |  |  |  |  |  |  |  |  |  |
| 35° - 49° |  |  |  |  |  |  |  |  |  |  |  |  |
| 50° - 64° | 1 |  |  |  |  | 1 | 1 | 1 | 1 | 1 |  | 1 |
| 65° - 79° |  |  |  |  |  |  |  |  |  |  |  |  |
| 80° - 95° | 1 | 1 |  |  |  |  |  |  |  | 1 |  | 1 |
| Totals | 2 | 1 |  |  |  | 1 | 1 | 1 | 1 | 2 |  | 2 |

The characteristics of antler gravers appear to be: smooth antler polish on both aspects of the bit edge and the dorsal and bulbar facets of the bit, particularly on ridges; striations running at right angles to the bit edge and at high angles to the bit axis; possible *MicroStep* scars on the opposite aspect of the bit edge.

Variations with Edge Angle

Variations of the edge angle do not, as was the case with use on other materials, result in any recognizable variation in the appearance of the microwear polish or striations.

If we compare the occurrences of scar types on high-angled (>65°) planing edges used on wood (table 1B) and antler (table 14B), it is apparent that stepped scars (and utilization damage, as well) are proportionately more common on the antler planes. But, examining table 19, which summarizes all uses on antler (except graving), we can observe the same "funneling" effect, the reduction in the diversity of scar types found as the edge angle increases, as can be seen on similar tables for wood- and bone-working (tables 17, 18).

Table 17

Wood Working* - Edge Angle and Utilization Damage Associations

| | LD | SD | MicroD | LS | SS | L Step | S Step | MicroStep | ½Moon | N |
|---|---|---|---|---|---|---|---|---|---|---|
| <35° | 2 12.5% | 10 62.5% | | 4 25.0% | 4 25.0% | 3 18.8% | 2 12.5% | | 11 68.8% | 16 |
| 35° - 49° | 2 14.3% | 7 50.0% | 1 7.1% | 4 28.6% | 4 28.6% | 2 14.3% | 2 14.3% | 2 14.3% | 7 50.0% | 14 |
| 50° - 64° | 1 8.3% | 3 25.0% | 1 8.3% | 4 33.3% | 6 50.0% | 1 8.3% | 5 41.7% | 1 8.3% | 2 16.7% | 12 |
| 65° - 79° | | | | | 1 25.0% | | 2 50.0% | 1 25.0% | | 4 |
| 80° - 95° | | | | | 1 16.7% | | | 1 16.7% | | 6 |
| Totals | 5 | 20 | 2 | 12 | 16 | 6 | 11 | 5 | 20 | 52 |

*Except boring and graving (N=8)

NOTE: The percentages are of the row N; for example, ½Moon breakages occurred on 50% of all wood working edges with angles between 35 and 49 degrees.

Table 18

Bone Working* - Edge Angle and Utilization Damage Associations

| | LD | SD | MicroD | LS | SS | L Step | S Step | MicroStep | ½Moon | N |
|---|---|---|---|---|---|---|---|---|---|---|
| <35° | 1 33.3% | 1 33.3% | | 1 33.3% | | | 1 33.3% | 2 66.7% | | 3 |
| 35° - 49° | 5 35.7% | 7 50.0% | | 8 57.1% | 6 42.9% | 2 14.3% | 7 50.0% | 7 50.0% | 2 14.3% | 14 |
| 50° - 64° | 3 50.0% | 1 16.7% | | 3 50.0% | 4 66.7% | 1 16.7% | 4 66.7% | 3 50.0% | | 6 |
| 65° - 79° | 1 25.0% | 1 25.0% | | 1 25.0% | | 2 50.0% | 3 75.0% | 3 75.0% | | 4 |
| 80° - 95° | | | | | | 1 50.0% | 1 50.0% | 1 50.0% | | 2 |
| Totals | 10 | 10 | | 13 | 10 | 6 | 16 | 16 | 2 | 29 |

*Except boring and graving (N=6)

NOTE: Percentages are of row N.

## Traces Left by the Working of Some Plant Materials

Although this study is concerned with the microwear traces likely to be found on Lower and Middle Paleolithic implements, an examination of implements from neolithic sites in Germany and Syria showing the classic "sickle-" or "corn gloss" was undertaken for completeness' sake and to check the conclusions of Witthoft (1967), who provided a good description of the distinctive features of corn gloss and an explanation of its causes. Witthoft listed the distinctive features of corn gloss as: (1) a very smooth, highly reflective surface, (2) a "fluid" appearance, (3) "filled-in" striations, and (4) "comet-shaped pits."

*Table 19*
*Antler Working\* - Edge Angle and Utilization Damage Associations*

|        | LD | SD | MicroD | LS | SS | L Step | S Step | MicroStep | ½Moon | N |
|--------|----|----|--------|----|----|--------|--------|-----------|-------|---|
| <35°   |    |    |        |    |    |        |        |           |       |   |
| 35° - 49° | 1 | 1 | 1 |    | 2 |   |   | 1 | 2 | 2 |
| 50° - 64° |   |   |   | 1 | 1 | 1 | 1 | 1 |   | 1 |
| 65° - 79° |   | 1 |   |   |   |   |   | 1 | 2 | 2 |
| 80° - 95° |   |   |   |   |   |   |   | 1 | 2 | 3 |
| Totals | 1 | 2 | 1 | 1 | 3 | 1 | 3 | 6 | 2 | 8 |

\*
Except boring and graving

Witthoft claimed that corn gloss was the result of the spread of plant opal (from the phytoliths in grasses) over the harder flint surface by the same mechanism whereby iron oxide rouge is spread over harder gemstones during lapidary polishing. This spreading of plant opal, which flows due to frictional pull and frictional heat, results in the fluid appearance of the polish surface and especially the filled-in striations. As only grasses are supposed to contain sufficient plant opal to allow this type of intense polish, corn gloss on an implement is a sure sign that the implement was used on grass, that is, as a sickle.

The examination of thirteen sickle blades from the Linear Bandkeramic site of Hienheim (Bavaria) and seven sickle blades from the Pre-Pottery Neolithic site of Abu Hureyra (Syria), all showing (to the naked eye) glosses of various extent, confirmed Witthoft's description. Plate 54 shows a typical area of corn gloss, with a smooth surface, comet-shaped pits, and a filled-in striation. The fluid appearance of the polish is better seen at lower magnification and is difficult to photograph, but I concur with Witthoft's description. The striations on all the archeological sickle specimens were generally situated at a low angle (<30°) to the working edge. On every specimen, a few odd striations could be found running at higher angles, but the majority of them indicated a direction of use roughly parallel to the edge: in other words, a cutting motion, rather than a chopping motion, was employed. The "tails" of the comet-shaped pits ran parallel with the striations and pointed away from the edge--therefore opposite to the direction of use. Plate 55 shows the corn gloss developed on an experimental flint sickle blade used by M. Newcomer for reaping grass. The method of use involved gathering bunches of grass stems into the hand and cutting them free with a slicing motion of the sickle. The tool was used for about three hours, in the course of which approximately 1500 handfuls of grass were cut.

Wood polish is, as noted above, somewhat similar to corn gloss in that it is bright and smooth. But wood polish lacks the filled striations and comet-shaped pits and never covers as extensive an area as corn gloss. Corn gloss, even when it is weakly developed, is brighter and can be seen, much more so than wood polish, to be the thick addition of material to the flint microsurface. The above statements are also true of the polishes found on experimental implements used for cutting other, slightly harder plant materials-- such as bracken stems, in the case of implement no. 13 of the blind test (pl. 62); and bamboo stems, in the case of exp. 101 (pl. 56).

## Measurement of Polish Differences

Once it became clear that the microwear polishes produced by use on different materials were distinctive in appearance, an attempt was made to acquire some quantitative measurements of their differences.

The WILD M20 microscope camera is equipped with a light meter which measures the average amount of light available in the field of view and gives a reading in microamperes of current (from the photocell). Thus, one reading that can be made is the average amount of light reflected from a standard area of the polished surface under normal light-field (LF) illumination, that is, the "brightness" of the polish. Since with LF illumination, one can limit the area lit by closing a diaphragm to the central portion of the field of view, the standard area from which measurements were taken was defined by allowing the edges of the circle of light to touch the corners of the 35 mm photo grid projected by the camera eyepiece at 200 magnification. The standard diameter of this circle of light is 280 microns. The use of a smaller standard area cut the variation in light intensity so severely that, given the crudity of the microampere scale on the meter, discrimination was impossible. A larger standard area gave better discrimination, but since most microwear polishes, even on extensively used specimens (except corn gloss), seldom covered a large enough area of the microsurface to fill even the 280 micron diameter area, use of a larger area made it virtually impossible to compare the measurements on different polishes.

A somewhat less reliable measure of the "roughness" of a polish can be obtained by measuring the light reflected from the polish under Dark Field (DF) illumination. Under DF illumination, smooth, polished surfaces arranged perpendicular to the optical axis reflect very little light, while irregular, rough polish surfaces reflect a good deal. Crudely, then, smooth polishes give low readings on the meter, and rough polishes give high readings. However, the ground color of the flint affected the DF readings much more severely than the LF readings. This problem was partially solved by "norming" the DF data by subtracting the mean of the DF readings of an implement's unpolished surfaces from the mean of the DF readings from the polished surfaces. Since the unpolished surfaces are always rougher than the polished surfaces, it follows that this measure will be a negative quantity and that smooth polishes will show high, and rough polishes low, *negative* readings. Regrettably, with DF illumination, there is no possibility of reducing, by means of a diaphragm, the lighted area, and this means that the DF reading had to be taken from the whole field of view of the microscope at 200X. The number of experimental implements with areas of complete polish large enough to provide reliable, comparable measurements using the whole field of view was very small.

The results of these two measurements are displayed as a scatter diagram (fig. 19). The hide polishes are in the lower left corner of the graph, where expected, meaning that they are relatively dull and rough. The measurements from neolithic sickle blades place the corn glosses in the upper right corner, where expected, meaning that they are bright and smooth. The three wood-polish data points represent the lower corner of the true range for wood polish. The LF and DF difference measurement on wood polish are artificially low, as it proved difficult to create, even by quite prolonged use, areas of polish comparable in extent with those of corn gloss and the hide polishes. However, the wood-polish points are in the "correct" position vis-à-vis the other polishes.

Because of the technical problems involved in simply getting the raw measurements and finding large enough areas of polish, this method of distinguishing polishes is not likely to be useful as a research tool in its present form--that is, for distinguishing between

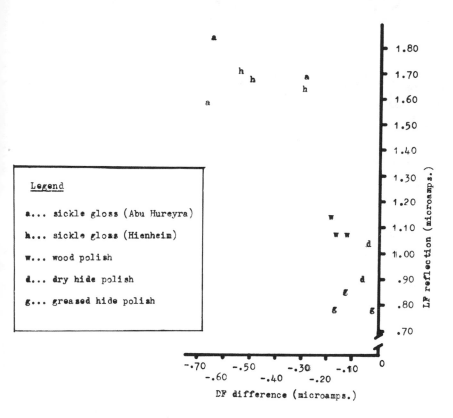

Figure 19.  Light reflection measurements on various microwear polishes.

polish types on archeological specimens.  Besides, to obtain a complete set of measurements on just a single piece can take up to an hour, involving the taking of several separate measurements for averaging and the adjustment of the piece so that the plane of the polished or unaltered surface coincides as closely as possible with the focus plane of the microscope.  The purpose of these measurements was to objectify some of the distinguishing features of these microwear polishes--an aim which met with moderate success.  Not only do these polishes appear different from one another, but they are *measurably* different.

## A "Blind" Test of Microwear Analysis

At the suggestion of M. Newcomer of London University, a lithic technology specialist who was highly skeptical about the reliability and validity of functional interpretations based on microwear analysis, a "blind" test of the validity of microwear analysis was arranged.  Dr. Newcomer manufactured a set of flint tools using simple debitage and retouch techniques and then used them to perform specific tasks on materials of his choosing, recording the details carefully.  After an initial cleaning in detergent and hot water, these tools were presented to me for microwear analysis.  The aim was to see the degree of agreement between the inferred uses, as determined by microwear analysis, and the actual uses of this sample of fifteen implements.  I recleaned all of these implements by immersing them in warm NaOH and HCl solutions.  The results of this test are presented as follows.  After the number of the implement is Dr. Newcomer's brief description of the tool's use (material worked, actions, length of use) and his "comments," which give a fuller description of its use. This is followed by a section headed "microwear analysis," giving the entirely independent findings of the microscopic examination and the writer's brief interpretation of the implement. Finally, a section headed "discussion" examines the agreement between the actual and the inferred use.

| NUMBER | TOOL | MATERIAL | ACTION | TIME |
|--------|------|----------|--------|------|
| 1 | Clactonian notch | Wood | Whittling | 18 minutes |

*Comments.* Notch made with single blow of hammerstone. Material worked was ash sapling cut six months before the experiment, c. 18 mm in diameter. Tool held in bare hand and used to whittle a long, tapering point by pulling tool toward operator, sometimes with ventral surface upward and sometimes dorsal upward.

*Microwear analysis.* Fig. 20:1. On either side of the center of the notch are areas of faint polish rounding the edges. This polish, though weakly developed, is bright and smooth, and, therefore, is probably wood polish.

Most of the striations and abrasion tracks observed were hammerstone scratches associated with the center of the notch on the bulbar aspect. Two other striations were found on the bulbar aspect associated with the areas of polish and edge damage; these run at relatively low angles to the edge. This may indicate that the implement was used for cutting a roughly circular object, for example, a branch or stem with a diameter less than 40 mm.

The utilization damage was found, like the polish, on either side of the center of the notch. The damage consisted of *MicroD* scars on both aspects of the edge with some *MicroStep* scars on the bulbar aspect.

The final interpretation of this piece is: activity--possibly cutting; material worked--wood.

*Discussion.* The worked material was identified correctly; however, the inferred activity is wrong. Newcomer's notes indicate that the distal end of the tool led during the use movement, which explains why the striations ran at low angles to the edge. It was the angle of these striations and the equal distribution of utilization damage on both aspects which led to the misinterpretation of the method of use of this piece.

| NUMBER | TOOL | MATERIAL | ACTION | TIME |
|--------|------|----------|--------|------|
| 2 | Flake | Wood | Chopping | 21 minutes |

*Comments.* Tool held in bare hand, sometimes at proximal end and sometimes at distal. Material worked was ash cut six months before the experiment, c. 30 mm in diameter, chopped to rough point with the tool. Tip of wood point held on pine anvil, which was sometimes struck by tool.

*Microwear analysis.* Fig. 20:2. There is only one small area of polish, which occurs on the proximal portion of the bulbar aspect of the working edge. It is bright and is probably wood polish, but it is also somewhat rough, which makes it impossible to be certain.

The striations, which are quite common along the edge, run in two different directions. The majority run at right angles to the working edge, and since these are present on both edge aspects, the most likely use is chopping (the edge opposite the working edge would be battered if this implement were a wedge). The few parallel striations may represent a secondary use of this same edge or, more likely, a few cutting strokes executed between chopping strokes to clear the cut area.

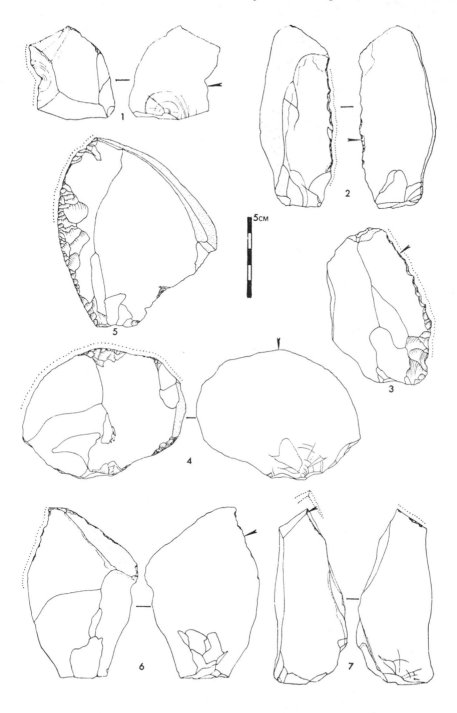

Figure 20. "Blind test" implements, nos. 1-7. (Stippling indicates portion of the edge actually used; arrows indicate where photomicrographs were taken.)

The utilization damage consists of *LS*, *SS* scars, and ½*Moon* breakages found on both aspects, and *L Step* scars found only on the dorsal aspect of the working edge. At first glance, one might be inclined to interpret this implement as a saw because of the presence of a number of ½*Moon* breakages on the edge. However, these breakages can arise from other uses, like chopping, whittling, and wedging.

The final interpretation of this piece is: activity--chopping; material worked--wood.

*Discussion.* The interpretation of this piece based on microwear analysis is correct in all respects.

| NUMBER | TOOL | MATERIAL | ACTION | TIME |
|---|---|---|---|---|
| 3 | Denticulate | Wood | Sawing | 12 minutes |

*Comments.* Tool made by retouch with hammerstone. Tool held in dry leather pad to protect hand. Material was ash cut in March 1976, c. 25 mm in diameter. Two circular cuts almost all the way through sapling made in 7 and 5 minutes, respectively.

*Microwear analysis.* Fig. 20:3. There are only a few minute patches of polish along the retouched edge, and these are not enough to provide a certain diagnosis. The polish is smooth and bright, so the worked material could be wood (or possibly antler).

As one might expect from the morphology of this piece, the numerous striations present on both aspects of the edge, running parallel to the edge, indicate that this implement was used as a saw.

Along most of the working edge, utilization damage could not be distinguished from the small types of retouch scars. On the extreme distal portion of the working edge, a ½*Moon* breakage occurs, and a short area of *MicroD* and *MicroStep* scars were found on the dorsal aspect. These scars are probably utilization damage.

The final interpretation of this piece is: activity--sawing; material worked--possibly wood.

*Discussion.* Despite the uncertainty over the interpretation of the microwear polish, the inferred and actual use agree in all respects. The weak development of the polish is probably due to the fact that the wood worked was hardwood (which generally produces less polish than softwood), seasoned (which also limits the production of polish), and principally because the implement was only used for 12 minutes.

| NUMBER | TOOL | MATERIAL | ACTION | TIME |
|---|---|---|---|---|
| 4 | Flake | Meat | Cutting | 44 minutes |

*Comments.* Tool slightly retouched with antler hammer to remove irregularities on working edge. Tool held in bare hand, thumb on bulb. Material was raw breast of lamb, complete with ribs, weighing 2 lbs. 9 oz. Cutting done on pine anvil, which tool cut into frequently. Tool also hit ribs often and was used to cut gristle off ends of ribs.

*Microwear analysis.* Fig. 20:4, pl. 57. There is a bright, rough polish, sometimes showing a greasy luster, along the distal edge on both edge aspects. This polish is sometimes similar in appearance to that found on no. 13, though, in the present case, it is confined to the extreme edge. The most likely worked material is vegetable matter, with meat a second possibility.

There are a few striations and abrasion tracks which demonstrate a use-movement parallel to the working edge--that is, cutting or slicing.

The utilization damage (other than in the retouched areas) consists primarily of very minute ½Moon breakages and SS scars on both edge aspects, with some MicroD scars on the dorsal aspect.

The final interpretation is: activity--cutting (knife); material worked--unknown (possibly vegetable matter or meat).

*Discussion.* The inferred activity is correct, but not the worked material. The ambiguous character of the microwear polish is, no doubt, the result of the working edge striking the pine plank used as a cutting board. This contact with the plank left a bright "wood polish" which became mixed with the "meat" (and possibly "bone") polish on the same edge. Although meat was considered as a possible worked material, it was believed unlikely in the end, because of the brightness of the polish on many areas of the edge. This test was particularly useful and provides some important cautionary information.

| NUMBER | TOOL | MATERIAL | ACTION | TIME |
|--------|------|----------|--------|------|
| 5 | Sidescraper | Fat | Scraping | 31 minutes |

*Comments.* Tool retouched with antler hammer. Held in bare hand with thumb on bulb. Material was fresh, raw, pork fat, and tool was used to remove fat from skin, holding skin on pine anvil. Tool cut through skin occasionally and hit anvil. Tool pulled toward worker and accumulated fat removed with fingers.

*Microwear analysis.* Fig. 20:5. There are no wear traces to be found on this implement, except a few, small, isolated patches of a faint, bright polish inside some of the flake-scar depressions on the dorsal aspect, which probably result from retouching with an antler hammer.

This piece was probably unused.

*Discussion.* It is obvious that the scraping of fat, which is almost a pure lubricant, leaves very few traces, if any, even after prolonged use. A reexamination of this implement, even with knowledge of which area of the edge was used, failed to locate any unequivocal microwear traces other than the scattered patches of polish mentioned above.

| NUMBER | TOOL | MATERIAL | ACTION | TIME |
|--------|------|----------|--------|------|
| 6 | Flake | Wood | Whittling | 14 minutes |

*Comments.* Tool retouched slightly on right edge with hammerstone to remove projections. Held in pad of dry leather. Material was billet of pine cut at least 5 years ago, c. 20 mm in diameter, whittled to very acute point on pine anvil, which tool contacted only rarely. Tool pushed with thumb on bulb.

*Microwear analysis.* Fig. 20:6, pl. 58. The microwear consists of a weakly developed polish on the bulbar aspect of the distal left lateral edge, accompanied by a few striations running at right angles to the edge. The polish, though faint, is bright and smooth and is a wood polish (pl. 58).

The utilization damage along this edge consists of SS and MicroD scars on the dorsal aspect, LS scars on the bulbar aspect, and some ½Moon breakages on both aspects.

The interpretation of this portion of this piece is: activity--whittling; material worked--wood.

There is, however, a second area of microwear polish on the small cusp of the distal end of the flake. The polish, which is found on both aspects, is bright, rugged, and is possibly bone polish. On the dorsal surface of the cusp, there are a great number of relatively minute striations which run primarily in two directions relative to the bit axis (approximately 60° to the axis and approximately 280° to the axis). This may mean that this bit or cusp was used for graving. The worked material may have been bone, but, under certain circumstances, wood can produce a similar microwear polish. This portion of the implement may be interpreted thus: activity--graving; worked material--wood or bone.

*Discussion.* The interpretation of the one edge of this implement as a wood-whittling knife is correct, and the interpretation of the wear on the distal cusp is more correct than wrong. The worked material, in this case, is probably the very seasoned wood of the pine anvil, which can leave a rougher polish than fresh wood (see discussion section on implement no. 7). The graving interpretation reflects the fact that the cusp came into contact with the cutting board, while the implement was moving roughly parallel with the long axis of the flake. At the end of a whittling stroke, it is common, especially when whittling to a point, briefly to change the direction of the stroke from a whittling stroke to a quick, slicing movement in order to remove the wood shaving. Such strokes were executed with this piece, and it is quite likely that when the projecting cusp came into contact with the anvil at the end of the whittling strokes, it cut (or graved) a short groove into the wood surface while moving parallel to the long axis of the flake.

| NUMBER | TOOL | MATERIAL | ACTION | TIME |
|--------|------|----------|--------|------|
| 7 | Flake | Wood | Drilling | 10 minutes |

*Comments.* Flake with strong, burinlike distal end used in bare hand, thumb on bulb. Material was pine board, 1 inch thick, at least 10 years old. One hole cut by boring from both sides to meet in middle.

*Microwear analysis.* Fig. 20:7, pl. 59. The wear traces found on this implement are situated in a complicated pattern on its distal end, which has been divided into three areas for convenience of description.

Area 1: The sparse polish present along the bit edge is probably bone polish, as it is rough and somewhat bright. There are numerous striations associated with the polish which run primarily at high angles to the edge. The edge damage consists of *LS* and *SS* scars.

A faint area of polish can be seen on the dorsal bit corner and extends along the right lateral edge a short way. On microelevations of the bulbar bit corner are patches of polish with a strong directional character. Again, this polish is probably the result of working bone. The direction indicated by the linear features of the polish is approximately 75° to the flake axis. There are also a number of overlapping *MicroStep* scars.

Area 2: A faint polish rounds this edge. The polish is not easily identifiable but is probably bone polish. A couple of short striations on the bulbar aspect indicate a direction of use approximately 60° to the edge. The utilization damage consists of *MicroStep* scars on the dorsal aspect and *L* and *S Step* scars on the dorsal aspect of the edge.

Area 3: The polish rounds the edge here but is most intense on the lateral aspect of the edge. The polish is smoother than the other polishes but is probably bone polish as well. Striations occur on both aspects of this edge and are oriented at right angles to the edge.

The utilization damage consists of a series of *S Step* and *SS* scars on the dorsal edge aspect.

Area 1 is interpreted as a burin used for graving bone; area 2 as an edge used briefly for planing bone; and area 3 as an edge used for scraping bone.

*Discussion.* The inference of the worked material is wrong. The microwear polish on this

specimen, especially on the bit edge, is unlike normal wood polish.  It may be that the
relatively old age of this wood has so altered its texture that it produces an "abnormal"
wood polish which, if true generally, is an interesting fact.

Most of my woodworking experiments were conducted with fresh or only slightly seasoned
(6 months old) wood, while this experiment was conducted on wood "at least 10 years old,"
not, perhaps, a likely material to be encountered in Lower Paleolithic circumstances.  Well-
seasoned wood of most temperate types is very difficult to work with unground flint edges,
and the seasoning of wood only becomes advantageous when the woodworking technology is relatively well-developed, involving complex joinery.  Even in primitive technologies, the repair of simple wooden tools and utensils, intially shaped from unseasoned wood, after they
have been in use for some time, would mean that some working of seasoned wood is likely to
occur.  Nevertheless, when the damaged tool is a simple one, like a spear or a digging
stick, and the damage is extensive, like a broken or split tip, it would be easier and
quicker to make a new implement from fresh wood than laboriously to rework the intractable
old seasoned one.  Thomson (1964: 408) gives an example of the repair of a damaged digging
stick by an Australian aborigine (it is not clear from his account how old the stick was,
but the implication was that it was not newly made).  However, even in this case, the stick
was repointed by charring and grinding, not by scraping or whittling with a sharp stone
edge.  All the wooden implements described by Thomson were made from unseasoned wood.
Driftwood, which might be well seasoned, was used by some primitive peoples, but usually
because they lived in treeless environments, like the Eskimo.  In the Upper Paleolithic,
particularly in the then-cold and sparsely forested regions of northern and eastern Europe,
the working of driftwood may have been quite common and, therefore, microwear polish of the
type found on implement no. 7 might be a fairly common occurrence, but this is speculation
as far as I am concerned.

Even in the making of wooden bows by some American Indians, a product greatly improved
if made from seasoned wood (Pope 1925: 58), the shaping of bow commonly took place while
the wood was still green (Goldschmidt 1951; Kelly 1932; Hoffman 1896).  Swanton (1946: 577)
quotes an account of bow-making on the Carolina coast that states that the shaping was done
wile the wood was still green because it became so difficult to cut when seasoned.  What
is clear from a number of ethnographic accounts of bow-making in aboriginal America, in
which the condition of the wood being worked was specifically mentioned, is that as much of
the shaping and reduction of the bow was done within a few weeks of cutting if possible,
whether the bow was finished immediately or after a period of seasoning.

To return to the piece under consideration, if the various edges showing wear traces
had been considered as a whole, the activity inferred for this tool might not have been so
far off target.  But since the three areas showing microwear traces are actually separated
from each other by areas of unaltered edge, the fact that they all resulted from a single
use instead of three separate uses was not immediately apparent.  After it had been decided
that area 1 was used as a graver, the traces on the other areas could only be explained by
referring them to other activities.

| NUMBER | TOOL | MATERIAL | ACTION | TIME |
|--------|------|----------|--------|------|
| 8 | Truncation | Meat | Cutting | 28 minutes |

*Comments*.  Tool made by retouch with hammerstone.  Used in bare hand with index finger
usually on retouch.  Material was raw lamb, sliced into small chunks on pine anvil, which
tool frequently contacted.

*Microwear analysis.* Fig. 21:8, pl. 60. The polish occurs on both aspects of the left lateral edge. It is rough, greasy, and dull--meat polish--though there are some areas of brighter, smoother polish on the distalmost portion of the working edge. The striations are of the narrow, deep type most commonly found on meat-cutting edges, and run parallel to the working edge.

The utilization damage consists of *MicroStep* scars irregularly distributed along the dorsal aspect, with *MicroD* scars distributed on both aspects of the working edge.

The polish, striations, and utilization damage all confirm that this implement was used for cutting meat. The brighter polish on the distal working edge may indicate a secondary use.

*Discussion.* The interpretation of this piece, deduced from the microwear analysis, is correct. The brighter polish is, of course, the result of the implement's cutting through the meat into the pinewood cutting board.

| NUMBER | TOOL | MATERIAL | ACTION | TIME |
|--------|------|----------|--------|------|
| 9 | Flake | -- | -- | -- |

*Comments.* The flake was unused, and the retouch on the left edge occurred spontaneously.

*Microwear analysis.* Fig. 21:9. There are no apparent striations, microwear polishes, or utilization-damage scars on this piece. This implement was unused.

*Discussion.* There is no discussion necessary--the inference is quite correct.

| NUMBER | TOOL | MATERIAL | ACTION | TIME |
|--------|------|----------|--------|------|
| 10 | Flake | Hide | Cutting | 23 minutes |

*Comments:* Tool slightly retouched on right edge with hammerstone to remove projections. Held in bare hand, thumb on bulb. Material was hide from forehead of two freshly killed oxen, and tool was used to slice hide into strips. Tool often cut into pine anvil, having also cut through hair on outside of skin.

*Microwear analysis.* Fig. 21:10. There are no unequivocal traces of use to be found on this implement. It is possible that there is some microwear polish, perhaps meat polish, along the distal right lateral edge, but it is impossible to be certain. No striations or abrasion tracks could be found on this edge. The edge damage found along this edge consists of *SS*, *SD*, and *MicroD* scars on the dorsal aspect and a few small ½*Moon* breakages on both aspects; this may be utilization damage.

The edge damage located on the proximal portion of the right lateral edge is probably spontaneous retouch.

This piece could have been used briefly as a meat knife, but that is a guess, not an interpretation.

*Discussion.* The guess about the function of this implement is nearly correct, but for all the wrong reasons. The actual working edge of this implement is the distal corner of the left lateral edge. A reexamination of this area of the edge revealed that there is, indeed, a microwear polish on both aspects of this edge quite comparable to polishes found on experimental fresh-hide scrapers. There were a number of fine striations associated with this polish running at about 30° (or slightly less) to the flake axis. How was this polish overlooked? The answer is simple--carelessness. The whole circumference of the flake was examined, except for a small area (about 6 mm long) on the distal corner of the left lateral edge. The reason it was not examined was that some small, metal (brass) scratches could be

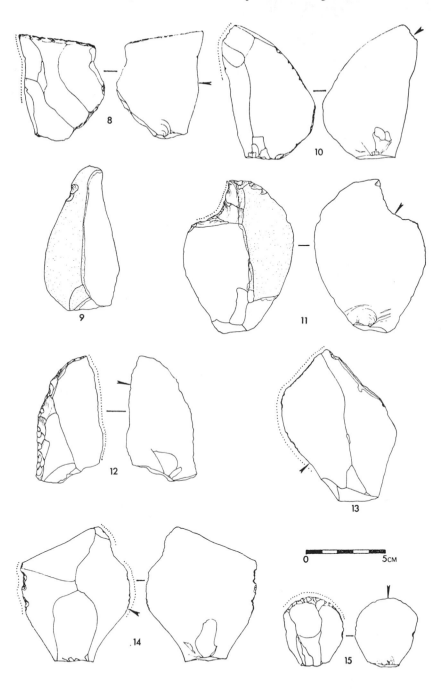

Figure 21.  "Blind test" implements, nos. 8-15.

seen, with the naked eye, leading directly to this corner on the bulbar aspect. Because of these metal scratches, it was assumed that the small ½Moon breakages in this area were the result of some careless handling which had allowed that portion of the edge to come in contact with metal. Therefore, it was further assumed that whatever traces (if any) were originally in that area would have been carried away with the damage spalls and that it was unnecessary to examine that area of the edge. Unfortunately the small ½Moon breakages were, of course, utilization damage, and the polish in this area was unaffected by whatever caused the metal scratches. The suggested possible meat polish seen on the right lateral edge may actually be the result of rubbing with the hand during use.

| NUMBER | TOOL | MATERIAL | ACTION | TIME |
|--------|------|----------|--------|------|
| 11 | Retouched notch | Wood | Scraping | 13 minutes |

*Comments.* Tool retouched with hammerstone. Held in bare hand, thumb on bulb. Material was ash cut six months prior to the experiment, c. 15 mm in diameter. Tool used to reduce diameter of shaft, pushing and pulling.

*Microwear analysis.* Fig. 21:11, pl. 61. A well-developed microwear polish is found inside the concave scraper edge, predominantly on the bulbar aspect, but on the dorsal aspect as well. The polish is bright but uneven, with a few curiously smooth pockmarks. This is probably antler polish, but wood cannot be ruled out. Only one striation could be found, on the bulbar aspect and running at right angles to the edge. The placement of the polish on the bulbar and dorsal aspects suggest that the bulbar face of the implement was held at an angle of greater than 35° to the surface of the worked material and led during movement. Utilization damage could not be isolated from the smaller components of the retouch.

The final interpretation of this piece is: activity--scraping; worked material--antler (or wood).

*Discussion.* The inferred activity is correct. As for the worked material, wood and antler polishes can often be quite similar to each other (cf. p. 56). Indeed, after the first examination of this implement, wood was thought the more likely worked material, but subsequent reexamination changed this impression, unfortunately.

| NUMBER | TOOL | MATERIAL | ACTION | TIME |
|--------|------|----------|--------|------|
| 12 | Backed knife | Frozen meat | Cutting | 23 minutes |

*Comments.* Tool retouched with hammerstone. Held in bare hand with thumb on dorsal surface. Material was raw, frozen lamb shoulder, allowed to thaw for one hour, and sliced into small pieces, first cutting strips off bone, then slicing on pine anvil, which tool hit often.

*Microwear analysis.* Fig. 21:12. Small, scattered area of polish can be found on both aspects of the distal left lateral edge. These polish areas, as sparse as they are, are bright and smooth, suggesting that this implement was used on wood. The numerous striations and abrasion tracks, which are more common on the dorsal aspect, indicate a use-movement parallel to the edge.

The utilization damage is composed primarily of ½Moon breakages, which become progressively larger toward the distal end. There are also some *S Step* and *SS* scars scattered along the dorsal aspect of the distal section of the working edge.

It seems likely that this implement was used to cut or saw (?) wood. The main difficulty with this interpretation is the relatively mild nature of the utilization damage, considering the thinness of the working edge (edge angle = 20°). The wood worked (if it was wood) must have been of a fairly soft variety.

*Discussion.* This implement was misinterpreted because the meat polish produced by frozen meat is quite faint (reexamination had determined that it is just present), while the wood polish is quite striking. The wood polish is, of course, the result of the implement's cutting into the pine anvil, and to that extent there is some accuracy in the proffered interpretation. It seems that the cutting of frozen meat produces microwear polish more slowly than unfrozen meat. This is probably because when a flint edge is cutting through soft, unfrozen meat, the meat engages relatively large areas of the flint surfaces on the two edge aspects, while, when cutting hard, frozen meat, only the edge is actually engaged by the meat.

| NUMBER | TOOL | MATERIAL | ACTION | TIME |
|---|---|---|---|---|
| 13 | Flake | Bracken | Cutting | 26 minutes |

*Comments.* Tool held in bare hand, thumb on bulb. Material was growing bracken (*Pteridium aquilinum*), cut through in two to three slices. 500 stalks cut.

*Microwear analysis.* Fig. 21:13, pl. 62. There is an extensive polish present on both aspects of the left lateral edge, which extends several millimeters back from the edge, indicating deep penetration. The polish is quite bright, but sometimes greasy and rough (fig. 140f). I am unfamiliar with this polish, but the depth of penetration suggests a soft material. The worked material might be meat, but meat polish is never as bright as this and, since it develops so slowly, has never been seen to cover as extensive an area on any of my experimental pieces. The worked material is, therefore, more probably some vegetable material.

Only two striations could be found on the dorsal aspect, which indicate a use-movement parallel to the long axis of the flake--that is, cutting or slicing.

The utilization damage consists of scattered *MicroStep* scars on the dorsal aspect, a few *SS* on the bulbar aspect, and a series of minute ½*Moon* breakages on both aspects of the working edge.

The final interpretation of this piece is: activity--slicing; worked material--unknown, but probably vegetable matter.

*Discussion.* The inferred use of this implement agrees perfectly with the actual use. The worked material was deduced from the fact that other vegetable materials (for example, wood and grass) produced very bright polishes (namely, wood polish and corn gloss); therefore, since this polish was bright, the worked material was thought likely to be of a vegetable origin, though it was not one with which the author had experimented.

| NUMBER | TOOL | MATERIAL | ACTION | TIME |
|---|---|---|---|---|
| 14 | Flake | Rabbit | Skinning | c. 45 minutes |

*Comments.* Tool held in bare hand in various positions. Material was fresh, mature rabbit. Skinning done on pine anvil. Left edge used to cut off forefeet, right edge used for fine cutting. Skin cut into 1-inch strips on pine anvil after removal from rabbit.

*Microwear analysis.* Fig. 21:14, pl. 63. There are two areas showing wear traces on this piece--one on the right lateral edge, and one on the left lateral edge.

On the right lateral edge, there is a considerable amount of polish on both aspects. This polish is dull, "greasy," and rugged and is, in all likelihood, a meat polish (pl. 63). The striations present are of the narrow, deep type (common on meat-cutting edges) and run parallel to the long axis of the flake. The utilization damage consists of *SS*, *MicroD*, *MicroStep* scars, and small ½*Moon* breakages on both aspects of this working edge.

On the left lateral edge, there are scattered areas of meat polish on both edge aspects. The striations and abrasion tracks, which are larger than those on the right edge, run parallel to the edge proximally, and at right angles to the edge distally. The utilization damage is more severe on this edge than on the right lateral edge, consisting of *SS* and *S Step* scars irregularly distributed on the dorsal aspect; *LS* and *LD* scars on the bulbar aspect; and *SD*, *MicroStep*, and ½*Moon* scars on both aspects. This indicates that the left edge was probably used for cutting through or breaking a joint, while the right edge was used for cutting through meat only.

Since there are two used edges on this piece, they will be summarized separately. Right lateral edge: activity--slicing; worked material--meat. Left lateral edge: activity--cutting; worked material--meat, cartilage, ligament, and bone.

*Discussion.* The inferred use agrees very satisfactorily with the actual use. The different functions of the right and left lateral edge were distinguished with remarkable accuracy.

| NUMBER | TOOL | MATERIAL | ACTION | TIME |
|---|---|---|---|---|
| 15 | Endscraper | Bone | Scraping | 11 minutes |

*Comments.* Tool retouched with antler hammer. Held in bare hand, thumb on dorsal surface. Material was fragment of raw ox metapodial, skinned out ten months before the experiment. Tool used to scrape point on bone splinter by pushing down length of splinter. Bone point held on pine anvil, which tool often hit. Task unfinished, since tool needed sharpening.

*Microwear analysis.* Fig. 21:15, pl. 64. A well-developed microwear polish was found on the central portion of the distal scraping edge. The polish is bright, somewhat smooth, and scored with numerous striations, some shallow, some deep, running at right angles to and across the edge. The polish is found on both aspects of the edge--continuously on the bulbar aspect, and on the microelevations of the dorsal aspect. This fact, and the orientation of the striations, indicate that the body of the implement was held at approximately a right angle to the worked surface; in other words, it was a scraper.

The polish itself, however, is of an unfamiliar type (pl. 64). Its brightness could indicate use on wood, or this feature and its bumpiness could indicate use on antler. But the presence of so many narrow striations suggested that this tool was used on fresh hide (perhaps after drying a day or two). All my experiments involving the working of wet or fresh hide were conducted on small hare hides and did not result in particularly prolonged use. Any comparison of this polish with the polishes found on fresh hide scrapers involves a considerable amount of extrapolation, which is an unreliable method of polish identification. However, the polish on this implement is very similar to that shown in a photograph in Semenov's *Razvitiye Teknikiye* (1968: fig. 50 g), which he considered to be the result of hide scraping. One cannot exclude the possibility that this polish is an antler polish, which is certainly a similar polish (especially on scraping edges), but the general distribution of the polish over the microtopography and the presence of so many narrow striations tends to argue against this possibility.

No utilization damage could be clearly distinguished from the retouch scars on the dorsal aspect of the working edge, and no damage scars were found on the bulbar aspect.

The final interpretation of this piece is: activity--scraping; worked material--possibly hide, less likely antler.

*Discussion.* The inferred activity is correct, but the inferred worked material is wrong. The second possible worked material that was considered, antler, is closer to being correct.

The identification was made on the basis of extrapolation from experimental data of uncertain relevance, and comparison with a (not very good) photograph of Semenov's, neither of which were adequate to the task. The reason why such a polish was not produced in the previous bone-scraping experiments may be that Dr. Newcomer conducted his scraping on a piece of bone nine months old. Almost all my experiments on bone working have been conducted on cooked bone or fresh bone no more than a couple of weeks old (most no more than a few days old, fresh or cooked). The reason for this limitation was that bone which had been left exposed for three to four weeks on an outdoor workshop area was found to be hard to work and extremely destructive of tool edges, so that working edges quickly became too dull for continued use before much work could be completed. However, the bone worked in this experiment, although old, was not dry; it had been protected from exposure to the elements and therefore from the solvents and temperature fluctuations that cause degreasing and destruction of bone collagen. It is reasonable to question whether bone was likely to be so protected on Lower and Middle Paleolithic living floors. In caves and rock shelters, perhaps, bone would be sufficiently protected from the elements and temperature fluctuations to remain in a tractable state for months, but, at open sites, the bone would probably deteriorate rapidly. A hunting and gathering existence would surely imply that a constant supply of easy-to-work, fresh bone was readily available, and there would be little compulsion to use any old bone, no matter what its condition. Whatever the likelihood of old but still tractable bone being worked in the early stages of the Paleolithic, the distinctive polish produced by this experiment indicates that the variability of bone polishes is greater than previous experiments had indicated.

## General Conclusions and Discussion

The results of the test have been tabulated below, in most cases, by scoring 1 for a correct inference and 0 for an incorrect inference. Of course, such scoring is merely a convenient method of summarizing the results of the test, and nothing more. Nevertheless, one must decide whether one wishes to know how correct the inferences based on microwear analysis were or how wrong they were. How should implement no. 6 be scored, for example, where two separate uses were inferred (whittling and graving) from microwear traces that actually resulted from only one use? Should one subtract credit from the score given for the correct inference--in which case, the apparent number of correct inferences would total to less than the actual number of such inferences--or should one ignore the incorrect inference (graving) because the actual use of the piece (whittling) was correctly inferred? There is also the question of how one should "score" implement no. 14, on which the left and right edges were used for different tasks which were correctly inferred. In the tabulation below, correct inferences have been emphasized; thus, no. 6 has been scored only once--as a set of correct inferences--whereas no. 14 has been scored as two sets of correct inferences. If there had been an implement, like no. 14, which had two separate edges used for two different tasks, but had been missed or incorrectly inferred, then that implement would have scored as two sets of incorrect inferences. Also, partial credit has been allowed for determinations of the worked material, like those for nos. 4 and 11, where a firm decision between two possible materials (one of which was correct) could not be confidently made.

It is obvious from these results that the more specific the information sought about the precise function of an implement, the more difficult it is to provide accurately. There is a logical, stepwise relationship between the inference of the used area, the

| No. | Area | Action | Material | | Total |
|-----|------|--------|----------|---|-------|
| 1 | 1 | 0 | 1 | | 2 |
| 2 | 1 | 1 | 1 | | 3 |
| 3 | 1 | 1 | 1 | | 3 |
| 4 | 1 | 1 | 0.5 | | 2.5 |
| 5 | 0 | 0 | 0 | | 0 |
| 6 | 1 | 1 | 1 | | 3 |
| 7 | 1 | 0 | 0 | | 1 |
| 8 | 1 | 1 | 1 | | 3 |
| 9 | 1 | 1 | 1 | | 3 |
| 10 | 0 | 0 | 0 | | 0 |
| 11 | 1 | 1 | 0.5 | | 2.5 |
| 12 | 1 | 1 | 0 | | 2 |
| 13 | 1 | 1 | 1 | | 3 |
| 14a | 1 | 1 | 1 | | 3 |
| b | 1 | 1 | 1 | | 3 |
| 15 | 1 | 1 | 0 | | 2 |
| | | | | | |
| Totals | 14 | 12 | 10 | = | 36 |
| Total possible | 16 | 16 | 16 | = | 48 |

method of use (or action), and the worked material. If the used portion of the tool cannot be isolated (as was the case in no. 10), then, of course, no further correct inferences about the tool's function can be made. Although it is not necessary to reconstruct the method of use or activity in order to infer the worked material, as the latter can usually be determined from the microwear polish itself, it is helpful to know the method of use as a check against possible misinterpretation of the microwear polish. For example, if one identifies an ambiguous microwear polish as hide polish but finds that the implement was used as a chopper, then obviously one thinks again about the identification of the polish. In all, eight working edges (on seven implements) were correctly identified (or, in the case of no. 9, shown to be absent), their method of use correctly reconstructed and the material they were used to work correctly identified--in other words, their functional interpretation was completely correct.

It is important that, as well as considering the general success of this experiment in microwear analysis and the vindication of the methods used, as represented by the successful inferences, the errors be examined in detail to see what information they may provide about the limitations of the technique and any lessons that they may disclose for future work.

Of the two errors in the isolation of the used areas, only one (no. 5) can be assigned to a real limitation of method or technique, since the misplacement of the used area on no. 10 was simply the result of carelessness. The lack of any apparent wear traces on no. 5, even after a thorough reexamination, indicates that scraping (or, for that matter, cutting) fat is unlikely to leave wear traces recoverable by the methods used in this study, though there may be traces observable with the higher magnifications obtainable with the scanning electron microscope. It may be, of course, that such a use leaves no traces whatever--in which case, we are up against a common archeological limitation and not one peculiar to microwear analysis. The misinterpretation(if that is the word) of no. 10 is the result of

simple, but not excusable, human error.  There is little doubt in my mind that if the used
area of this implement's edge had been examined, then the correct interpretation of its
function would have followed.

The inference of the method of use (or action) of an implement relies upon the evidence provided by the utilization damage, the orientation and distribution of linear wear
features (like striations), and the location and extent of the areas of microwear polish.
When these features are not present, or are ambiguous, errors in interpretation will obviously arise.  On no. 5, there were no wear traces of any kind present (except for those interpreted as antler-hammer marks) so, obviously, it was impossible to make any inferences
about this implement's action during use.  The guess made about the action of no. 10 was
substantially correct, but, since it was based on the wrong evidence, it must be counted as
an error.  The action of no. 1 was misinterpreted because the only striations (from utilization) present ran at low angles to the edge (unlike the high angles usually found on
whittling or planing edges), and the microwear polish was found on both edge aspects, which
is a trait most common on sawing and cutting edges and uncommon on whittling edges in my
experiments, where the polish tends to occur predominantly on only one edge aspect.  This
uncharacteristic distribution of the polish is the result of the tool's being employed with
the dorsal and the bulbar edge aspects alternately in contact with the wood surfaces.  This
method of whittling is seldom possible with most unretouched edges, where only one aspect
(usually the bulbar) is flat enough to serve as the contact aspect.  The interpretation of
no. 7 was the result of a failure in the logic of inference--because the three areas showing traces of use, although in close proximity, were separated by small areas of unworn
edge, they were interpreted separately, rather than as the result of a single use.  Nevertheless, the number of errors for this aspect of microwear interpretation is probably a
reasonable reflection of the percentage of similar errors one would expect to make when
studying prehistoric implements.

From my point of view, the inference of the worked material was complicated in this
test by Dr. Newcomer's use of a wooden cutting board (particularly in the butchering experiments) and the fact that the woodworking experiments and the one bone-working experiment were conducted on aged or seasoned materials.  The use of the cutting board led to
the errors in the identification of the worked material for nos. 4 and 12, where the mixture of the wood and meat polishes confused the issue, although the two polishes were distinguished from one another on no. 8.  While there is no doubt that a cutting board or
platform is of considerable assistance in some tasks, especially hide scraping or hide cutting, one might argue that its use in butchering tasks has more to do with modern standards
of cleanliness than with any increase in efficiency.  There is a certain amount of ethnographic evidence that animals were often butchered by hunter-gatherers on the ground (for
example, see fig. 1 in Gould et al. 1971), or on their own hides (Mandelbaum 1941: 193;
Gifford 1936: 265), or, at best, on a bed of foliage (Gifford 1936: 265).  A reexamination
of some of the Hoxne implements, initiated in light of the information provided by the
present test, confirmed the presence of wood polish on some of the hide-cutting knives, but
no such traces were found on any of the meat or butchering knives.

The polish found on no. 7 was misidentified as bone polish because of its rugged appearance, but this polish was the result of working a piece of cut wood at least ten years
old.  While not inconceivable, it seems very unlikely that such well-seasoned wood would
have been worked in Lower Paleolithic times.  And because of the relative intractability
of seasoned wood in general, compared with freshly cut wood, when working with stone tools,

it is unlikely that wood seasoned for more than a month or two at the most was commonly worked in the earlier periods of prehistory--certainly there was no obvious advantage to Paleolithic man. The microwear polish on no. 11 was also misidentified as antler polish, and this is indeed an error likely to occur when prehistoric collections are subjected to microwear analysis, since these two polishes are, under certain conditions, virtually indistinguishable. Since the materials to be worked in this test were not agreed upon beforehand, I had no way of knowing that there were to be no antler-working experiments. Had these test implements been, instead, from a known Lower Paleolithic context, a period from which evidence of antler-working is on present evidence so rare as to be almost nonexistent, all ambiguous polishes of the type seen on no. 11 would have been unhesitatingly identified as being the result of woodworking. But there is little doubt that confusion of wood and antler polishes could cause errors when dealing with later prehistoric implements from periods and regions where antler-working is known to be common. We may conclude from the error made in the identification of the polish on no. 15 that the variability of bone polish is much greater than could be expected from the results of the experiments reported above. However, the piece of bone that was worked was several months old, which may explain why working it produced an uncharacteristic (but nevertheless distinctive) polish. As was the case with the experiments using seasoned wood, we may ask whether it is likely that Paleolithic men would have worked such a material. While the percentage of fully correct interpretations of approximately 62% is enough to demonstrate the validity of these methods and techniques, it is probable that if the test implements had actually been from a Paleolithic site, where one would have some prior knowledge of the limited range of materials (in a limited range of conditions) likely to have been worked, then the percentage of correct identifications would have been much higher, perhaps as much as 80% but more likely around 70-75%.

The results of this test confirm that, with the use of high-magnification and the careful study of all types of microwear traces, one can almost always isolate the used portion of the tool and reconstruct its movement during use, as well as, in the majority of cases, determine exactly which material was being worked. On the pieces which were correctly interpreted, the accuracy of the reconstruction was sometimes very satisfying to the author: for example, the distinction made between the two different uses of the right and left edges of no. 14. The results of this test also serve as a partial confirmation of the distinctiveness of the various microwear polishes, since it was the character of the polishes found on the test implements that provided the basis for the inferences concerning the worked material.

Without undermining the encouraging results of this test for microwear analysis, the errors of inference made in the course of it have provided some valuable lessons and, indeed, some useful new information. The results of the microwear analysis on implements from Hoxne and Clacton were reviewed in light of these lessons, and the new information, with the result that the slightly tentative interpretation of some implements from Hoxne as "plant-gathering knives" became more certain, and evidence of the use of cutting boards in hide cutting at Hoxne was discovered.

Finally, this test prompts me to challenge other microwear analysts, using approaches different from those outlined in this thesis, to undertake similar tests of the validity of their functional inferences.

## Experiments with Hand Axes

In addition to the experiments already described, which were conducted with flakes and chopper-cores, four experiments were conducted with replicas of hand axes. The four implements were made by Peter Jones, an accomplished young student of experimental flint-knapping at Oxford, using hard-hammer flaking to rough out the shapes and soft-hammer flaking to finish the pieces. Three of these hand axes had approximately similar dimensions (that is, $L$ about 100 m, and $B$ about 60 mm; figs. 22, 23, 24), while one was slightly larger ($L$, 126 mm; $B$, 72 mm; fig. 25). Four different activities were undertaken with these implements: digging, cutting meat, scraping and cutting fat from a hide, and cutting through or breaking bone joints. All four hand axes were microscopically examined before as well as after use.

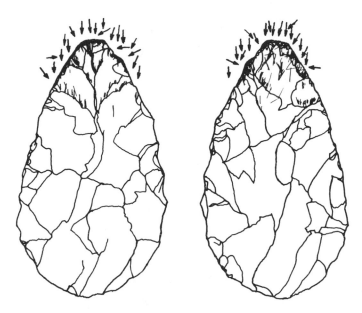

Figure 22.  Experimental hand ax used for digging (exp 32).

The first implement (exp. 32) was used for digging into some sandy, alluvial topsoil as if grubbing for roots. The tip of the implement was inserted with a push and then slightly twisted to loosen the soil. After ten minutes of digging, very little abrasion had taken place, but a few shallow striations were found within 25 mm of the tip, and running predominantly parallel to the implement's long axis. On the tip, the edges showed signs of crushing. After twenty minutes of use, the edges of the tip were crushed, and there were numerous striations on both aspects, some quite deep. Most striations and abrasion tracks ran parallel to the tool axis, but a few, particularly on the lateral edges near the tip, ran at high angles to the axis (fig. 22). These latter striations were, no doubt, the result of the twisting, "spading" movement during use. The parallel striations were found on the proximal, up-curving sections of the flake scars. In addition to edge-crushing and striations, a severe abrasion "polish" at the tip, and eroding flake scar ridges up to 3 mm distant from the tip, was observed. This abrasion polish is very rough (pl. 65), not unlike dry hide polish, but lacking the diffuse linear traces of that type

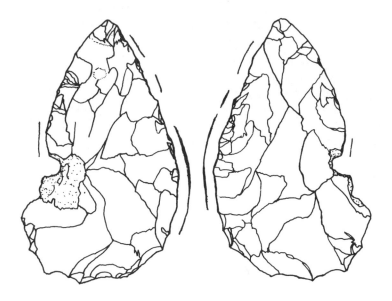

Figure 23.    Experimental hand ax used for cutting meat (exp 155).

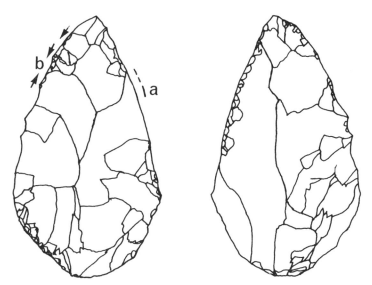

Figure 24.    Experimental hand ax used for removing fat from hide (exp 156).    (a) scraping edge; (b) cutting edge.

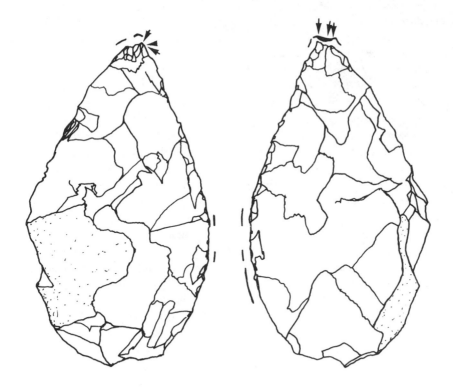

Figure 25.  Experimental hand ax used for breaking bone joints (exp 157).

of microwear polish and much more rugged.  Even after repeated cleaning in NaOH and HCl
baths, small, iridescent mineral particles could still be seen resting in pits and depressions in the polished area and, it appears, these were sometimes incorporated in the abrasion polish itself (pl. 65).  This abrasion polish can be detected easily by the naked eye.
The severity of the damage and the microwear traces left by digging should make them quite
easy to identify, if they occur, on archeological implements.

The second experimental hand ax (exp. 155; fig. 23) was used for cutting up several
pounds of meat (venison, in fact).  The work was accomplished with a unidirectional cutting
motion, using the left edge of the implement (when observed from aspect 1).  The resultant
microwear consisted of a faint meat polish on both aspects of the working edge.  It was
most developed on the convex medial portion of the working edge.  There were no striations
to be seen on any portion of the used edge.  On the right edge (opposite the working edge),
there was a small area of faint polish, affecting both aspects, adjacent to the area of
preserved cortex.  This polish was evidently caused by contact with the hand during use,
since this part of the edge never came into contact with the meat.  Not enough of this
polish was present to enable one to isolate any distinguishing features; microwear caused
by contact with the hand during use was also extremely rare on the rest of the experimental
implements.  No utilization damage could be distinguished from the smaller retouch scars
on the working edge.  Other than the problem of isolating utilization damage from the retouch, the traces found on this piece were exactly similar to those found on experimental
flakes used for meat cutting.

The third hand ax replica (exp. 156; fig. 24) was used for scraping and cutting fat away from a section of pig hide of approximately 150 sq cm. This task was accomplished by using the right edge (observing aspect 1) with a scraping action, aspect 1 leading during movement, and using the left edge for cutting with a sawing action. The only traces left by the scraping on the right edge were a small area of bright, greasy polish on aspect 1 of the right edge, which rounds the edge. The only traces left on the left edge were a number of deep striations and abrasion tracks running parallel with the edge and distributed on both edge aspects. These are undoubtedly the result of contact with the soil when the hide was accidentally cut through, since the experiment was carried out on the open ground. No traces of a microwear polish were found, however, on the left "cutting" edge: this is because the amount of hide cutting was insufficient for a hide polish to develop.

The fourth experimental hand ax (exp. 157; fig. 25) was used for cutting through and breaking the joints in a section of the spinal column of a cow. Some cutting and sawing was done using the right edge (observing aspect 1), while the tip was inserted between the joints and twisted, prying the vertebrae apart. The latter activity eventually removed the tip and left a slightly concave area of shallow, invasive damage scars on aspect 1 of the tip. Associated with the damaged tip were areas of bone polish (pl. 66) more intense on aspect 2 but clearly present on aspect 1 as well. A few deep, narrow striations occurred with the polish: running at right angles to the long axis of the implement on aspect 1 and parallel to it on aspect 2. A weakly developed bone polish, the result of the cutting and sawing activity, was found on both aspects of the proximal portion of the right edge. No striations or utilization damage could be distinguished in this area.

These hand axes proved to be perfectly adequate tools for accomplishing the various tasks undertaken in these experiments, though the implement employed for removing fat from the back of the hide (exp. 156) showed a tendency to cut through the hide, and its working edge had its efficiency quickly reduced by the rapid accumulation of fatty tissue, which had to be removed periodically in order to continue working. Also, a larger hand ax than that used in experiment 32 would probably have been more suitable for use as a grubbing or digging tool. Two points are clear as a result of these experiments: (1) the wear traces that are produced on hand axes by various uses do not differ significantly from those that occur on comparably used flake tools; (2) the severe wear traces left by digging should be easily recognizable on fresh archeological specimens, if they occur on them at all.

Since very few hand axes were included among the archeological specimens studied in the second part of this thesis, the experiments using replica hand axes were not taken any further. It was sufficient to know, for immediate purposes, that the microwear traces found on used hand axes were fully comparable with those found on experimental flake tools used for the same tasks.

## The Experimental Program:  Conclusions

There are several important conclusions that can be drawn from this study of natural wear and the traces found on the experimental implements. Some of these conclusions are methodological and technical, addressing the related questions of how one should go about studying microwear and what equipment one should use. Others are conclusions of fact, whose application provides the background for the microwear analysis of archeological specimens.

It is clear that all ranges of magnification, from what can be seen with the naked eye to very high optical magnifications, must be employed in the study of implement function.

The most interesting and informative features of microwear patterns cannot be observed, let alone studied, if too low a range of magnifications is used.

The value of the microscopic study of experimentally made and used implements should be clearly apparent. Such a study should be an essential first step in microwear study. The value of such an experimental framework is greatly enhanced if it is based upon the particular materials likely or known to have been available and if it takes into account usages likely to have been employed at the archeological sites to be studied.

The most important discovery made in the course of these experiments is that the microwear polishes formed by various worked materials have distinctive appearances and are, indeed, distinguishable from one another. It has also been determined that some of these polishes are not merely different, but measurably different. The likely consequence of these facts is that not only should the methods of use of archeological implements be determinable, but the actual material on which they were used should also be inferable in many or even most cases, given that the artifacts are in a suitable condition for study. The results of the blind test demonstrate that this can be done with reasonable confidence. There are a few convergences, however, that may present some difficulties: use on meat may not always be distinguishable from use on fresh, wet hide; use on wood may not always be distinguishable from use on soaked antler, unless the microwear polish is well developed; bone and antler saws will sometimes be indistinguishable from one another. But these few problems should hardly effect the overall ability of the microwear analyst correctly and fully to interpret flint implements in functional terms, and there may be other kinds of evidence to help him choose between alternative identifications.

A study of the summary tables for the various experimental uses (tables 17-19) should make it clear that many variables other than the material worked and the method of use--for example, the angle of the edge and the depth of insertion into the material (which can be the same for a variety of uses on a variety of materials--will affect the type and size of the utilization damage formed. This means that utilization damage alone cannot serve as a sensitive index of function. Also, utilization damage can too rarely be distinguished from the smaller components of retouch scar patterns. It is really only distinguishable from other kinds of edge damage when it is found in association with traces of true microwear (particularly, the microwear polishes). However, once one is reasonably certain that the damage on the edge is utilization damage, then it can serve as a useful check on an interpretation already based on the microwear traces and may also provide useful information about the manner in which the implement was used. For example, if one finds meat polish and striations parallel to the edge on an implement, but the associated edge damage is much heavier than one would expect from the cutting of meat alone, then one can better describe the implement as a "butchering knife," which has been in contact with bone or has cut through joints, than as simply a "meat knife," used only for cutting up flesh.

Finally, it is clear that the "natural" and "technological" effects can in almost every case be reliably distinguished from the microscopic traces left by human use. Natural traces not only appear different to microwear traces, but generally affect those portions of an implement that are never affected by microwear. Technological effects are less randomly distributed, since they are generally the result of purposeful activity, but they are usually limited in their microscopic manifestations to sporadic areas of abrasion, that would never, alone, be taken as a firm indication of use.

4. THE SELECTION OF ARCHEOLOGICAL COLLECTIONS FOR MICROWEAR STUDY

The experiments described in the preceding chapter were designed with the idea that
the results would be applied to the microwear analysis of assemblages from British Lower
Paleolithic sites. This concentration on the Lower Paleolithic came about for the following reasons:

1. I wished to break new ground both in methods and in material, and most of the
previous microwear analysis had been conducted on Upper Paleolithic implements.

2. Most of the British Upper Paleolithic sites had been badly disturbed by unscien-
tific excavations in the late nineteenth century; recent excavations at some of these
sites by several excavators, principally J. Campbell (1978), were only able to recover
small numbers of implements, which would be unsuitable as samples for microwear analysis and not necessarily representative of the original assemblages.

3. British Middle Paleolithic sites are rare and poor in remains of all kinds, so no
suitable assemblages of this type were available.

4. This left the Lower Paleolithic, a period that has been of personal interest to me.

There were several criteria employed in the selection of assemblages for microwear analysis
that were meant to insure that the implements studied would retain microwear traces, would
be adequately documented, and would have been unaffected by postexcavation damage.

For an assemblage to be suitable for microwear analysis, the majority of its implements must be in extremely fresh condition, that is, unaffected by any form of natural abrasion. This condition is best fulfilled by only studying collections from archeological deposits judged to be in primary context. This restriction means that assemblages from the
vast majority of British Lower Paleolithic sites were unsuitable for microwear analysis as
assemblages, since they were in secondary contexts (see Roe 1968, concerning Acheulean assemblages; and Wymer 1968, concerning Clactonian assemblages). Only two sites were thought
to contain Clactonian assemblages in probable primary context--Swanscombe (Lower Loam) and
Clacton-on-Sea (the golf course excavation site). Only six Acheulean sites were thought to
contain assemblages likely to be in primary context--Caddington, Bowman's Lodge, Gaddesden
Row, Round Green, Stoke Newington, and, after recent excavations, Hoxne.

As well as being wholly unabraded, the implements must not be affected by heavy white
patination, as this destroys the microsurface of implements and, consequently, most of the
really informative wear traces. Some of the implements from Caddington were so affected
(Roe 1968: 9), making them unusable for any microwear study.

In order that the results from any microwear study may be checked against supplementary data of the kind referred to in chapter 1 and so that such results could confidently be given archeological significance, it is important that the assemblages employed be recently excavated by modern scientific methods involving the recovery of all flaked material and faunal remains, and using three-dimensional recording procedures.  This requirement eliminates otherwise acceptable assemblages, like Caddington, Stoke Newington, Bowman's Lodge, and Gaddesden Row.

The postexcavation treatment and storage of the implements must also be considered.  If implements are stored in boxes and drawers in contact with one another, "box damage" of various types will occur, mainly edge damage and scratching.  While these traces can be distinguished relatively easily from true utilization damage and microwear, they may nevertheless remove or seriously alter any true wear traces.  Unfortunately, most of the collections made before 1960 in Britain and, indeed, in many other countries, were stored in such a fashion and would, therefore, be unsuitable for intense study (although there may be useful information that can still be obtained from them).  However, the implements from the recent excavations of the classic Lower Paleolithic sites of Swanscombe (by J. Waechter), Clacton, and Hoxne (by J. Wymer and R. Singer) were carefully stored.  The implements from Swanscombe and Hoxne were individually bagged in plastic or paper bags, while those from Clacton were carefully set in cotton wool, well separated from each other, in boxes.  The artifacts in these three collections also met the other conditions indicated above.

Finally, it was crucial that any collections meeting the above criteria should be available for study.  Since it was desirable that the collections be brought to Oxford for study because the necessary facilities and equipment were concentrated here, more than simple professional courtesy was required from the people with the relevant collections at their disposal.  Fortunately, my work met with the most encouraging interest and continued assistance from the late J. Waechter (excavator of the Swanscombe Lower Loam industry) and from R. Singer and J. Wymer (excavators of the Clacton Golf Course and Hoxne sites).  There are certainly other series of artifacts in Britain that may be suitable for microwear analysis (High Lodge, for example), but, for one reason or another, these were not available for study.

Thus, the three assemblages finally submitted to detailed microwear analysis for this study were the "Clactonian" material from the Swanscombe Lower Loam, the Clactonian industry from the Clacton Golf Course site, and the Acheulean assemblages from the recent excavation at Hoxne.  All of these collections were from (in the judgment of the excavators) primary context sites, were relatively unpatinated, had been carefully excavated using modern methods, had been carefully stored after excavation, and could be made available for thorough study over a prolonged period.

5.  A MICROWEAR ANALYSIS OF FLINT ARTIFACTS FROM THE
    GOLF COURSE SITE, CLACTON-ON-SEA (ESSEX)


## History and Stratigraphy

The Lower Paleolithic exposures in and around Clacton-on-Sea (Essex) have been the
subjects of investigations since the beginning of this century.  All of these are exposures
of sediments which fill an ancient river channel (or channels) of Mid-Pleistocene age.
Hazzledine Warren (1914, 1922, 1955) collected flint implements from various exposures,
principally on the now-inaccessible "Foreshore" area just southwest of the Clacton Pier,
from before the World War I until about 1950 (Singer et al. 1973).  Warren recognized the
distinctiveness of the industry, calling it "Mesvinian" after an industry found in the
Pleistocene river-gravels of Mesvin, Belgium, at the suggestion of the Abbé Breuil.  The
industry was rechristened Clactonian, and Clacton became its type site when it was clear
that the implements from Mesvin were "in a derived condition" and mixed with other industries (Oakley and Leakey 1937).  The first systematic excavation in the Clacton Channel
deposits was conducted by K. P. Oakley and M. Leakey in 1934 (Oakley and Leakey 1937).  The
material analyzed in the present study was obtained during the most recent excavations,
which took place in 1969 and 1970 under the auspices of the University of Chicago, depart-
ment of anatomy (Wymer and Singer 1970; Singer et al. 1973).

The stratigraphy of the University of Chicago excavations showed little similarity to
the earlier exposures along the Foreshore, but could be correlated with the 1934 excavation.
The sequence recorded can be summarized as follows (from Singer et al. 1973):  (1) topsoil
and subsoil: 10-30 cm thick; (2) brown fissile clay, stony clay: 60-70 cm thick; (3) whit-
ish, variegated marl with occasional shelves, interdigitated with shelly sand: 60 cm thick
(in one restricted area of the surface of the marl, there is a shallow deposit of gravel
containing patinated implements--this is known as the "gravel spread on top of the marl");
(4) gravel in variable clayey-sand matrix: gray clay with stone inclusion: 50-60 cm thick;
(5) London clay.

The artifacts analyzed here were recovered from the marl (3) and gravel (4).


## Condition of Artifacts

Only implements in the freshest condition were suitable for microwear analysis, so
attention was concentrated on the implements classed by the excavators (on the basis of
simple observation), as "mint," or "sharp."  It became apparent that most implements in
sharp condition (see Singer et al. 1973: 27) were not suitable for analysis, as they

usually showed signs of slight natural abrasion and severer forms of weathering. Even implements classed as "mint" sometimes showed signs of natural abrasion (especially deep soil
movement striations) that rendered them unreliable pieces for microwear analysis. Every
implement which showed, under examination, natural abrasion or severe weathering and patination was excluded from further consideration. The mere presence of a few oddly distributed
edge-damage scars, which may have resulted from the original settling of the deposits and
very slight movements within them under the pressure of overlying sediments, was not considered sufficient criterion for excluding a piece. These scars can be the result of use
and do not obscure or substantially remove true microwear traces, as do natural abrasions
and weathering. Most implements excluded because of natural abrasion, and so on, were rejected after an examination with the naked eye. Of the 312 implements picked out as suitable for examination under the microscope, 64 (50 from the gravel, 14 from the marl) were
later excluded for reasons of natural abrasion. The breakdown of the remaining implements
is as follows:

*Marl* (including the gravel spread on top of the marl)

| | |
|---|---|
| unused | 87 |
| probably used | 3 |
| used | 14 |
| | 104 |

| | |
|---|---|
| percentage of total with use traces | 13.46 |
| percentage of total with use traces plus probably used | 16.35 |

*Gravel* (including the contorted gravel)

| | |
|---|---|
| unused | 112 |
| used | 32 |
| | 144 |

| | |
|---|---|
| percentage of total with use traces | 22.22 |

Though the percentage of used implements is smaller for the marl than the gravel, this is
not a significant difference.

## Description of Used Pieces

Since only forty-six pieces from Clacton show undoubted traces of use, it is possible
and desirable to give a brief description of each, with its microwear traces. The artifacts are listed according to functional categories within the stratigraphic units of the
gravel and the marl. The dimensions are given to the nearest mm, and the measurements
were taken by the methods outlined in chapter 3. The grid coordinates, depth (in meters),
and catalog number are all as assigned by the excavators.

MARL

### Wood-whittling or planing

CL 1534: L45 B48 Th13 B/L 1.067 Th/b .271; coordinates 617 153 depth 1.62; pl. 67.

A corner-struck triangular flake of unpatinated, dark gray flint. There are two
areas of the edge showing microwear and associated utilization damage: (1) the
distal left lateral edge, edge angle 26°, with a convex shape, showing wood polish
on the dorsal aspect only but confined to the very edge, and on the bulbar aspect
a small area of *SD* scars accompanied by two small ½*Moon* breakages; (2) distal
right lateral edge or tip, edge angle 31° and straight edge shape, with wood
polish on the dorsal aspect only and associated with some *MicroDeep* damage on the
same aspect. The striations found on the bulbar aspect of the left lateral edge

(none were found on the right lateral edge) run at about a 60° angle to the edge. The implement was probably held this way during use so that more of the edge was engaged during a whittling stroke; therefore, because of the increased friction, the cutting would have been slower and more controllable. This fact and the relatively mild nature of the utilization damage, given the thinness of the two working edges, imply that the whittling done with this implement must have been of a fairly delicate nature.

CL 80:    L49 B59 Th28 B/L 1.204 Th/B .4756; coordinates 513 148 depth 1.02; fig. 26, pl. 68. A left, cortex-backed irregular flake of a gray flint; the large dorsal facet is a thermal fracture. The microwear traces occur on the right lateral edge on the bulbar aspect. The slightly concave edge has an angle of 34°. The microwear traces consist of a wood polish on the bulbar aspect, more developed away from the center of the concavity, with a single shallow striation on the dorsal aspect. The associated edge damage consists of *SD* scars, perhaps creating the slight concavity on the dorsal aspect.

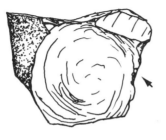

Figure 26.   CL 80.

## Wood scraping

CL 1034:  L33 B56 Th14 B/L 1.697 Th/B .250; coordinates 665 184 depth 1.08; fig. 27. A right cortex-backed side-struck flake. The wear traces occur on the left lateral edge, which is nearly straight (very slight concavity). The microwear traces consist of two small patches of wood polish on the bulbar aspect disposed on raised points of the microtopography near the edge. The polish in both cases is more intense on the proximal side of these raised features, indicating movement during use away from the center of the piece--for example, scraping. Other than these two slight patches, there are no areas of polish at the edge; this is probably because the utilization damage carried the forming polish away. The associated edge damage, occurring on the dorsal aspect, consists of a continuous run of *SD* and *S Step* scars, with two *LS* scars in the center of the edge. The *LS* scars may be retouch, but such invasive scars rarely occur in wood-scraping experiments.

Figure 27.   CL 1034.

CL 977:   L32 B36 Th8 B/L 1.125 Th/B .222; coordinates 641 184 depth 1.88; fig. 28.
          A small, retouched flake of brown, banded flint, which conjoins CL 578 (position
          550 213 depth 1.53), from the top of the gravel. The wear traces are associated
          with the retouched notch. A very lightly developed polish, probably wood polish,
          occurs on the dorsal aspect of the retouched edge (edge angle 80°); however, an
          intense polish has formed on a ridge, running between the dorsal and bulbar as-
          pects, formed by the intersection of the platform and the retouched notch (see
          fig. 28). Handling of the implement indicates that when scraping with the dorsal
          edge of the notch, this ridge is brought into full or partial contact with the
          worked material. Nevertheless, this polish is not unequivocally wood polish--it
          is bright, relatively smooth, but there is a slight roughness to the polish that
          is unlike wood polish. Since the concave shape of the used edge and the incon-
          clusive evidence of the dorsal polish argue for this implement's use on wood, I
          suggest the ridge polish is a wood polish which has been subject to slight chemi-
          cal weathering. The edge damage forming the notch is undoubtedly retouch, and it
          is impossible to distinguish the small components of the retouch from what might
          be utilization damage.

Figure 28.  CL 977 (conjoins with CL 578).

CL 399:   L37 B50 Th10 B/L 1.3514 Th/B .200; coordinates 543 159 depth 1.09.
          A trapezoidal flake struck from a rolled cobble (possibly retouched). The micro-
          wear consists of a wood polish on the left-canted distal edge on the bulbar as-
          pect. On the dorsal aspect of the working edge is a continuous area of SS and
          MicroStep scars. These are most probably retouch because the SS scars are rela-
          tively large (1.5 mm long) and uniform in size. Also, the unretouched, unused
          portion of the distal edge shows the bulbar aspect curving up to the relatively
          flat dorsal surface. If the whole distal end were like this originally, it would
          not have been a particularly efficient edge for scraping in the manner the micro-
          wear indicates, but would have required retouching of the edge in just the place
          and in the direction the edge damage occurs. However, wood-scraping edges tend
          to be "self-retouching" during use if the original edge is as thin as this one.
          The edge damage and bulbar surface form an angle of 60°. The edge is straight.

## Wood sawing

CL 683:   L50 B49 Th16 B/L .980 Th/B .326; coordinates 554 274 depth 1.12; fig. 29, pl. 162.
          This flake was classified by the excavators as being "slightly rolled," although
          it was boxed with mint/sharp implements. In fact, it is quite fresh (once lime
          encrustations have been removed) but is made of a light brown, variegated, coarse-

grained, cherty flint which does not have the obviously "sharp" look of the other
implements, which were made with dark, fine-grained, homogeneous flint. There is
a polish on both aspects of the right lateral edge, which is bright but has a
rough appearance due almost certainly to the coarseness of the flint--otherwise it
is a wood polish. The edge damage consists of alternate *LD*, *LS*, *SD* scars on both
edge aspects. In the polish there are shallow abrasion tracks and striations
parallel to the edge, indicating a sawing or cutting movement during use. The
edge is straight, and its edge angle is 25°.

Figure 29.  CL 683.

CL 168:    L77 B46 Th23 B/L .597 Th/B .500; coordinates 484 152 depth .751.
           A long, right cortex-backed flake. The microwear, which consists of extremely
           well-preserved wood polish, covers both aspects of the proximal left lateral edge,
           which is slightly convex. The indications of direction in the polish indicate a
           movement roughly parallel to the edge, that is, sawing. The edge damage consists
           of small ½Moon breakages, which experiments show very commonly result when sawing
           with thin (low-angled), unretouched edges, and a few *MicroD* and *MicroS* scars ran-
           domly distributed on both aspects of the used edge. The task involved here must
           have been a delicate one, since the edge is thin (edge angle 28°) and the edge
           damage is relatively slight, while the polish is well developed.

Wood chopping/adzing
CL 1578:   L193 B74 Th46 B/L .796 Th/B 622; coordinates 479 233 depth .94; fig. 30, pl. 70.
           A large chopper-core with only four flake removals; it was originally a slightly
           rolled cobble. There is a slight wood polish on the distal edge of aspect 1 (see
           fig. 25) and a small patch of wood polish on the same aspect where the ridge be-
           tween the two flake scars meets the edge. These areas of polish are accompanied
           by *MicroD* and *MicroS* edge damage. On aspect 2, a small area of *MicroStep* damage
           is opposite the main polish area. Aspect 1 is flatter than aspect 2, and the as-
           pect 2 flake scars form a steep angle with the general implement axis. In other
           words, aspect 1 is the bifacial equivalent of a ventral surface. The edge is com-
           plexly shaped, but the main area of wear is straight. The edge angle is 45°. Be-
           cause of the unifacial placement of the microwear polish and the delicateness of
           the edge damage, this implement is more likely to have been used as an adze than
           as a chopper. The delicateness of its edge damage is no argument against its use
           as a chopping-adzing tool, since experiments show that with a sturdy edge, adzing
           fresh wood will often not create any large utilization damage, even after consider-
           able use.

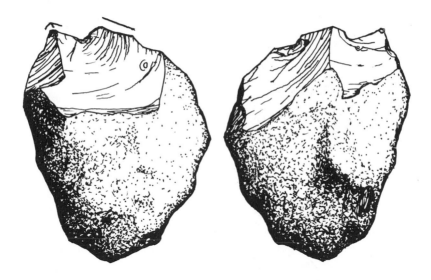

Figure 30. CL 1578.

## Wood boring

CL 405:   L63 B50 Th34 B/L .794 Th/B .680; coordinates 449 194 depth .96.

A large, chunky, thermal flake with a cusp formed between two Clacton notches. On the dorsal surface of the cusp there is a small patch of faint polish, probably wood, on a piece of edge just proximal of the area affected by edge damage. The ventral surface (thermal-fracture surface) of the cusp shows *MicroStep* damage to the cusp tip and central ridge. The dorsal surface shows some shallow scalar damage at the cusp tip. The edge damage of the cusp is so similar to that formed on an experimental wood borer used for less than 150 strokes that, with the small patch of probable wood polish, one can confidently interpret this piece as a wood borer.

## Meat knives

CL 78:   L31 B50 Th13 B/L 1.613 Th/B .26; coordinates 55S-195, 60S-320 cutting V depth 1.92; fig. 31, pl. 71.

Side-struck flake retouched with Clacton notch. There is a meat polish on both aspects of the right lateral edge. The polish on the bulbar aspect is more intense, while that on the dorsal is more extensive. There are a series of tiny *SD* scars on the bulbar aspect on the distal end of the concavity. While this is morphologically not what one might expect a meat knife to look like, it may have been an *ad hoc* tool or have been used for a special butchering task, like cutting through joint ligaments. It has undeniably been used for a relatively long time (2000 strokes?). The edge angle is 42°.

Figure 31.  CL 78.

CL 395:   L61 B26 Th16 B/L .426 Th/B .615; coordinates 541 151 depth 1.15; fig. 32, pl. 72.
          Bladelike flake with backing retouch on left lateral edge. A meat polish is dis-
          cernible on both aspects of the right lateral edge for the proximal 2/3 of the
          edge length. There are several minute striae scattered over this polished area.
          At the very tip, there are two parallel striae that probably did not result from
          use. These are similar to the striae caused by soil movement, in that their
          grooves are not smooth and they are relatively deep; however, they are much nar-
          rower than such striae and lack the U-shaped cross-section typical of soil-
          movement striae. The edge is straight, and the edge angle is 40°.

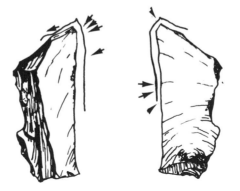

Figure 32.  ·CL 395.

CL 11:    L26 B29 Th9; coordinates cutting VII depth 1.00.
          Small retouch flake with cortex on dorsal. Microwear polish is disposed on both
          aspects of the dorsal platform edge as well as extending along the bulbar plat-
          form edge from the right lateral edge to the point of percussion. The polish is
          most developed along the dorsal platform edge, decreasing in intensity as one
          nears the center of the platform. This is a meat polish, although rather dull.
          Some shallow striations on the platform indicate a direction of use at an angle
          to the edge, although a slicing action could have caused them if the implement
          was canted slightly during use. Because of the polish along the bulbar edge of
          the platform, it is clear that, in spite of its small size, this piece was used
          after it was detached. The edge is convex, and the edge angle is 55°.

CL 328:   L91 B56 Th25 B/L .615 Th/B .446; coordinates 467 158 depth .60; fig. 33.
          A large flake with a steep back on right edge. The microwear consists of an ex-
          tensive area of meat polish, most extensive on the left distal corner and extend-
          ing down the left lateral edge. The polish is more pronounced on the bulbar as-
          pect. There are a large number of very minute striae in the polish, whose general
          orientation indicates a movement during use parallel to the left lateral edge.
          The edge angles vary along the used edge between 32° and 45°; the average 38° is
          used for all comparisons. The edge shape for the used area is generally convex.
          It is clear that this implement was used for a considerable period of time com-
          pared to the others.

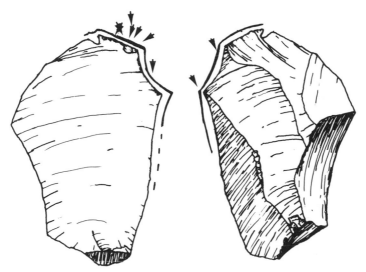

Figure 33.  CL 328.

Meat cleaver?

CL 1544:  L76 B65 Th32 B/L .855 Th/B .492; coordinates 588 169 depth 1.631.
          Thick, corner-struck flake with backing retouch on right lateral edge. Two faces
          of the dorsal surface are slightly water abraded (before detachment from a core).
          On the bulbar surface of the left distal end edge, there are a number of short
          abrasion tracks running at an angle to the edge. These are accompanied by some
          LS edge damage. At a few points in the center of this bulbar edge, there are
          areas of slight polish, like meat polish, in an early stage of formation. One
          cannot be sure that the abrasion tracks are related to the possible meat polish.
          If they are, then this implement is a butchering chopper or cleaver; if they are
          not, then we can only say that this implement was used briefly on meat.

Possibly used pieces

CL 678:   L51 B42 Th13; coordinates 578 131 depth 151.
          Flake from rolled cobble of brown, banded flint. Microwear consists of a few
          striae on the left lateral edge, bulbar aspect. The most distal striation is very
          narrow and somewhat deep, the more proximal striations are broader and quite shal-
          low. The direction of the striae indicates a direction of use parallel or at a
          slight angle to the edge. There are no traces on the dorsal surface--no polishes

and no edge damage. This implement appears to have been used for cutting, but the material cannot be determined in the absence of polish or utilization damage. Broad striae of the type found on proximal portion of the edge commonly result during woodworking--but not the narrow striations on the distal portion of the edge. Narrow striations are commonly seen on hide- and meat-working edges, but not broad striae. The possibility exists that this implement was used for cutting in the preparation of some plant material. The edge angle is 55°, and the edge is a complex shape.

CL 1527: L41 B40 Th11; coordinates 487 232 depth .84 (gravel in marl).
    Mottled, white-patinated flake. This piece is likely to have been used, even though the evidence is somewhat equivocal. The *SD* damage along the dorsal right lateral edge seems to be a typical utilization edge damage, although such effects can be caused by minor soil movements. On the bulbar right lateral edge are several narrow striations disposed parallel to the edge. The patination effects obscure any polish that might have been present. Both the edge damage and the striations are commensurate with a use like cutting or sawing, but the material worked cannot be determined. The edge is convex, and the edge angle is 32°.

GRAVEL

### Wood whittling or planing

CL 1480: L64 B62 Th21 B/L .969 Th/B .339; coordinates 653 160 depth 2.25; fig. 34, pl. 73.
    Large, partially cortex-covered flake with retouch on right lateral edge. The microwear consists of a small area of wood polish and several long striations concentrated at the center of the concavity formed by retouch on the bulbar aspect of the right lateral edge. No utilization edge damage can be isolated from the small elements of the retouch on the opposite dorsal surface of the used edge. The striations indicate two directions of use at different angles to the edge, but most of the striations are oriented at high angles to the edge. The edge is concave, and the edge angle is 72°.

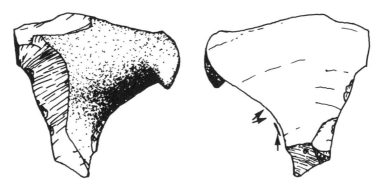

Figure 34.  CL 1480.

CL 1225: L54 B45 Th18 B/L .833 Th/B .400; coordinates 431 202 depth 1.82; fig. 35, pl. 74.
    Retouched, snap-backed flake. The left lateral edge has been steeply retouched and then notched distally. There are some incipient cones on the bulbar surface several millimeters from the retouched edge which imply that the maker (or user)

was trying to make at least one more notch proximally similar to the one present distally. The distal notch was used for whittling wood, as evidenced by the fact that on the bulbar aspect of the distal edge of the notch, there is a clear wood polish. On the dorsal aspect of this edge, opposite the polish, there is a series of small *SD* damage scars. At the proximal edge of the notch scar, a short cusp protrudes from the general line of the edge, and on the bulbar aspect of the edge is another small patch of wood polish. The edge is concave, and the edge angle is 30°.

Figure 35.  CL 1225 (hatched areas indicate recent breakages).

CL 689:  L46 B63 Th37 B/L 1.370 Th/B .587; coordinates 659 241 depth 1.05; fig. 36, pl. 75.
Shatter-piece retouched in concavity. Along a biconcave section of the ventral edge, an intense wood polish has developed. There are a few patches of wood polish on the dorsal aspect at the extreme edge, on the ridges of the utilization and retouch scars. A few shallow striations can be seen in the ventral polish running at roughly right angles to the edge; similar shorter striations were found at the very edge on the dorsal aspect. Because the polish is more extensive on the ventral surface, and because of the direction and length of the associated striations, this implement is interpreted as a wood plane. If one could say definitely that the edge damage on the dorsal aspect contained relatively large utilization-damage scars, then this implement could have been used as a scraper as well. Indeed, some of my wood-planing experiments showed that it was often efficacious to use the planing edge, like a scraper, for a few strokes in order to remove a knot which was preventing efficient planing. This procedure usually left a few microwear traces but especially it caused some *S Step* and *MicroStep* utilization edge damage (since a "planing" edge is, by definition, a steep-angled edge) on what would otherwise have been a virtually undamaged edge. Because of the size of most of the damage scars on this piece, there can be little doubt that this edge has been retouched. It is impossible to say whether this retouch was original modification or resharpening. The edge angle is 90°.

CL 112:  L100 B51 Th23 B/L .510 Th/B .451; coordinates--none recorded; from cutting VIII "Contorted clay and stone," no depth recorded.
A right cortex-backed flake. This flint has been weathered, which means there is some dissolution of the microsurface. However, since a microwear polish presents less surface area to the dissolution process, it is well preserved in relation to

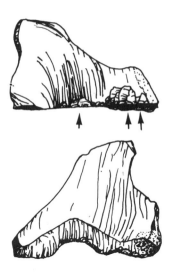
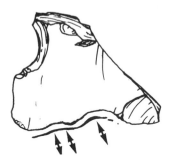

Figure 36.  CL 689.

the rest of the flint surface, and the polish patches are "raised" or "pedestaled" above the general level of the microtopography. The polish is undeniably wood polish and disposed on the bulbar aspect of the distal left lateral edge. Its placement and a few directional features in the polish indicate whittling, with a movement roughly at right angles to the edge. There is no edge damage, which is not unusual in view of the high edge angle (56°) and the featureless, straight edge. It is interesting to note that this particular piece, if the user were right-handed, must have been used with a toward-the-user movement because the wear is placed so distally on the left lateral edge, otherwise there is no convenient grip for an away-from-the-user movement. Of course, the opposite would be true if the user were left-handed.

CL 262:  L43 B37 Th11 B/L .861 Th/B .297; coordinates 455 149 depth 1.23.
Small, semirectangular flake with nibbling retouch on right lateral edge. The microwear is a wood polish disposed on the bulbar aspect of the straight distal edge. There is no microwear associated with the edge damage (*SD* and *SS*) on the adjacent right lateral edge. Associated with wood polish, on the bulbar aspect, are two broad, shallow, damage scars, as well as several very minute scars of a similar morphology. There are few indications of direction in the polish and no striae, but the placement of the polish and the confinement of the utilization damage to the bulbar aspect indicate an insertion of the edge at roughly right angles to its own axis--in other words, planing or whittling. The edge angle ranges from 50° to 70°; the median 60° is used for comparisons and statistical purposes.

CL 234:  L37 B61 Th23 B/L 1.649 Th/B .377; coordinates 493 144 depth 1.39; fig. 37, pl. 76.
Side-struck flake with right cortex back. This piece shows a wood polish on the bulbar aspect of the distal edge. The polish is confined to the very edge, but

there are a number of shallow striae leading away from the edge at a slight angle
to it.  On the dorsal aspect of this edge, there is a continuous line of edge damage consisting of *SS* and *S Step* scars.  The edge is straight, and the edge angle
is 38°.

Figure 37.  CL 234.

CL 1563: L83 B60 Th34 B/L .723 Th/B .567; coordinates 585 155 depth 1.67; fig. 38, pl. 77.
A large, cortex-covered flake with steep end retouch.  The microwear is disposed,
as one might expect, on the retouched distal end, and it consists of a very faint
wood polish on the bulbar aspect accompanied by a number of shallow striae running
into the interior of the implement (one 20 mm long) roughly parallel with its long
axis (pl. 77).  The polish is placed on the distal side of some small raised features of the microtopography, confirming what is suggested by the length and
placement of the striae, namely, that the working edge was pushed into the worked
material.  The length of the striae indicates that the bulbar surface was held at
a very low angle to (if, indeed, it did not rest on) the worked material--in this
case, wood.  On the dorsal aspect, in the hollow of one of the retouch scars, near
the edge, are two shallow striae of the same type as found on the bulbar aspect.
These seem likely to have been caused by the wood shavings curling away in front
of the edge during use.  On the bulbar aspect of this edge, there are several
broad, shallow, flake scars, including one particularly large one, that are commensurate with its use as a plane.  Finally, in the center of the dorsal cortex
is a large protuberance that serves as an excellent handhold for planing.  The
edge angle is 79°.

## Wood scraping

CL 1104: L41 B43 Th19 B/L 1.049 Th/B .442; coordinates 555 164 depth 1.88.
A small, chunky flake with a left cortex back.  The microwear consists primarily
of short, shallow striae on the dorsal aspect of the distal end edge with a very
faint but bright polish at a few points on the very edge.  The polish is probably
wood polish, although too little survives to be certain.  The shallow striae certainly suggest woodworking, as does the associated edge damage (*SD* and *S Step*)
found on the bulbar aspect.  All these patterns taken together indicate a wood
scraper.  The edge is straight, and the edge angle is 90°.  It is interesting to
note the alternate notches on the butt, creating an "Aterian tang"; however, these
are likely to have resulted from alternate flaking on the core prior to the de-
tachment of this flake.

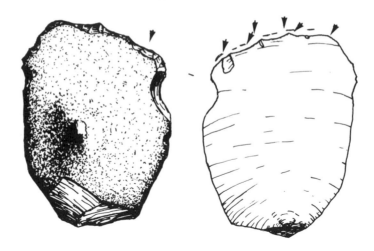

Figure 38.  CL 1563.

CL 1643: L71 B50 Th18 B/L .704 Th/B .360; coordinates 608 213 depth 1.93; fig. 39, pl. 78.
Denticulate implement, bifacially retouched, right cortex-backed. The principal
microwear trace is a line of wood polish rounding the bulbar aspect of the distal
end edge. There are a few short striae associated with this polish, situated on
the bulbar aspect, which run at relatively low angles to the edge. On the bulbar
aspect of the left lateral edge, opposite the most distal of the notches forming
the denticulated edge, is a single narrow striation at a right angle to the lateral edges. There are similar striations in the hollow of the most distal notch on
the dorsal aspect. These two dorsal striations are situated a few millimeters
from the edge; one runs parallel to the edge, the other at nearly right angles to
it. The *SD* and *SS* edge damage, following the convexity of the distal notch's dorsal edge, is possibly utilization damage, since the damage resulting when the
notch was removed would probably not cover such a large section of the edge. Most
of the edge damage on the dorsal aspect of the end is too large to be utilization
damage and is therefore retouch, but the small components of the damage pattern
probably include some utilization damage. This implement was probably used for
more than one task, but only the wood scraping with the distal end is easily isolated. The angle of that edge is 90°, and the edge is straight.

## Wood chopping or adzing

CL 1518: L73 B60 Th50 B/L .822 Th/B .833; coordinates 652 163 depth 2.09; fig. 40, pl. 79.
A chopper-core with traces of four flake removals. In the center of this implement's edge, wood polish is situated on both edge aspects. On the aspect that
shows more polish, there is a short, shallow striation disposed parallel to the
tool's long axis. There are various edge-damage scars, ranging from broad, shallow scars four millimeters wide to the tiniest step scars. Many of these scars
are situated at the respective points of percussion of the larger flake removals
and are likely to have resulted during the shaping (if it was purposefully shaped)
of the implement; other scars undoubtedly resulted when the piece was used to chop
wood. The edge angle ranges between 58° and 61°; 60° is used in comparisons and
the statistical analyses.

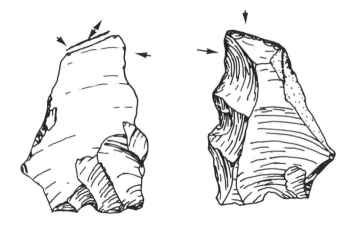

Figure 39.  CL 1643.

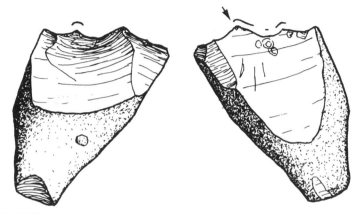

Figure 40.  CL 1518.

CL 1485:  L91 B50 Th61 B/L .549 Th/B 1.22; coordinates 534 179 depth 1.82; fig. 41, pl. 80.
A massive, thick, right cortex-backed flake.  There are patches of wood polish on
both aspects of the left lateral edge, on the distal margins, and ridges of utilization damage scars.  Indications of direction in the polish (see pl. 80) and a
few shallow striae on the dorsal aspect indicate movement during use at right angles to the edge (and flake axis).  The edge damage consists of *SS* and *Step* damage
on both edge aspects, amounting to a light crushing, particularly on the more projecting parts of the edge.  The edge slope is complex, and the edge angle is 85°.

CL 638:  L79 B75 Th36 B/L .949 Th/B .480; coordinates 525 242 depth 1.51; fig. 42.
A large, end-retouched flake.  The only microwear is extremely sparse, but there
is a bright polish on the bulbar aspect of the distal end edge, which is probably
wood polish.  The edge damage on the dorsal aspect of the curved end is associated
with, in every case, the larger retouch removals and tends to be large (*L* and *S*
*Step*, *LS*, and so on).  It is unlikely to be utilization damage.  On the bulbar aspect, however, associated with the faint polish, are some small, broad, shallow
scars, and in the center of the end curve is a large, shallow, trapezoidal flake

removal, indicating a greater force than mere planing.  It seems reasonable to interpret this implement as a wood adze.  The edge angle is 67°.

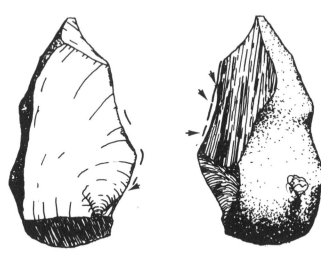

Figure 41.  CL 1485.

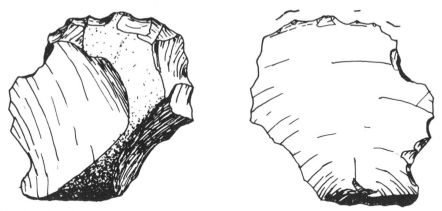

Figure 42.  CL 638.

Wood boring

CL 320:   L40 B36 Th12 B/L .900 Th/B .33; coordinates 482 152 depth 1.43; fig. 43, pl. 81.
A triangular, retouched thermal flake.  The bit shows wood polish on the ventral edges, accompanied by *MicroStep* edge damage.  The dorsal edges of the bit show some *MicroStep* scars that are probably utilization damage.  A fine example of a wood borer.

Figure 43.  CL 320.

CL 92:    L97 B60 Th42 B/L .619 Th/B .700; coordinates 526 146 depth 1.21; fig. 44, pl. 82.
          A large, crude biface, classified by Singer et al. (1973: pl. I,6) as a "proto-
          handaxe." The microwear pattern, consisting of wood polish and a few short striae,
          is confined to the first centimeter of the tip. The polish is most intense on the
          dorsal aspect of the left lateral edge and the dorsal ridge, and less intense on
          the ventral aspect of the right lateral edge. The first 1.3 centimeters of the
          ventral right lateral edge show an edge damage consisting of larger retouch scars,
          grading down to S Step scars at the extreme edge. There is S Step and MicroStep
          damage on the dorsal left lateral edge and the dorsal ridge. The placement of the
          edge damage and the polishes indicate a one-way rotary movement which, viewing the
          implement from the end-on, is counterclockwise, or, from the view of the user,
          clockwise. This almost certainly indicates that the user was right-handed, since
          this movement of the left wrist is awkward and less powerful than a counterclock-
          wise movement.

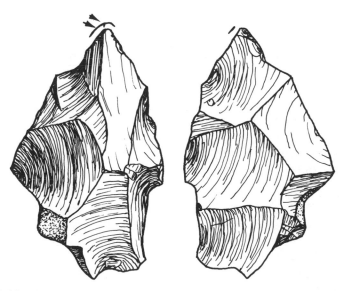

Figure 44.  CL 92.

Hide scraping

CL 1194: L51 B44 Th18 B/L .863 Th/B .409; coordinates 448 203 depth 1.87; fig. 45, pl. 83.
A side- and end-retouched flake. The microwear traces consist of several striations on the bulbar aspect of the right distal end edge and a clear hide polish
(pl. 83) on a small retouched convexity of the left lateral edge. This hide polish appears primarily on the bulbar aspect but has also rounded the edge and so
appears on the dorsal aspect as well. The diffuse linear traces in the polish indicate a working movement at right angles to the edge, with the implement held at
a high angle of attack. This implement was used for scraping hide: the polish
is more similar to dry hide and greased hide polish than to fresh hide polish.
Indeed, this polish is remarkably similar to, though less extensive than, the polishes seen on Upper Paleolithic endscrapers (author's observation). The distal
striations cannot be interpreted very precisely, nor can it be determined whether
they are the result of use or of handling during use. The edge angle is 72°.

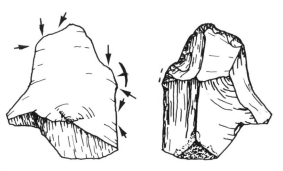

Figure 45.  CL 1194.

CL 1178: L76 B63 Th31 B/L .829 Th/B .492; coordinates 551 185 depth 2.13.
A large, end-retouched flake. The microwear traces occur opposite each other on
the bulbar aspect of the lateral edges. Along the proximal half of the left lateral edge is a pronounced hide polish, confined to the edge on the bulbar surface,
rounding the edge, and continuing in a less intense pattern onto the dorsal aspect. On the bulbar aspect, the polish is accompanied by several long striae,
but on the dorsal aspect, there are myriads of narrow, deep striae. The striae
on both edge aspects run at right angles to the edge. Almost directly opposite
the hide polish, on the bulbar aspect of the right lateral edge, is an area of
somewhat different polish, probably wood polish, as it is bright and smooth, which
may be from a brief use as a whittling knife or could perhaps have resulted from
hafting. Associated with it is an *LS* scar. There is no edge damage associated
with the leather polish. The edge angle of the left lateral edge is 70° and that
of the right lateral is 45°.

CL 613:  L52 B35 Th21 B/L .673 Th/B .600; coordinates 560 208 depth 1.64; fig. 46, pl. 84.
Flake with endscraper retouch. There is a clear, fresh hide polish around the
bulbar aspect of the curved end. This polish is interrupted in two places, which
correspond to areas where large, final flake scars occur on the dorsal edge, implying an attempt at resharpening. There are no striations; however, there are
some indications of direction in the polish which indicate movement of the

implement during use at right angles to the edge.  The edge is convex, and the
edge angle ranges from 68° to 83°, so 76° is used for all comparisons.

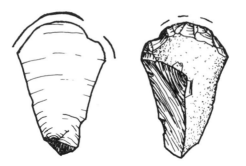

Figure 46.  CL 613.

## Hide or meat (?) cutting

CL 643:  L65 B78 Th30 B/L 1.200 Th/B .385; coordinates 634 101 depth 1.26.
A large, side-struck flake.  The microwear consists of a rough, intense polish
with some resemblance to both hide and meat polish on both aspects of the distal
left lateral edge.  There are a few striae on both aspects, indicating a direction
of movement parallel to the edge.  On the bulbar aspect, the polish is terminated
by an area of *LS* and *SS* edge damage.  The severity of the polish argues for its
being caused by use of the implement on hide.  The edge angle is 35°, and the edge
shape at the concentration of wear is convex.

## Bone boring

CL 1552:  L51 B54 Th8 B/L 1.059 Th/B .333; coordinates 619 158 depth 1.88; fig. 47.
Cortex-covered flake with retouched distal cusp.  The microwear consists of a polish on both aspects of the cusp principally on the dorsal edge and on right
(viewed dorsally) bulbar edge.  The polish is a well-developed bone polish with
no indication of direction.  On the dorsal aspect near the ridge is a blurred
striation running roughly parallel with the bit (and flake) axis.  The cusp is
scarred with *MicroShallow* scalar and *MicroStep* scars on all projecting edges and
ridges.  The distribution of a few of the larger of these scars and the intensity
of polish on the right bulbar cusp edge suggest a clockwise movement during use
which, as argued when discussing CL 92, indicates a right-handed user.

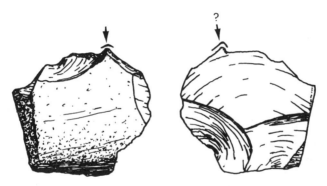

Figure 47.  CL 1552.

## Bone graving (?)

CL 783:    L49 B33 Th13 B/L .673 Th/B .394; coordinates 442 142 depth 1.36; fig. 48.

The principal microwear pattern occurs on the straight, "screwdriver" tip of this implement, and consists of a beveled area, canted dorsally, showing a clear bone polish. Situated on the dorsal aspect proper, just adjacent to the bone-polish area, are a few short abrasion tracks, at right angles to the bit edge, which are deeply "gouged" into the microsurface. On the bulbar aspect of this tip are a number of *SS* scars. All these features indicate a movement during use at right angles to the small bit edge with the dorsal aspect leading, that is, like a burin. On a true burin, the axis of the bit edge would lie at nearly 90° to the plane of the bulbar surface; on this implement, the axis of the bit edge lies nearly parallel to the bulbar surface. The abrasion tracks could have been caused by contact with sand grains on the bone surface; the edge angle of the bit is 39°.

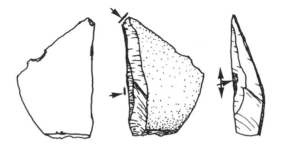

Figure 48.    CL 783.

There is also an area of associated microwear and edge damage on the left lateral edge. The microwear consists of two sets of roughly parallel striations running at right angles to each other. The greater number run parallel to the edge. They are situated just above a set of *L* and *S Step* scars; the edge angle here is 88°. There is a small, shallow notch on the bulbar right lateral edge formed of *SD* damage. It is possible that this damage, as with the striations and stepping scars on the left lateral dorsal edge, relates to handling or even hafting.

## Meat-cutting and butchering

CL 124:    L58 B39 Th23 B/L .6724 Th/B .589; coordinates 488 195 depth 1.48; fig. 49, pl. 85.
A left cortex-backed flake with a "spontaneous retouch" notch on end. The microwear is situated on both aspects of the right lateral edge and consists of a faint meat polish. It is accompanied by *MicroDeep* scalar and *MicroStep* edge damage mainly on the dorsal aspect, but a few scars occur on the bulbar aspect. The edge is straight, and the edge angle is 42°.

CL 734:    L83 B61 Th26 B/L .735 Th/B .426; coordinates 476 213 depth 1.81; fig. 50.
Thick, left cortex-backed flake with large flake removed from bulbar surface. The microwear is distributed on the distal right lateral edge and consists of a typical meat polish on both edge aspects. There are a few striations in the polish, the majority of which run roughly parallel to the edge, some of which run at a high angle to the edge. The edge damage associated with the polished area consists of discontinuously distributed *SS* and *S Step* scars, there being slightly

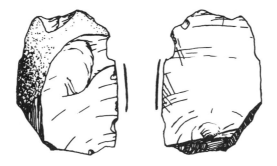

Figure 49.  CL 124.

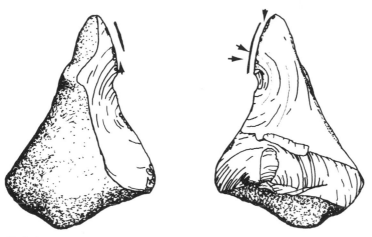

Figure 50.  CL 734.

larger scars on the dorsal aspect compared to the bulbar.  There is a continuous run of 15 mm of *SS* scars on the dorsal face of the left lateral edge, on the proximal side of the edge convexity caused by the removal of the bulbar flake.  This is followed proximally by about 4 mm of *SS* damage on the bulbar face.  This second area of edge damage is unaccompanied by any polish or striations.  The edge showing microwear is convex in shape, and the edge angle is 38°.

CL 1008:  L68 B54 Th22 B/L .794 Th/B .407; coordinates 522 214 depth 1.82; fig. 51, pl. 86. A notched left cortex-backed flake.  The microwear pattern consists of a meat polish on the bulbar aspect of distal left lateral edge.  A few striations in the polish indicate a direction of movement at a high angle to the existing edge but more or less parallel to the flake axis.  There are a few striae 1 to 2 cm from the edge on the bulbar aspect that may or may not be related to the use of the piece.  Also on the bulbar aspect, there are a few *SS* scars associated with the polish.  On the dorsal aspect of this edge, in the concavity of the notch, are scattered *SS* scars, and where the ridge between the notch and the dorsal face meets the edge, a quantity of *MicroStep* damage occurs on the distal side of the ridge.  It seems that the implement was used after the notch removal, although I think most of the polish formed before its removal, implying that this implement was resharpened during use. The edge angle is 42°.

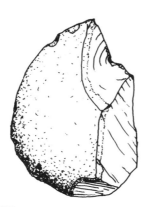

Figure 51.  CL 1008.

CL 671:  L41 B44 Th17 B/L 1.073 Th/B .3864; coordinates 502 279 depth 1.52; fig. 52, pl. 87. A small, right cortex-backed flake. The microwear pattern consists of a meat polish disposed on both aspects of the left lateral edge, with no striations. Edge damage consisting of *MicroD* and very minute *MicroStep* scars occurs irregularly on both aspects of the same edge in association with the polish. The edge angle is 38°, and the edge is convex.

Figure 52.  CL 671.

CL 1254:  L58 B44 Th14 B/L .759 Th/B .318; coordinates 546 201 depth 1.97; pl. 88. Right cortex-backed flake, with additional bifacial "blunting" retouch to right lateral edge. The microwear consists of one small patch of meat polish on the bulbar aspect of the left lateral edge and a shallow striation directly opposite on the dorsal aspect. The edge damage consists of *SS* and some *S Step* scars, mainly occurring on the bulbar aspect of the used edge. On the distal part of the left lateral edge (2 cm beyond the microwear and other edge damage) is an area of *LS* and *SS* scarring which is probably retouch rather than utilization damage. The edge is convex, and the edge angle is 40°.

CL 113:  L70 B67 Th29 B/L .957 Th/B .933; coordinates none cutting VIII depth level 5. Right cortex-backed, end-retouched flake. There are two areas of microwear on this implement: (1) a meat (or fresh hide) polish with large numbers of striations on both aspects of the left lateral edge, and (2) a similar polish on the

bulbar aspect of the retouched distal edge with no striations or indication of
direction. The striae on the left lateral edge make it clear the general direction of use was parallel to the edge. The polish on the distal edge may have resulted from scraping fresh hide, but, in the absence of any clear directional
clues, we cannot be sure. Certainly the left lateral edge was used for cutting
meat or fresh hide. The used edges are both convex; the left lateral edge angle
is 45°, and the distal edge angle is 90°.

## Unknown worked materials

CL 1551: L37 B39 Th8 B/L 1.054 Th/B .205; coordinates 618 156 depth 1.80; fig. 53.
Small, end-notched irregular flake. The microwear consists of a faint, rough polish on the bulbar aspect of the distal notch edge. There is a single short abrasion track in the polish, running at a high angle to the edge. In the right bulbar corner is a long, broad striation which curves from an angle of about 45° to
the flake axis to about 90° to the flake axis. On the dorsal aspect of the distal
edge, there is a considerable quantity of *MicroStepping* in the center of the concavity, but whether this is utilization damage or the smaller components of retouch is difficult to determine. The edge angle is 90°. This implement is undoubtedly a scraper but of what cannot be rigorously determined. It is likely the
material worked was wood, but this is just a guess.

Figure 53. CL 1551.

CL 1362: L43 B53 Th24 B/L 1.233 Th/B .453; coordinates 648 242 depth 2.21; fig. 54.
Thick, cortex-covered flake. The microwear traces are found on the bulbar aspect
of the distal edge and consist of a smooth polish accompanied by numerous narrow
striations running roughly at right angles to the edge. On the dorsal aspect of
this edge is an area of *L* and *S Step* scars which is not completely coincident with
the bulbar microwear. The *L Step* damage suggests a hard material--like wood,
bone, or antler--and the smoothness of the bulbar polish suggests wood, but the
huge number of narrow striae are not compatible with normal use on wood. It may
be that the implement was used for scraping wood in circumstances that involved
the introduction of considerable quantities of clay and silt-sized grit (widest
track approximately 3.30 microns) between the implement and the wood. The edge
is straight, and the edge angle is 90°.

CL 578: L48 B41 Th16 B/L .854 Th/B .390; coordinates 550 213 depth 1.53; fig. 55.
Flake with retouch of left lateral edge, conjoins with CL 977 (from the marl)--
this flake is recorded as being from the "top of the gravel." The microwear consists of a very slight polish and a few very short striations disposed on the bulbar aspect of the left lateral edge. The few striations could be hammerstone
scratches produced when the edge was retouched. The polish is present in such

small quantities that it is impossible to determine its character. The retouching
of the left lateral edge effectively renders it impossible to distinguish any
utilization damage on the dorsal aspect. It is most likely that the morphology
of the used edge suited it best for wood planing or scraping, but there can be no
certainty about this. The edge is straight, and the edge angle is 75°.

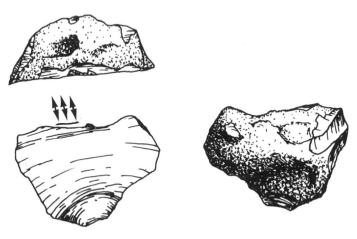

Figure 54.    CL 1362.

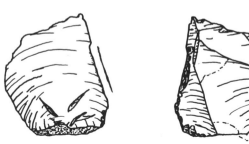

Figure 55.    CL 578.

CL 1559: L31 B34 Th14 B/L 1.096 Th/B .412; coordinates 616 159 depth 1.93.
        A small, thick, left cortex-backed flake.  The microwear consists of a number of
        relatively long, narrow striae on both aspects of the right lateral edge.  These
        striations are mainly on the dorsal aspect (there is only one striation on the
        bulbar) and are set some distance from the edge.  They run at nearly a right angle
        to the right lateral edge.  On the distal portion of this edge, on the bulbar as-
        pect, are a few irregular edge-damage scars of the *SS* and *S Step* type.  Along the
        curving left lateral edge on the bulbar aspect are some *LD, LS, SS,* and *S Step*
        damage scars, covering an area of 11 mm.  These flake scars could be the result of
        battering with a hammer of antler, bone, or hard wood, so it is probable that this
        implement is a wedge.  The mildness of the edge damage, and the distance from the
        working edge at which the striae are found, indicate this was a "secondary" wedge,

that is, a wedge inserted into an already opened split-crack to widen it. Without any microwear polish, which experiments have shown does not always appear on wedges, it is impossible to say what material was being worked. The edge angle is 43°.

CL 1217: L42 B56 Th14 B/L 1.333 Th/B .250; coordinates 536 247 depth 1.54.
Side-struck flake. The only microwear consists of an area of shallow striations on the bulbar aspect of the left lateral edge. The bulbar aspect of this edge is shaped by a series of *LS* scars which are probably retouch. Alternate to the dorsal *LS* is a short area of *SD* and *SS* damage on the bulbar aspect of the proximal left lateral edge. The edge angle is 40°, and the edge is convex.

CL 1636: L50 B52 Th14 B/L 1.040 Th/B .269; coordinates 615 187 depth 1.96; fig. 56.
Irregular, right cortex-backed flake. The microwear consists of a faint matt polish which is disposed on the bulbar aspect of the left lateral edge. There are two areas of polish, separated by a central cusp of the left lateral edge. The dorsal edge damage coincident with these polish areas consists of *SD* and *S Step* damage on the proximal side of the cusp and *S Step* damage on the distal side. This damage is probably all utilization damage and indicates a scraping motion during use. The polish is probably a hide polish, but it is so faint and of so ambiguous a character that it is difficult to be certain. The slight concavity of the edges at the points where the polishes appear would mean that, if this piece were used for hide scraping, the worked materials would have been slightly convex in shape, which might occur if the hide were draped over a log. American Indians scraped hides, especially small ones, using a log or plank for support (Driver 1961: 173). The use of a wooden support, like a log, would account for the relatively extensive utilization damage on this piece being associated with a hide polish. The edge angle varies between 45° and 52°, the average being about 48°.

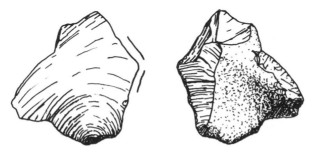

Figure 56. CL 1636.

## Associations between Wear Traces and Tool Morphology at Clacton

### Use and Edge Angle

We might suspect that certain edge angles are more suitable for certain tasks than others, although it is true that almost any simple task can be achieved with any edge angle. For example, one might, in a pinch, use a penknife blade to do any number of tasks

for which it is not particularly intended, at the same time recognizing that it is simpler
and more efficient to use the right tool for the right job, and our Paleolithic ancestors
were likely to have recognized this as well. Besides, stone tool users are less likely to
be caught without the "right tool" than the metal tool user of our own society, because
edge modification in the stone age involved only a few retouch blows to achieve a different
edge angle or, with an abundance of raw material in England at least, the easy manufacture
of another implement altogether.

A glance at table 20 suggests a few associations between the use to which an implement
edge was put and the angle of that edge. In the category of wood whittling/planing, there
is some suggestion of a bimodal distribution, with edge angle values clustering around
acute edges (<35°) and steeper values (60° - 90°), no doubt corresponding to our conception
of whittling using acute edges and planing using steep edges. It seems that for wood chopping and adzing, steeper-angled edges were employed--although, with such a small sample, it
is difficult to know whether this is significant. Although there are only two cases of
wood sawing, both the implements involved had acute edges (the actual values are 25° and
28°), and this is probably significant. The values for wood scraping show a definite clustering in the steep-angle region. The same applies, less certainly with such a small number of cases, to hide scraping.

*Table 20*
*Clacton, Use and Edge Angle (counting edges)*

|                              | <35° | 35°-49° | 50°-64° | 65°-79° | 80°-95° | Totals |
|------------------------------|------|---------|---------|---------|---------|--------|
| Wood whittling/planing       | 4    | 1       | 2       | 2       | 1       | 10     |
| Wood chopping/adzing         |      | 1       | 1       | 1       | 1       | 4      |
| Wood sawing                  | 2    |         |         |         |         | 2      |
| Wood scraping                |      |         | 1       | 1       | 3       | 5      |
| Hide scraping                |      |         |         | 2       | 1       | 3      |
| Meat cutting/butchery**      |      | 10      | 1       |         |         | 11     |
| Scraping, material unknown   |      | 1       | 1       | 1       | 2       | 5      |
| Other*                       | 1    | 3       | 1       | 1       |         | 6      |
| Totals                       | 7    | 16      | 7       | 8       | 8       | 46     |

*borers, N=4, not included.
**includes hide cutting (N=1).

The most striking clustering is shown in the ten meat knives, whose actual values have
only a 10° range. This is surprising, since meat is such an unresistant material. However,
if we consider that a number of these edges show utilization damage patterns much more severe than those that result when cutting through meat alone, then there is a possible reason for this strict selection of edge angles. Paleolithic man (or woman) was his (or her)
own butcher; cutting up animals involved cutting tissues and structures much more resistant
than meat--like ligaments, tendons, bone and joint tissues--which would quickly dull even
the less acute edges by edge damage. Besides, cutting meaty tissues with a very acute edge
results in a greater amount of utilization damage than does cutting with an only moderately
sharp edge, and edge damage means that sharp little pieces of flint are going to be scattered around the areas of the cuts. While it is difficult to imagine Clactonian man being
so fastidious about a few pieces of flint in his meat, if he hit hard tissue or cartilage

with an edge of 25° during some vigorous cutting, he would have rendered the surrounding tissues fairly unpleasant to eat because of the large number of sharp flint pieces (about a millimeter in diameter) that would have broken off the tool's edge. An edge angle of about 40° is much more resistant to edge damage in that situation, but is still sharp enough to be an efficient slicing edge for deep insertion into the worked material.

The scrapers for which the worked material is unknown (although wood is suspected for most of them) show, as well, a tendency toward steeper edge angles. Little can be said about the other implements for which the material worked is unknown.

## Use and Edge Shape

Just as it could be anticipated that certain edge angles would be more appropriate for particular uses, so we might also expect that certain edge shapes would be more appropriate for certain tasks and that this would be reflected in the association between the shape of used edges and their microwear patterns.

An examination of table 21 shows us that there is not, in fact, a clear relationship between the utilization and the final edge shape. The wood-whittling and planing implements seem evenly distributed between the three principal edge shapes. The same is true of wood chopping and adzing. However, the fact that the two wood saws have a straight and a convex edge, respectively, is probably significant. In an earlier edge-damage study of flakes from Caddington (Keeley 1978), several flakes with ½Moon edge damage (which occurs commonly during sawing) were found to have convex or straight edges in almost every case. The "preferences" for wood scraping seem to be for either straight or concave edges, while those for hide scraping are for convex and straight edges.

*Table 21*

*Clacton, Use and Edge Shape (counting edges)*

|  | Convex | Straight | Concave | Complex | Total |
|---|---|---|---|---|---|
| Wood whittling/planing | 4 | 3 | 3 |  | 10 |
| Wood chopping/adzing | 1 | 1 | 2 |  | 4 |
| Wood sawing | 1 | 1 |  |  | 2 |
| Wood scraping |  | 3 | 2 |  | 5 |
| Hide scraping | 2 | 1 |  |  | 3 |
| Meat cutting/butchery* | 7 | 2 | 2 |  | 11 |
| Boring, wood and bone |  |  |  | 4 | 4 |
| Scraping, material unknown |  | 2 | 3 |  | 5 |
| Other | 3 |  | 1 | 2 | 6 |
| Totals | 18 | 13 | 13 | 6 | 50 |

*
includes hide cutting (N=1).

It is the meat knives which show the closest association with a morphological characteristic, as the majority of meat knives have convex edges. Two implements have straight edges, and the two implements with concave edges have both been retouched with a Clacton notch, which creates the concavity, while none of the other working areas are on a retouched edge. It is quite likely that, prior to resharpening, the two implements with concave edges may have had convex or straight edges as well. One has only to think of a hunting knife, or even a butcher's knife, to understand why a convex edge is common. And anyone

who has had to resharpen such knives will know that it is the convex part of the blade
which takes the most resharpening because it receives most of the wear.

The scrapers for which the worked material cannot be determined occur on either
straight or convex edges. Since three of the five edges are suspected of having been used
on wood, it is not surprising that the preferences are the same as the wood scrapers. And
four of the six implements in the miscellaneous category are borers, which, not surprisingly, show their wear traces on a retouched cusp.

<u>Use and Blank Size</u>

One question that can be asked about the used pieces is Is there any consistency in
the selection of blanks from the flaked material available? In the gravel, the used flakes
are, on average, longer, broader, and thicker than the unused flakes (figs. 57 and 58)--to
be precise, they average 10 mm longer, 5 mm broader, and 6 mm thicker. The differences in
each case are statistically significant, but it is the magnitude of the differences that is
important. The nine used flakes from the marl constitute a very poor comparative sample
statistically speaking and, consequently, the differences, which run in the same direction
as in the gravel (that is, for larger used pieces) are so small that the internal variation
overwhelms them. But, in any case, such crude general calculations do not tell us much
about the selection of blanks for particular uses.

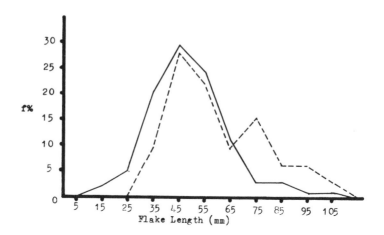

Figure 57. Clacton--histograms of used and unused flake lengths. Solid line=unused
flakes; broken line=used flakes.

Turning to the relationship between blank length (both flakes and cores) and particular uses, examination of table 22 shows that there are indeed some correlations. Wood
whittling/planing implements tend to be around 45 mm long (and though it is not readily apparent from the table, the planing implements--that is, those with higher edge angles--
tend to be longer). The wood choppers and adzes, as might be expected, are relatively
long. Wood scrapers tend to be short, while the hide scrapers are usually about 10 mm
longer than the wood scrapers. Meat knives seem to be on longer blanks, but the pattern
is unclear.

As the lengths used in table 22, especially the flake lengths, are not necessarily a
good reflection of the length of the piece in relation to the used edge, table 23 shows

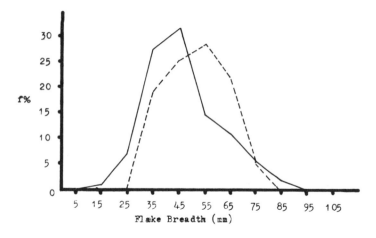

Figure 58.  Clacton--histograms of used and unused flake breadths.  Solid line=unused flakes; broken line=used flakes.

*Table 22*

*Clacton, Use and Blank Length (counting edges)*

|  | <40 mm | 40-49 mm | 50-59 mm | 60-69 mm | 70-79 mm | >80 mm | Totals |
|---|---|---|---|---|---|---|---|
| Wood whittling/planing | 1 | 5 | 1 | 1 |  | 2 | 10 |
| Wood chopping/adzing |  |  |  |  | 2 | 2 | 4 |
| Wood sawing |  |  | 1 |  | 1 |  | 2 |
| Wood scraping | 3 | 1 |  |  | 1 |  | 5 |
| Hide scraping |  |  | 2 |  | 1 |  | 3 |
| Meat cutting/butchery** | 2 | 1 | 2 | 3 | 1 | 2 | 11 |
| Scraping, material unknown | 1* | 2* | 2 |  |  |  | 5 |
| Other | 1 | 4 | 2 | 1 | 1 | 1 | 10 |
| Totals | 8 | 13 | 10 | 5 | 7 | 7 | 50 |

\* suspected use on wood.
\*\* includes hide cutting (N=1).

the association between use and the longest dimension measured parallel to the working edge.  The results are not very different, though the number of observations increases by two instances because two pieces have more than one working edge.  But it is clear that relatively long blanks were chosen for meat knives as opposed to, for example, short ones for wood scrapers.

Since the average Clacton flake, used or unused, tends to be about as broad as it is wide, the distribution of "raw" breadth ($B$) values virtually replicates the pattern seen on table 22, so no separate table has been included.  Even if we considered the relationship between the relative breadth ($B/L$) and use (table 24), we find little patterning, except around the total group mean.  The exceptions, again, are the meat knives, with a clustering of values around the narrower blanks, and the wood scrapers which were made on relatively broad flake blanks.

Table 23

Clacton, Use and Length Parallel to Used Edge (counting edges)

| | <40 mm | 40-49 mm | 50-59 mm | 60-69 mm | 70-79 mm | >80 mm | Totals |
|---|---|---|---|---|---|---|---|
| Wood whittling/planing | 1 | 1 | 4 | 3 | | 1 | 10 |
| Wood chopping/adzing | | | | 1 | 2 | 1 | 4 |
| Wood sawing | | | 1 | | 1 | | 2 |
| Wood scraping | 1 | 3 | 1 | | | | 5 |
| Hide scraping | 1 | | 1 | | 1 | | 3 |
| Meat cutting/butchery* | 2 | | 3 | 3 | 2 | 1 | 11 |
| Boring, wood and bone | 1 | | 2 | 1 | | | 4 |
| Scraping, material unknown | 1 | 2 | 2 | | | | 5 |
| Other | 2 | 2 | 1 | | 1 | | 6 |
| Totals | 9 | 8 | 15 | 8 | 7 | 3 | 50 |

*
includes hide cutting (N=1).

Table 24

Clacton, Use and B/L (counting edges)

| | <.600 | .600- .799 | .800- .999 | 1.000- 1.199 | >1.199 | Totals |
|---|---|---|---|---|---|---|
| Wood whittling/planing | 1 | 1 | 3 | 2 | 3 | 10 |
| Wood chopping/adzing | 1 | 1 | 2 | | | 4 |
| Wood sawing | 1 | | 1 | | | 2 |
| Wood scraping | | 1 | | 2 | 2 | 5 |
| Hide scraping | | 1 | 2 | | | 3 |
| Meat cutting/butchery** | 1 | 5 | 1 | 2 | 2 | 11 |
| Boring, wood and bone | | 2 | 1 | 1 | | 4 |
| Scraping, material unknown | | | 2 | 2* | 1* | 5 |
| Other | | 1 | 3 | 1 | 1 | 6 |
| Totals | 4 | 12 | 15 | 10 | 9 | 50 |

*
suspected use on wood
**
includes hide cutting (N=1).

The "raw" thickness values (Th) tell us very little, especially since there is so little internal variability in the Th measurements for the whole collection. However, if we consider the relative blank thickness (Th/B), cross-classified with use (table 25), some patterns emerge. The wood choppers are, of course, relatively thick. Wood scrapers are made on thin blanks, and hide scrapers on slightly thicker ones. Again, the meat knives show a remarkable clustering of values, in this case with 6 of the 10 values close to .400.

## Use and Retouch

Table 26 demonstrates that there is some reliance on retouched edges, particularly for certain uses, like scraping and planing of hide and wood, that require steep-angled, shaped edges. All the borers are on retouch-created or modified cusps. Other uses, like whittling and sawing wood, and cutting meat, not only do not require retouched edges but, in fact, may be more efficiently accomplished with an unretouched edge.

*Table 25*

*Clacton, Use and Th/B (counting implements)*

|  | <.250 | .250-.349 | .350-.449 | .450-.549 | .550-.649 | >.649 | Totals |
|---|---|---|---|---|---|---|---|
| Wood whittling/planing |  | 3 | 2 | 2 | 2 |  | 9 |
| Wood chopping/adzing |  |  |  | 1 | 1 | 2 | 4 |
| Wood sawing |  | 1 |  | 1 |  |  | 2 |
| Wood scraping | 2 | 1 | 2 |  |  |  | 5 |
| Hide scraping |  |  | 1 | 1 | 1 |  | 3 |
| Meat cutting/butchery** |  | 3 | 6 |  | 2 |  | 11 |
| Boring, wood and bone |  | 2 |  |  |  | 2 | 4 |
| Scraping, material unknown | 1* | 1 | 1* | 1* |  |  | 4 |
| Other |  | 3 | 2 | 1 |  |  | 6 |
| Totals | 3 | 14 | 14 | 7 | 6 | 4 | 48 |

\*
suspected use on wood
\*\*
includes hide cutting (N=1)

*Table 26*

*Clacton, Use and Retouch (counting edges)*

|  | Unretouched | Retouched | Totals |
|---|---|---|---|
| Wood whittling/planing | 6 | 4 | 10 |
| Wood chopping/adzing | 1 | 3 | 4 |
| Wood sawing | 2 |  | 2 |
| Wood scraping | 2 | 3 | 5 |
| Hide scraping | 1 | 2 | 3 |
| Meat cutting/butchery* | 8 | 3 | 11 |
| Boring, wood and bone |  | 4 | 4 |
| Scraping, material unknown | 3 | 2 | 5 |
| Other | 5 | 1 | 6 |
| Totals | 28 | 22 | 50 |

\*
includes hide cutting (N=1).

## Conclusions

The impression received from the tabulations above is of an industry with little formalization of types, in which flakes were selected from debitage for particular uses mainly
on the basis of their edge angles and edge shapes, with only loose attention to blank size
and general shape. The general results of the above cross classifications may be summarized as follows:

Wood-whittling knives and planes: Made on blanks 40-50 mm long and with about the
same breadth; no regular *Th/B* value association (even if we distinguish between whittling knives and planes); of course edge-angle values for whittling knives are by
definitions acute (between 25°-45°), and all planes are distinguished by high edge
angles (all actually greater than 72°); no particular associations with edge shapes;
whittling knives have unretouched edges, planes have retouched edges.

Wood choppers and adzes: The blanks are chopper-cores (2) or large flakes (2); no consistent edge shape or edge angle associations; 3 of 4 have retouched edges.

Wood saws: Just two examples, whose only common morphological characteristics are their acute edge angles (25° and 28°) and the fact that the edges are unretouched.

Wood scrapers: Blanks are short (<49 mm), relatively broad ($B$>1.00), and relatively thin ($Th/B$<.449); edge angle values are high (>60°) and edges are straight or concave; some retouched, some not.

Hide scrapers: Only three examples, whose common characteristics are steep edge angles (>72°) and straight or convex edges, but little else.

Meat knives: No particular blank-length association, but slight clustering of values of length parallel to the working edge between 50-69 mm; preference for narrower blanks ($B/L$<.799) and slightly thin blanks ($Th/B$<.449); 10 of the 11 meat knives have edge angles between 35° and 45°; 7 of 11 have convex shaped edges, and 8 (or 9 if we include CL 734) are on unretouched edges, the others have been resharpened rather than retouched. These implements form a remarkably consistent group.

Scrapers, worked material unknown: Three of these scrapers (CL 1551, 578, and 1362) were suspected of being used on wood, and it is interesting, even considering the small numbers involved, that, in terms of morphological characteristics, they fall within the limits of the wood scrapers--having high edge angles (common to both wood and hide scrapers, although the hide-scrapers values tend to be slightly lower), convex and straight edges, and blank lengths ranging from 37 to 48 mm. The implement suspected of being a hide scraper (CL 1636) is more problematical; the only characteristic it shares with the hide scrapers is its blank length.

## Choppers or Cores?

Of the 22 cores in fresh condition found at Clacton, only 2 showed definite signs of use. Many of the "chopper-cores" claimed by Singer et al. (1973: 34) to show signs of use have, in fact, been damaged by slight but definite rolling or, more usually, by soil movements. It is significant that the proportion of chopper-cores with "signs of use" drops from 83% in the gravel to 20% in the marl (Singer et al. 1973: 35), which is what one would expect if these "signs of use" were actually the result of rolling and/or contortions of the deposit. One cannot, of course, rule out the possibility that true choppers were made at Clacton but used and abandoned away from the site. Such implements would be less likely to be recognized and recovered as isolated finds, as they are less obviously the work of man than a hand ax found in a similar situation. However, it seems reasonable to conclude, from the evidence in hand, that Clactonian cores were primarily a source of usuable flakes, rather than implements in their own right, although true choppers were occasionally manufactured and used.

### Horizontal Distribution

## Gravel (fig. 59)

Because the implements were deposited at such varying depths in the gravel, it is difficult to rely on the distribution plan for the gravel as a whole for indications of horizontal clustering, but if the gravel is broken down by arbitrary levels, then the

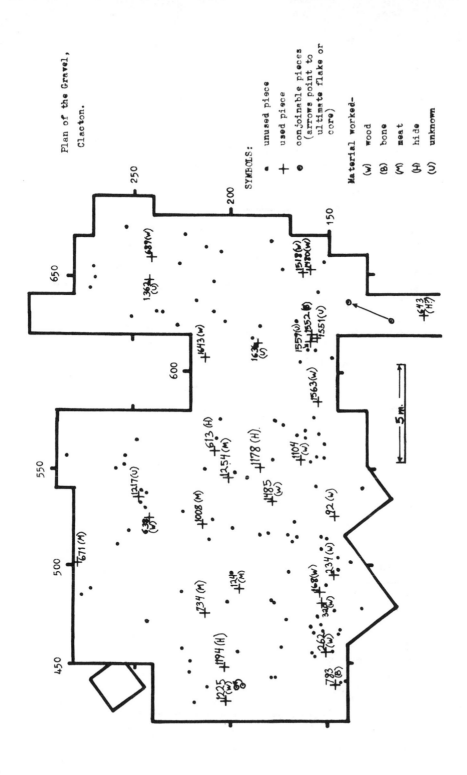

Figure 59. Plan of the Gravel, Clacton.

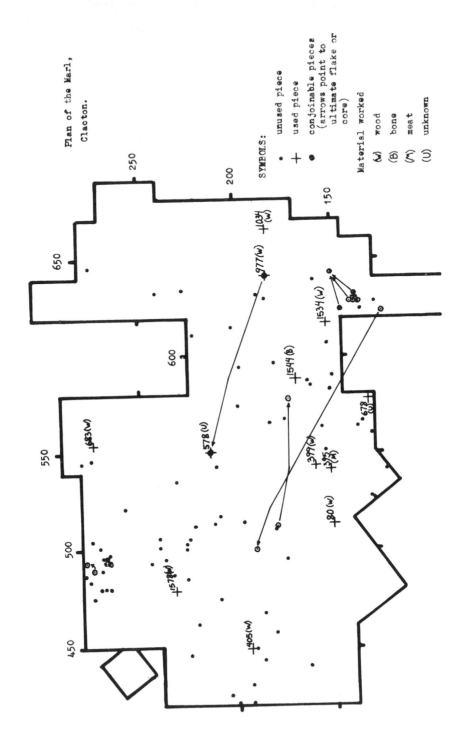

Figure 60. Plan of the Marl, Clacton.

number of pieces at each level becomes so small that no pattern can be distinguished. Besides, some groups of conjoinable pieces come from the top of the gravel *and* the bottom of the marl, which indicates that this interface is not a strict subdivision in archeological terms. Again, Singer et al. (1973) note "after the overlying Marl had been removed and while the gravel was still saturated, it was impossible to walk upon its surface without sinking several centimeters into it. Such conditions may well have existed during the time of the Clactonian activity, and movement by men or animals over this surface would have affacted the original bedding" (p. 19). It is clear that we cannot place much reliance on any horizontal distributions in the gravel.

One observation worth mentioning is that while 11 of the 21 woodworking implements were found south of the 180 centimeter line (that is, close to the ancient South Bank), the hide scrapers or meat knives were all found north of this line (see fig. 59). It may be that, if the Clactonians were in occupation along the South Bank, more noisome activities like butchering and hide preparation had taken place closer to the water and several meters from the area where the inhabitants spent more time. There is no correlation with the distribution of bone fragments, however, and the distribution of implements may be an effect of sampling.

Marl (fig. 60)

The small number of pieces involved show no particular clustering or concentration.

## Conclusions

The microwear analysis of flint artifacts from both the gravel and the marl indicates that a whole range of activities took place within the excavated area. These included butchery of animals, woodworking, hide preparation, and, surprisingly, in view of the traditional assessment of Clactonian technology and material culture, some bone boring and perhaps even graving. This broad range of activities suggests that this site may have been an occupation area and not a specialized activity site.

The investigation of the relationships between the functions of the implements and their morphology suggests that the main concerns of the "Clactonians" in selecting a blank (core, flake, or shatter-piece) for use were with its edge angle and edge shape. As often as not, the retouching of flakes was done for the purpose of blunting certain edges of the blank to make it more comfortable to hold in the hand, rather than to alter the shape or angle of the utilized edge.

## 6. A MICROWEAR ANALYSIS OF FLINT ARTIFACTS FROM THE LOWER LOAM AT SWANSCOMBE (KENT)

### History and Stratigraphy

Swanscombe is a Paleolithic site with a long history of scientific investigation, starting with the excavations of Smith and Dewey (1913, 1914) in 1912, followed by the discovery of fragments of a human skull by Marston (1936), and subsequent excavations by the Swanscombe Committee of the Royal Anthropological Institute (1938). The discovery in 1955 of another piece of the Swanscombe skull (Wymer 1955) resulted in another series of excavations (Wymer 1964, 1968). The implements used in the present study were recovered during the most recent excavations into the Lower Loam and Lower Gravel by J. Waechter et al. (1969, 1970, 1971, 1972).

The basic sequence at Swanscombe was established by Smith and Dewey (1913) and runs as follows from the top downward:

Upper Gravel
Upper Loam
Upper Middle Gravel
Lower Middle Gravel
Lower Loam
Lower Gravel
Thanet Sand

The majority of the implements used in this study came from the body of the Lower Loam, which, in some places, was nearly 2 m thick. But a number of the implements came from the "midden" layer, which is a sandy deposit, containing considerable quantities of broken mammal bones associated with flint implements, found at the junction of the Lower Gravel and the Lower Loam (Waechter et al. 1971: 60).

In the body of the Lower Loam, a "knapping floor" was discovered, containing 24 conjoinable flakes (Waechter 1971: 48; Newcomer 1971b). Some of these flakes were shattered so that "a total of 90 flakes and fragments" were conjoined (Newcomer 1971b: 51). None of these conjoined flakes were available for microwear analysis during the period of this study. However, it seems quite unlikely that the conjoinable flakes, which were found within a few centimeters of each other, and some of which were shattered, were ever used: they are more likely to be simple knapping debris.

### Condition of the Implements

In total, 267 pieces were examined and disappointingly the majority of these implements (*N*=201) were found to be unsuitable for microwear study. Most of these rejected pieces were small chips which had been subject to water-abrasion. A number of the larger pieces showed a "glaze" on their surfaces which may have been the result of abrasion by wind-borne silt (although water transport cannot be entirely ruled out). This glaze was more common on rejected implements from the Midden layer. Some of the pieces were excluded simply because they had been so heavily patinated ("weathered" would probably be a more accurate term) that there could be little hope of any microwear traces being preserved on their surfaces. However, most of the remaining 66 implements that were submitted to microwear examination were unpatinated and fresh and had extraordinarily sharp edges.

## Description of Used Pieces

Of the 66 fresh pieces from the Lower Loam and Midden at Swanscombe, only 4 implements showed definite traces of use. The description of these implements follows. The specimen numbers are those assigned by the excavators, and all measurements given are given in millimeters.

SC 69-A2-61:   L51 B32 Th17 B/L .628 Th/B .531; pl. 89.

Small flake with blunting by bipolar retouch on the distal right lateral edge. The microwear consists of a greasy meat polish (pl. 89), found on both aspects of the distal left lateral edge, accompanied by a few narrow, deep striae running at a low angle to the edge on the dorsal aspect. The utilization damage consists of irregular *LD* and *SD* scars on the bulbar aspect, *L Step* and *S Step* scars on the dorsal aspect, and two small ½Moon breakages in the medial portion of the left lateral edges. This flake, then, was used as a butchering knife; the larger utilization damage scars being the result of contact with bone or other hard tissues during use. The used edge is slightly convex, and the edge angle is 35°.

SC 71-B4-55:   L57 B44 Th11 B/L .772 Th/B .25; fig. 61, pl. 90.

A partially right cortex-backed, rectangular flake. The microwear traces occur on the distal portion of the left lateral edge, on both aspects of the edge. The striations run parallel to the edge. The utilization damage consists of a series of ½Moon breakages along this same edge. The microwear polish is relatively bright but quite pitted (pl. 90). It is a bone (or possibly antler) polish (compare with pls. 34, 53). While it would seem that the functional interpretation of this implement as a bone (or antler) saw is relatively straightforward, it does encounter some difficulties. The first is that the utilization damage on such a thin edge (edge angle 33°), is not as severe as one would normally expect to find on an antler or bone saw. The other difficulty is the rarity (or nonexistence) of sawn bone in the Lower Paleolithic. There is a record of a piece of antler found in the "Early Mousterian" levels at Hoxne by Reid Moir with a supposed saw cut on it (Moir 1926: 160, fig. 10). The photograph of it is not particularly illuminating. Nevertheless, there is nothing about the shape or placement of this "cut" as shown in Moir's photograph that indicates it is not a saw-cut. There can be little doubt that this implement was used with a sawing motion and came into substantial contact with bone (or possibly antler) during utilization, but the exact nature of its use on bone is not certain; it may be a butchering knife. The shape of the edge is convex.

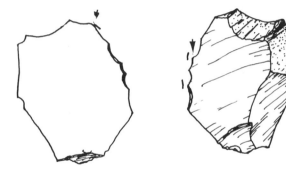

Figure 61.   SC71-B4-55.

SC 71-C3-71:   L116 B114 Th37 B/L .921 Th/B .319; fig. 62, pl. 91.

A very large, right cortex-backed flake with some possible blunting retouch
on the right lateral edge. The microwear traces consist of some broad, shallow striations on both aspects of the distal left lateral edge. There are no
traces of a microwear polish. The utilization damage occurs as *LS*, *SS*, and
*S Step* scars on the bulbar aspect, and *SD*, *L Step*, and *S Step* scars on the
dorsal aspect of the working edge. This implement appears to be a flake-
chopper, but, without a microwear polish, it is difficult to say what material
was being chopped. The type of striations present (broad, shallow) and the
mildness of the utilization damage argue for use on wood, but, in the absence
of a microwear polish, this is merely the most probable worked material. The
striations on the bulbar aspect of the working edge are more numerous and extend further into the body of the flake away from the edge, so that "adzing"
may be a better description of this implement's function than "chopping."
The shape of the working edge is slightly convex and has an edge angle of 52°.

This flake was found in association with a set of antlers still attached
to the facial part of the skull (Waechter 1972: 75). The antlers and bone
were very crushed, but the antlers were missing a couple of tines that had
been, it appeared, removed in antiquity. It is possible that this implement
was used to hack off the missing tines, but there is no way of telling from
the microwear traces if it was so employed.

SC 71-C3-81:   L42 B32 Th14 B/L .762 Th/B .438; pl. 92.

Small flake with small areas of cortex on left lateral edge and distal end
edge. The microwear consists of a bright but rugged polish (pl. 92) on the
dorsal aspect of the proximal right lateral edge. There are a few faint
striations on the bulbar aspect of this edge and some linear features in the
polish that indicate movement during use at right angles to the edge. The
utilization damage consists of some *MicroD* scars on the bulbar aspect of the
working edge. This implement is probably a wood-whittling knife. The roughness of the polish is probably the result of chemical weathering. This
weathering, which has not resulted in patination, has left the unpolished
flint microsurface pockmarked and very slightly smoothed. It is interesting
to note that the areas of the microsurface affected by the microwear polish

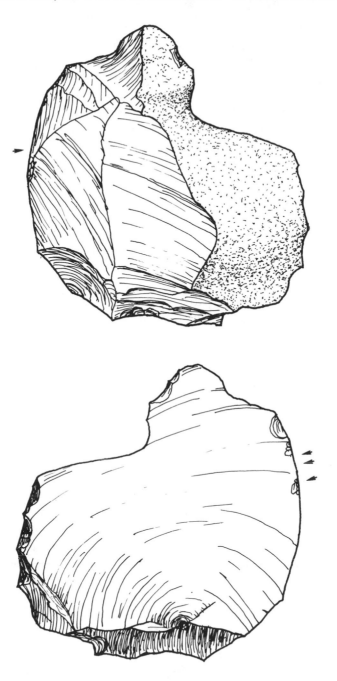

Figure 62.   SC71-C3-71.

have resisted, to some extent, this erosion simply because they present less surface area to the weathering agents than the originally grainy, unworn surfaces. This differential erosion of polished and unpolished surfaces had left the microwear polish areas minutely pedestaled above the unpolished areas. The brightness of the microwear polish, in addition to the evidence of the utilization damage and the direction of use, led one to suspect that prior to weathering it was a wood polish. The working edge is slightly convex, and the edge angle is 42°.

## Conclusions

With such a small number of implements involved, used and unused, it is difficult to say anything about the selection of flake blanks for use at Swanscombe or the associations between implement morphology and use. We can make a few superficial comparisons with the results obtained at Clacton (see chap. 5). The Swanscombe whittling knife (C3-81) fits in morphologically with those found at Clacton: it is on a flake between 40-50 mm long, its edge angle is between 25°-45°, and it has an unretouched working edge. The meat or butchering knife from Swanscombe (A2-61) also shares some morphological characteristics with similar implements found at Clacton: its length parallel to the working edge is between 50 and 69 mm; its *B/L* is less than .799; its edge angle is between 35° and 45°; its working edge is convex and unretouched. Since the material worked with the Swanscombe "flake-chopper" (C3-71) is unknown, it is not particularly meaningful to compare it with the wood choppers from Clacton, which have only their large size in common. It is interesting, nonetheless, that a large flake was used as a chopper, while none of the seven cores which were found to be in an acceptable condition for microwear analysis showed any signs of being used; two of the four wood choppers from Clacton also were large flakes. There are no bone saws from Clacton (or Hoxne), and the example from Swanscombe is, so far, unique, in the writer's experience.

Since the implements with microwear traces were found at several levels in the body of the Lower Loam and the small number of fresh unused implements among them was similarly distributed, it makes little sense to examine their horizontal distribution, or to make too much of the range of activities documented by the microwear traces. It does not seem likely, in view of the small number of flint implements recovered and the very small number of used pieces, that the portion of the Lower Loam so far excavated contains a single genuine "living floor." The Midden at the top of the Lower Gravel is probably just what its name implies--a rubbish dump where bones, antlers, and waste flakes accumulated. As Waechter has suggested, the true living floor may not have been far away.

## History and Stratigraphy

One of the best know Paleolithic sites in Britain is at Hoxne, which is also the type-site of the Hoxnian interglacial. It has been known since J. Frere (1800) found Paleolithic flint implements there in the last years of the eighteenth century. It played a part in the "discovery" of prehistory in the last century (Evans 1860; Prestwich 1860), and many excavations have been conducted there by various investigators since that time (Reid 1896; Moir 1926, 1935). The two most recent investigations at Hoxne by teams from Cambridge (West and McBurney 1954; West 1956) and the University of Chicago (Wymer 1974; Gladfelter 1976; Singer and Wymer 1976) have established the stratigraphy and chronology of the Hoxne deposits. The members of the University of Chicago team have greatly clarified the stratigraphy of the upper parts of the sequence and, most importantly for our purposes, have found archeological deposits which they were able to relate to the newly clarified stratigraphic sequence. The implements analyzed in the present study were obtained during the University of Chicago excavations in 1971-74. Prior to their work, many writers regarded the Hoxne artifacts as belonging to a single horizon.

The deposits at Hoxne are basically the result of the infilling of an interglacial lake which developed in a depression or basin in a till of the Anglian glaciation. The lake sediments are believed to be overlain by a periglacial deposit of the Wolstonian glaciation (although this has not yet been completely proved). The stratigraphic sequence may be summarized as follows (from Singer and Wymer 1976; Gladfelter 1976):

1.  *Glacial till* (fig. 63G).
2.  *Lacustrine clay-muds* (fig. 63E,F). There were a few flakes from the upper part of this layer which constitutes Archeological Layer 3 Main.
3.  *Detritus mud* (fig. 63D). It was from this layer that the flint implements constituting the "Lower Industry" came. The implements resting horizontally on the peaty detritus mud are designated as being from Archeological Layer 2 Main. The implements found lying at various angles in a "chalky, brecciated clay-mud" (Singer and Wymer 1976: 16) are designated as being from Archeological Layer 1 Main. However, these implements may not be in primary context. As Singer and Wymer (1976: 16) note: "The horizontal distributions of both levels are so similar that it is concluded that they have the same origin. A likely explanation is a mudflow from the steep lake sides, since disappeared. The condition of the

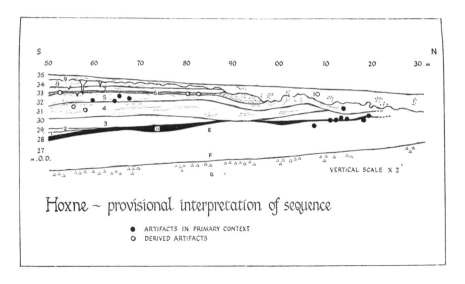

Figure 63. Hoxne section (from Wymer 1974).

material indicates it cannot have travelled far (- something in the order of 20-30 m) and it is accepted as a single contemporary industry." In the West cutting (as opposed to the Main cutting which has provided the basic sequence) an archeological deposit was found sandwiched between two clay layers, which is designated Archeological Layer 3 West. This layer is regarded by the excavators as a continuation of A.L. 2 Main (J. Wymer, pers. comm.).

4. *Reworked lake deposits* (fig. 63: 1,2,3).

5. *Fluviatile aggradation* (fig. 63: 4). From the upper, coarser deposits there are some derived implements.

6. *Floodplain silt* (fig. 63: 5). This layer contains flint implements which constitute Archeological Layer 6. The excavators regard these implements as being in primary context, and these make up part of the Upper Industry (Singer and Wymer 1976: 17).

7. *Coarse flint gravel* (fig. 63: 6).

8. *Laminated silts*, sands, and muds (fig. 62: 7, 8).

9. *Superficial deposit* (fig. 63: 9,10).

Implements were selected for examination from layers 3 (detritus mud) and 6 (floodplain silt).

### The Condition and Selection of Artifacts

The implements from the Lower Industry levels (A.L.'s 1 Main, 2 Main, and 3 West) were, in the main, in very fresh condition. The majority were unpatinated and, rarely, slightly stained. J. Wymer provided a selection of 75 pieces from A.L.'s 1 and 2 Main, while all the pieces from A.L. 3 West (*N*=408) were examined. This concentration on A.L. 3 West came about after comparison had been made between the 40 implements from A.L. 1 Main, 35 pieces from A.L. 2 Main, and a random sample of 131 implements from A.L. 3 West in regard to the relative proportion of implements which showed signs of abrasion and scratching by soil movements. The proportions were as follows:

|          | Fresh | Slightly Abraded | Abraded | Total |
|----------|-------|------------------|---------|-------|
| 1 Main   | 26    | 4                | 10      | 40    |
| 2 Main   | 18    | 5                | 12      | 35    |
| 3 West   | 93    | 16               | 22      | 131   |

In layer 3 West, the degree of abrasion was variable: most pieces were remarkably fresh; some were quite abraded, showing white scratches, extensive edge damage, and heavily abraded ridges; and only a few showed slight signs of abrasion on their dorsal ridges-- while in layers 1 and 2 Main, the degree of abrasion formed a continuum. This supports the contention of the excavators that these layers have been subject to transport, probably by soil movement (Singer and Wymer 1976: 16). The slight abrasion found on some implements in A.L. 3 West is probably the result of slight settlings and distortions of the deposit under the pressure of overlying sediments, rather than being the result of any actual transport. Besides, 21 of the 38 abraded and slightly abraded pieces from the layer 3 West sample do not, in my opinion, belong with the other pieces. Most of these are small, patinated chips (the fresh implements are unpatinated) which appear to be natural thermal and mechanical flakes from rolled flint cobbles. The larger pieces of these 21 "aliens" could easily be classified as small "eoliths" and are often thermal flakes with some mechanical scars on their margins. Had these pieces not been found in clear association with flints of undoubtedly human workmanship, they probably would not have been given a second glance. The abraded pieces from A.L.'s 1 and 2 Main are clearly implements which have subsequently been moved under pressure. It seems reasonable, then, to suppose that the implements from A.L. 3 West were in primary context, or that if they had been disturbed, they had not been moved more than very slightly.

The difference between A.L. 1 and 2 Main and A.L. 3 West, in terms of their relative proportions of abraded implements, is statistically significant. But since the pieces from A.L.'s 1 and 2 Main were selected, the bias for selecting fresh implements means that the real proportion of abraded pieces in these layers is undoubtedly higher.

Because of the excavator's doubts about the undisturbed nature of the material from A.L. 1 and 2 Main, and because of the undisturbed appearance of the pieces from A.L. 3 West, all fresh or mint implements from the latter were subjected to microwear analysis. Of the 408 pieces from this layer, 119 were judged unusable either because they had been subject to some natural abrasion (this includes the "abraded" and "slightly abraded" categories mentioned above) or, rarely, because they had been so heavily patinated or chemically weathered that microwear traces, if they had had them, could not have survived. This left 289 pieces that could be used in the analysis, of which 26 showed traces of use.

Of the 44 usable pieces from A.L.'s 1 and 2 Main, 2 showed signs of use, one from each of the Archeological Layers. One implement from the few fresh flakes (7) found in A.L. 3 Main (that is, in the top of the Lacustrine clay-muds) had traces of use. Additionally, 5 large bifaces from A.L.'s 1 and 2 Main were examined for traces of use. Of these implements, 4 showed traces of use and one, a hand ax, from 1 Main was too abraded for examination. This gives a total of 33 implements with traces of microwear from the analyzed portion of the Lower Industry.

As a further, perhaps contradictory, note on the undisturbed nature of the 3 West assemblage, I made a determined effort to find refitting pieces in this collection--with no success. All of the 408 pieces were laid out on a lab counter and worked on intermittently over 10 months in an effort to recover refits--this contrasts unfavorably with the Clacton material, where I found several refits, even though I had only small samples of the whole collection before me at any one time.

Unfortunately, the majority of the implements from the Upper Industry (A.L. 6) are not in mint condition and, as the excavators note (Singer and Wymer 1976: 17), "are patinated and have a faint lustre." Singer and Wymer attribute the patination to "surface exposure on a calcareous surface" and the luster to "the action of fine suspended sediment in flowing water" (1976: 17). It was, therefore, not practicable to submit implements from this layer to microwear analysis. Nevertheless, my curiosity about the sidescrapers which are a distinctive feature of this Upper Industry, led me to select 11 sidescrapers from the A.L. 6 collection that were less severely weathered than the majority of similar pieces, in hopes that some information about their functions might be recovered. Six of these implements were too heavily weathered to have retained any recognizable wear traces, but 5 of them did retain interpretable traces of use. In regard to the causes of their patination and luster, one need not posit a "calcareous surface," although there is independent evidence that such a surface may have existed (Wymer, pers. comm.), since it could as well have been caused by exposure to sunlight or exposure to certain chemicals released by plants, and the luster could have as easily arisen from contact with plant chemicals (Röttlander 1975: 108). The implements I examined were usually more heavily patinated on one face (most commonly, the dorsal face) than on the other, and some of the patinas were curiously mottled with diffuse brown lines that certainly suggest contact with plant roots. Only one of the pieces showed any definite signs of natural abrasion, but, then, these implements were selected for their freshness.

## Description of Used Pieces

Since only 38 of the pieces analyzed showed traces of use, it is possible to provide a brief description of each implement and its microwear traces. The artifacts are listed according to functional categories under the heading of each of the Archeological Layers involved--3 West, 1 Main, 2 Main, 3 Main, and 6. The grid coordinates, the height above ordinance datum (in meters), and the catalog numbers are all as assigned by the excavators. The dimensions are given in millimeters and measured as described in chapter 3.

## Archeological Layer 3 West (Lower Industry)

### Wood Whittling or Planing

HXN 4440:  L73 B37 Th17 B/L .506 Th/B .459; coordinates 349 203, 30.71 above O.D.; fig. 64, pl. 93.

Long, right-backed flake. The microwear consists of areas of wood polish on both aspects of the left lateral edge. The polish is heaviest on the dorsal aspect, and the polish on the bulbar aspect occurs mainly on the ridges between the utilization damage scars. There are no striations associated with either polish, but the few areas of polish in the dorsal utilization scars have a directional cast to them, indicating a movement during use approximately at right angles to the edge. The utilization damage occurs on the bulbar aspect of the edge and consists of small ½Moon, MicroD, and a few LS scars--these are all commensurate with a wood-whittling use. The more intense polish on the dorsal aspect indicates that this was the "contact" aspect, so, if a right-handed person were using it, it was probably used with an away-from-the-user movement. The edge is slightly concave, and the edge angle is 47°.

HXN 4599:  L54 B23 Th7 B/L .425 Th/B .304; coordinates 264 144, 30.67 above O.D.

A small, bladelike tip fragment. The microwear polish occurs principally on the

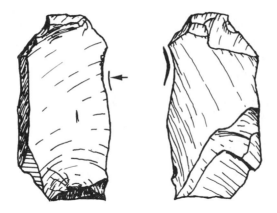

Figure 64.  HXN 4440.

bulbar aspect of the distal left lateral edge.  It is a bright, smooth polish
but has a slightly greasy luster.  Nevertheless, it is probably wood polish.
Thin patches of it occur on the dorsal edge aspect as well.  As with HXN 4440,
there are no striations, but the polish does have a directional cast, which runs
at right angles to the edge.  The edge damage consists of *MicroD* scars which
have been affected by the polish.  The bulbar aspect was undoubtedly the one in
contact with the wood during use.  The task was probably relatively delicate because of the smallness of the implement and because of the smallness of the
edge-damage scars.  The edge is slightly convex, and the edge angle is 62°.

## Wood Scraping

HXN 3958:  L33 B25 Th6 B/L .757 Th/B .24; coordinates 280 155 above O.D.

A small, triangular flake.  There is an area of wood polish on the dorsal aspect
of the left lateral edge but none on the bulbar aspect.  There are no indications
of the direction of use.  The *SD* and *MicroD* utilization damage scars distributed
solely on the bulbar aspect make it very likely that this implement was used for
scraping wood.  Because of the small size of this tool, it seems likely that the
task was a relatively delicate one, involving the working of a small shaft (about
10 mm in diameter) of wood.  The edge is straight, and the edge angle is 40°.

HXN 4200:  L65 B37 Th13 B/L .569 Th/B .351; coordinates 352 189, 30.42 above O.D.; fig. 65,
pl. 94.

A long flake with a removed bulb.  This implement had two functions:  as a
scraper and as a wedge.  On the dorsal aspect of the proximal right lateral
edge, there is an area of wood polish.  On the dorsal aspect of this same edge
is a series of *SD* scars with small patches of wood polish on the ridges between
them.  There are no striations, but, again, the placement of the polish and the
character of the utilization damage indicate scraping as the method of use.  On
the bulbar aspect of the distal portion of this same edge, there is another
series of *SD* scars (and a few *S Step* scars), but there were no associated microwear traces.  The edge is straight, and the edge angle is 35°.  It is possible
that this portion of the edge was used for scraping as well but, in the absence

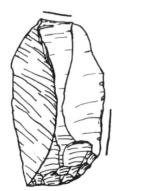

Figure 65.  HXN 4200

of any true microwear, one cannot be sure. Another area of wood polish was
found on the distal end edge (pl. 94). The polish is most intense on the distal
aspect of this edge, but there are a few traces of polish on the bulbar aspect
as well. The comparative rarity of polish on the bulbar aspect is probably due
to its being continuously carried away by the *S Step* and *MicroStep* utilization
damage scars that formed on that aspect. The reason that this edge is interpreted as a wedge is because the opposite end of the flake shows clear signs of
battering with a soft hammer. Since the dorsal aspect of the distal edge is
flat and the bulbar aspect is convexly curved, the "bit" would have a tendency
to turn toward the dorsal aspect as it was inserted. This accounts for the
utilization damage being on the bulbar aspect only. · This turning movement of
the bit would have increased the tendency of the implement to pry open any de-
veloping split in the wood. This turning tendency and the steepness of the edge
angle (60°) would have made this a very difficult implement to use as a primary
wedge (that is, a wedge used in initially opening the split in a material) but
would have suited it admirably for use as a secondary wedge (that is, a wedge
used to widen an already existing split). There are no clues as to which use
came first, scraping or wedging, but a logical sequence might have involved
wedging off of a piece of wood that was then "cleaned up" with the scraping
edge.

## Wood Chopping/Adzing

HXN 3576:   L63 B41 Th19 B/L .650 Th/B .463; coordinates 277 111, 30.83 above O.D.; fig. 66,
pl. 95.

A large, rectangular flake. The microwear occurs on the dorsal aspect of the
distal end edge and consists of a wood polish (pl. 95) and two striations (disposed at right angles to the edge). Opposite the polish, on the bulbar aspect,
is a series of *SD* and *SS* scars, and interrupting this series is a single ½Moon
breakage. This implement could have been used for whittling wood, but having
the working edge on the distal end would have made it awkward to use and,
surely, one of the lateral edges would have been more suitable. But the distal
edge would have been quite suitable for use as a light adzing tool, using short

Figure 66.  HXN 3576.

chopping movements with the dorsal aspect (in this case, the "contact" aspect) held at a low angle to the surface of the worked material.  Besides, such a large ½Moon breakage (5 mm width) is extremely rare on whittling edges.  The edge is slightly concave, and the edge angle is 42°.

Wood Wedging

HXN 3515:  L33 B34 Th10 B/L 1.030 Th/B .294; coordinates 364 194, 30.47 above O.D.; fig. 67.

Figure 67.  HXN 3115.

A rectangular, medial (?) fragment of a flake.  The microwear consists of wood polish situated on both aspects of the distal portion of the left lateral edge. The directional features of the polish run at right angles to the edge.  Co-existent with the polished area, on the bulbar aspect, is a heavy concentration of predominantly S Step scars running over a few earlier L Step scars.  Proximal from, and adjacent to, the polish area, on the dorsal aspect of the same edge, is a small area of LD and SS scars.  On the right lateral edge, directly oppo-site the working edge, is a battered area, which shows large, circular flake scars on the bulbar aspect, crushing of the edge itself, and some small, incipi-ent cones on the dorsal aspect.  These facts all point to the use of this imple-ment as a wedge on wood and suggest that it was driven in with a hammerstone. It has a few curious features, however.  It seems that the whole of the left lateral edge was not inserted into the wood but only the distal half.  There is a possibility that this implement was once longer, because the flake surface which forms the dorsal aspect of the distal edge may be the result of a break-age.  It has the appearance of a "burin" scar with its point of percussion on the working edge. Unfortunately, there is no negative bulb, and the character of the surface is sufficiently ambiguous to make this uncertain. Whether this is half of a larger implement that was broken in use or not, it seems likely that it was held between the thumb and forefinger, on its proximal half, and that the distal portion of the left lateral edge engaged the wood, while the distal portion of the right lateral edge received blows from a hammerstone. The working edge is straight, and the edge angle is 48°.

HXN 4597:   L55 B60 Th7 B/L 1.09 Th/B .116; coordinates 266 118, 30.56 above O.D.; pl. 96. Tip fragment of an irregular flake with a long, square-ended cusp, with recent breakages. The recent breakages (which may be excavation damage) have removed most of the right lateral edge, and a recent snap has removed the striking platform and bulb. The microwear occurs on both aspects of the square-ended cusp and is present in the form of a wood polish which is more intense on the dorsal aspect. Again, there are no striations, but the disposition of the polish suggests a movement parallel with the long axis of the piece. The utilization damage appears as *SD* scars on the dorsal aspect of the working edge. The extent of the microwear polish indicates, for use on wood, a relatively deep penetration into the worked material. It seems likely that this implement is the distal portion of a wedge or, less likely, a chisel, but without the missing portions of the flake, which would carry the traces of the hammer blows, it is impossible to be absolutely certain. The working edge is slightly convex, and the edge angle is 20°.

## Hide Scraping

HXN 3911:   L54 B44 T11 B/L .814 Th/B .25; coordinates 283 169, 30.55 above O.D.; fig. 68, pl. 98.

Figure 68.   HXN 3911.

A small sidescraper retouched on the left lateral edge. The microwear consists of a fresh hide polish (pl. 98) on the bulbar aspects of the left lateral edge and the distal end edge. While the polish can be seen mainly on the bulbar aspect of these edges, it does round the edge, but does not penetrate very far onto the dorsal aspects. There are no striations, but the presence and placement of some linear features in the polish indicate that the use-movement was a scraping one. The shape of the left lateral edge is complex, consisting of two slight convexities, but there is some polish even in the center of the concavity, although it is discontinuous. In this concave area, there are small areas of unworn edge which show the remarkable preservation of sharp flake edges that occur at Hoxne. The distal end edge is straight, and its edge angle is 58°. The edge angle of the retouched left lateral edge ranges from 47° to 58°, with the average about 55°.

HXN 4227:  L77 B60 Th25 B/L .779 Th/B .416; coordinates 297 137, 30.60 above O.D.; fig. 69, pl. 99.

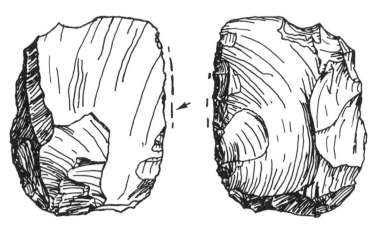

Figure 69.  HXN 4227.

A convex sidescraper on a thermal (?) flake (or shatterpiece). The sidescraper retouch occurs on the bulbar aspect of the right lateral edge. Most of the dorsal surface of this piece is formed by a thermal fracture, and most of the bulbar surface is formed by a fracture surface that may be thermal as well. The piece is backed and shaped bifacially by a series of scars, some of which were certainly struck with a soft hammer. The microwear consists of a hide polish occurring mainly on the dorsal aspect of the scraper edge (pl. 99), but rounding the edge and appearing on a few retouch scar ridges on the bulbar aspect. A single striation and some linear features of the polish indicate movement during use at right angles to the working edge. The edge is slightly convex, and the edge angle ranges between 40° and 45°, with the average around 42°.

HXN 4341:  L77 B46 Th11 B/L .597 Th/B .239; coordinates 311 170, 30.56 above O.D.; fig. 70. A long sidescraper with blunting retouch on the right lateral and distal end edges. The microwear polish occurs predominantly on the bulbar aspect of the left lateral edge, but shows up in a few spots on the dorsal aspect. The polish is clearly a hide polish and probably fresh hide. The striations and linear features associated with the polish indicate a direction of use at right angles to the working edge. There are a few striations running at low angles to the edge, distal from the area of polish, that are probably not related to function, though their cause is not clear. It seems that the working edge has been resharpened at some point in its working life. The initial retouch scars that formed the scraper edge, which had an edge angle of between 45° and 50°, seem to be the result of soft-hammer blows. But in the center of the working edge (as defined by the extent of the bulbar microwear polish) is an area of hard-

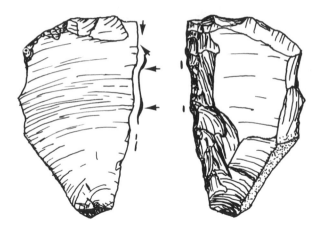

Figure 70.  HXN 4341.

hammer retouch scars which created an edge with an angle of approximately 65°.
The areas of the bulbar aspect showing the most intense polish are on either
side of the slight concavity created by the hard-hammer retouch, implying that
these are remnant areas of the original working edge.  This edge was used after
the resharpening for the same purpose as before--scraping fresh or wet hide.
The working edge, when viewed edge on, arches up toward the dorsal surface.
This fact, coupled with the central placement of the microwear traces on the
otherwise straight scraper edge, may point to the scraping of hides draped or
stretched over a round object, like a log, in the manner of a "beaming post"
(Driver 1961: 173).

HXN 4383:  L63 B60 Th16 B/L .952 Th/B .266; coordinates 330 165, 30.46 above O.D.; pl. 100.
A large, roughly rectangular soft-hammer flake.  Two areas show microwear traces:
the central portion of the right lateral edge and the distal portion of the left
lateral edge.  The microwear polish on the right lateral edge is definitely a
hide polish (pl. 100), with a few striations and linear features disposed at
right angles to the edge.  The hide worked was probably relatively dry.  The
polish rounds the edge and occurs primarily on the bulbar aspect.  In the center
of the working edge, on the dorsal aspect, there is a small concentration of
*MicroStep* and *S Step* scars.  Although this edge appears straight or even slightly concave in plan view, if viewed edge on, it bows substantially down toward
the bulbar surface in the center of the working edge.  The angle of this edge
is 70 .  The microwear polish on the left lateral edge is also probably a hide
polish but sometimes appears brighter than the polish on the opposite lateral
edge.  This polish appears on both aspects of the working edge.  Since it is
weakly developed, there are no linear features in the polish and there are no
associated striations.  The utilization damage associated with the microwear
consists of a few *LS* and *SS* scars on the bulbar aspect of the distal working
edge and *MicroD* and *MicroStep* scars on both aspects of the more proximal section
of the worn edge.  It seems probable that this edge was used for slicing hide

that had been laid on a piece of wood, which would account for the brighter
areas of microwear polish (that is, traces of wood polish superimposed on the
dominant hide polish) and the reltively large size of the utilization damage
scars.  The edge angle is 40°.

## Hide Cutting

HXN 4129:  L49 B52 Th8 B/L 1.061 Th/B .153:  coordinates 318 171, 30.50 above O.D.; fig.
71, pls. 106, 107.

Figure 71.  HXN 4129.

A tip fragment with hard-hammer blunting retouch on the distal and proximal corners of the left lateral edge.  It has probably a meat polish (pl. 106), but at
the very edge there is often a brighter polish that may be wood polish (pl. 107).
There are no striations, but there are linear features in the polish that indicate a movement during use parallel to the working edge.  Because the polish is
so intense (pl. 107), it is possible that it is actually a fresh-hide polish and
that this implement was used for cutting up fresh hide laid over a piece of
wood (cf. HXN 4383 above).  The utilization damage consists of *MicroStep* scars
on both aspects and *S Step* scars on the dorsal aspect of the left-hand portion
of the working edge.  On the convex curve of the right-hand part of this edge
is a series of very small ½*Moon* breakages.  The edge angle ranges between 30°
and 48°, with the average about 40°.

## Meat Cutting and Butchering

HXN 3491:  L80 B40 Th11 B/L .50 Th/B .275; coordinates 366 218, 30.65 above O.D.
A long, right cortex-backed flake, with a deep, retouched (?) notch on the distal left lateral edge.  The microwear consists of a sparse meat polish distributed on both aspects of the left lateral edge.  There are no actual striations,
but the disposition of the polish in relation to certain features of the microtopography suggests a use movement, cutting, parallel to the edge.  The utilization damage consists of some very small ½*Moon* breakages and *MicroD* scars on
both aspects of the proximal convexity of the working edge.  The edge is generally convex, and the edge angle is 31°.  There is no microwear associated with
the distal notch, the origin of which remains unclear.

HXN 3503:  L68 B60 Th14 B/L .882 Th/B .233; coordinates 357 215, 30.60 above O.D.; fig.
72, pl. 101.
A large butt fragment of a flake, with blunting by hard-hammer retouch on the

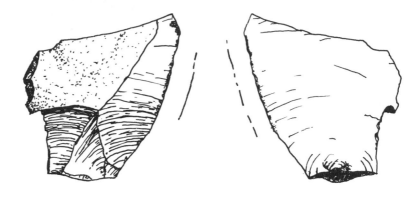

Figure 72.  HXN 3503.

left lateral edge.  The microwear consists of a sporadic meat polish (pl. 101)
along the distal two-thirds of the right lateral edge, observable primarily on
the bulbar aspect.  There are no striations or other indications of the direction of use associated with the polish.  The utilization damage consists of *SD*,
*S Step*, and *MicroD* and *MicroStep* scars irregularly distributed on both aspects
of the working edge.  This implement is undoubtedly a meat knife, the edge of
which has probably come in contact with harder materials, like bone, tendons,
or cartilage.  Perhaps "butchering knife" would therefore be a better description.  The edge is convex, and the edge angle is 34°.

HXN 3820:  L95 B46 Th12 B/L .484 Th/B .26; coordinates 292 177, 30.66 above O.D.; fig. 73,
           pl. 102.

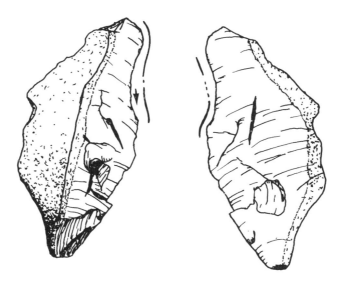

Figure 73.  HXN 3820.

A long, left cortex-backed flake. The microwear consists of a meat polish, with a pronounced greasy luster, on both aspects of the distal right lateral edge. There are a few striations and linear features in the polish that indicate a movement roughly parallel with the edge. The shape of the working edge is complex, consisting of two small convexities separated by a long concavity. The utilization damage occurs on the most distal convexity and is made up of very small ½Moon breakages. This is obviously a meat knife. The edge angle is, on average, 22°. This implement was found within a few centimeters of HXN 3821.

HXN 3821:  L101 B92 Th27 B/L .910 Th/B .293; coordinates 291 179, 30.70 above O.D.; fig. 74, pl. 103.

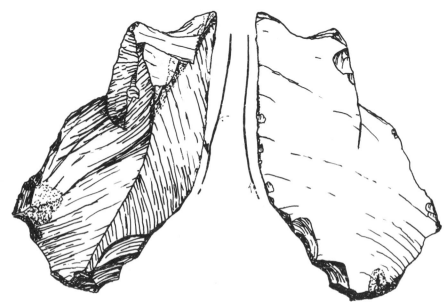

Figure 74.  HXN 3821.

A large, pointed flake with blunting by retouch along the proximal third of the right lateral edge and on a projection on the left lateral edge. The microwear pattern is composed of a clear meat polish on both aspects of the distal two-thirds of the right lateral edge. There are occasional patches of what appears to be bone polish (pl. 103) on microelevations along this same edge. There are a few striations of the narrow, deep type oriented at various angles to the edge, but most run roughly parallel with it. *S Step* and *MicroStep* scars are found sporadically along the dorsal aspect of the working edge. On the bulbar aspect, the damage is heavier, consisting of a continuous run of *LS*, *S Step*, *MicroD*, and *MicroStep* scars. This implement was probably used in butchering meat for cutting through joints or in some other way that brought it into repeated contact with bone. The edge is slightly convex, and the edge angle ranges between 60° and 66°, averaging approximately 62°. The heavy, hard-hammer retouch on the proximal portions of the lateral edges was undoubtedly intended to blunt them, and possibly to shape them and to facilitate handling. This implement was found within a few centimeters of HXN 3820.

HXN 4008:    L78 B44 Th13 B/L .564 Th/B .295; coordinates 306 151, above O.D.; fig. 75, pl.
             104.

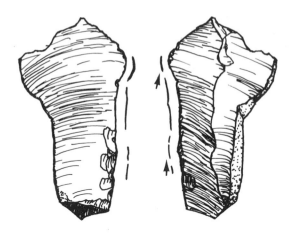

Figure 75.   HXN 4008.

A long, right cortex-backed flake with invasive bifacial retouch on the proximal
half of the left lateral edge.  The microwear consists of a very intense meat
polish found on both aspects of the left lateral edge.  In the proximal part of
this edge, the retouched area, there are small areas of what is probably bone
polish (pl. 104), very similar to the polish left by bone sawing.  There are a
few striations and linear features in the polish which show a use-movement parallel to the working edge.  This implement should be regarded as a butchering
knife rather than as purely a meat knife.  The retouch was probably intended to
strengthen the proximal edge for use in cutting through joints, and so on, but
it may have been a result of resharpening as well.  The edge is a complex shape,
mostly straight with a small distal convexity.  The edge angle is 40°.

HXN 4079:    L95 B57 Th10 B/L .600 Th/B .175; coordinates 331 196, 30.44 above O.D.; fig. 76,
             pl. 105.
             A long, pointed bladelike flake, with recent (excavation) damage on the distal
             right lateral edge.  The microwear occurs as a meat polish (pl. 105), with
             minute, narrow, deep striae on both aspects of the medial right lateral edge.
             This polish is most intense on the dorsal edge aspect.  The polish may have once
             extended further distally along this edge, but the excavation damage (the flake
             scars are recent and there are traces of metal associated with them) has removed
             the edge in that area.  The striations run at various angles to the edge.  The
             utilization damage consists of a few isolated *MicroD* scars on both aspects of
             the working edge.  Because of the orientation of the striations and the occur-
             rence of the microwear in the center of a slight concavity of the edge, it is
             possible that this implement was a knife used to cut off pieces of meat gripped
             between the teeth during eating (see Semenov 1964: fig. 42: 3).  The edge is
             slightly concave, and the edge angle is 35°.

HXN 4212:    L62 B42 Th12 B/L .677 Th/B .285; coordinates 355 188, 30.38 above O.D.; pl. 108.
             A left cortex-backed flake with hard-hammer blunting retouch on the proximal

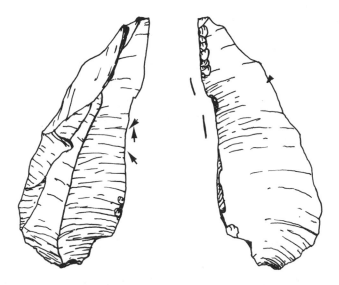

Figure 76.  HXN 4079.

portion of the left lateral edge and similar retouch removing the bulb and striking platform.  The microwear consists of a greasy meat polish (pl. 108) on both aspects of the distal two-thirds of the right lateral edge.  There are no striations or other indications of the direction of use.  The utilization damage consists of randomly distributed *SS* and *MicroStep* scars on both aspects of the working edge.  This implement was a meat knife.  The edge is slightly convex, and the edge angle is 42°.

HXN 4248:  L78 B56 Th14 B/L .717 Th/B .25; coordinates 287 121, 30.48 above O.D.; fig. 77.  A long, triangular flake.  The microwear polish occurs along the distal three-quarters of the left lateral edge and is a bright meat polish.  There are no

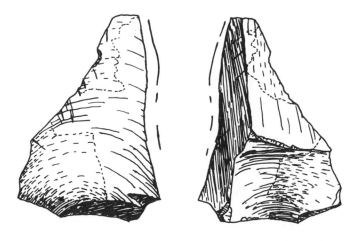

Figure 77.  HXN 4248.

indications of the direction of use. The utilization damage occurs primarily on the distal, slightly convex, third of the working edge. It consists of *MicroD* and *MicroStep* scars distributed irregularly on both edge aspects. It seems, given the distribution of the polish and the utilization damage, that this implement was used for cutting; therefore, it is a meat knife. The edge shape is complex being concavo-convex, and the average edge angle is 39°.

## Bone Chopping

HXN 4252:  L52 B71 Th45 B/L 1.365 Th/B .633; coordinates 299 138, 30.57 above O.D.; fig. 78, pl. 109.

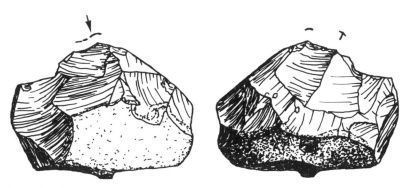

Figure 78.  HXN 4252.

A small, bifacial chopper-core. The microwear consists of a few patches of bone polish (pl. 109) on some high points on both aspects of the central portion of the chopping edge. There is a single striation running at a high angle (approx. 70°) to the long axis of the implement. The utilization damage is quite difficult to separate from the small scars resulting from the hard-hammer blows, but *L* and *S Step* scars are quite abundant in the area where the polish occurs. This implement was probably used for roughly chopping bone, possibly to get at the marrow. The edge is convex, and the edge angles range from 58° to 82°, with the average about 68°.

## Bone Boring

HXN 4198:  L49 B32 Th13 B/L .653 Th/B .406; coordinates 352 187, 30.43 above O.D.
A small, left snap-backed flake, with steep hard-hammer retouch on the right lateral edge. The microwear appears on the bulbar aspect and dorsal ridge of a robust cusp created by retouch on the right lateral edge and is a bright rough polish that is probably bone polish. There is one short abrasion track on one of the dorsal ridges of the cusp which runs at a right angle to the bit axis. There are some *MicroStep* scars on the bulbar aspect of the cusp. It seems likely, then, that this implement was used for boring bone, but why the user did not employ the perfectly good (if broken-tipped) trihedral end of this flake instead of creating a cusp by retouch is hard to understand.

## Plant Gathering or Cutting

HXN 3497:  L67 B58 Th13 B/L .865 Th/B .224; coordinates 363 208, 30.54 above O.D.; fig. 79, pl. 110.

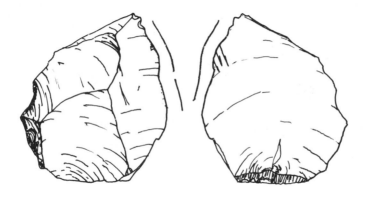

Figure 79.  HXN 3497.

A left retouch-backed flake.  On both aspects of the right lateral edge is a
very bright, very smooth microwear polish which is unlikely to be true corn
gloss but which must come from the working of a vegetable material (pl. 110).
There are no striations or directional indications associated with the polish,
but the extent of the polished area means it must have been the result of a
slicing motion.  The polish is, however, less extensive on the dorsal aspect.
The utilization damage consists of a few scattered *S Step* and *MicroD* scars on
both aspects of the working edge.  The shape of this edge is generally convex,
and the edge angle is 34°.

HXN 3518:  L74 B62 Th15 B/L .837 Th/B .241; coordinates 364 225, 30.44 above O.D.
A large, rectangular flake with some spontaneous retouch, or perhaps intentional
blunting, on a small area of the distal end edge.  The microwear polish appears
on both aspects of the distal half of the left lateral edge.  It is very bright
and very smooth, like the polish on HXN 3497 and must be the result of cutting
some plant material.  There are no clear indications of the direction of use,
but the extent of the polish on both aspects points to a slicing or cutting
method of use.  The utilization damage occurs as *SD* and *MicroD* scars on both
edge aspects but principally on the dorsal aspect.  The edge is convex, and the
edge angle is 42°.

HXN 4113:  L51 B44 Th15 B/L .862 Th/B .340; coordinates 335 189, 30.34 above O.D.; fig. 80,
pl. 97.
A left cortex-backed flake.  The microwear consists of a bright, smooth polish
on both aspects of the proximal right lateral edge.  On the bulbar aspect, there
are some short, narrow, deep striations, some of which run parallel to the edge,
and others of which run at about a 30° angle to it.  The utilization damage is
made up of *MicroD* scars on both aspects and some *MicroStep* scars on the bulbar
aspect.  Despite what is very likely wood polish, the interpretation of the implement is not easy.  Although the striations indicate a movement roughly parallel to the edge, it cannot be a wood saw because the utilization damage is too
small.  It could have been used for making shallow cuts along the grain of fresh
wood or for cutting through the bark on a branch preparatory to peeling it off.

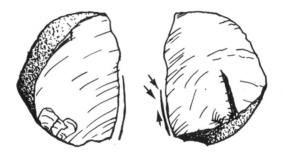

Figure 80.  HXN 4113.

It is also possible that this implement was used for cutting some soft material,
like meat or vegetable matter, that left no wear traces, on a wood cutting
board.  It is also conceivable that the material worked was some woody vegetable
material, like bracken stems.  The edge is slightly convex, and the edge angle
is 40°.

## Use Unknown

HXN 3822:  L77 B59 B/L .766 Th/B .220; coordinates 291 179, 30.70 above O.D.
A large, right snap-backed flake.  The only possible trace of wear on this implement is a single, narrow, deep striation on the bulbar aspect of the left
lateral edge.  Normally this would not be considered as sufficient evidence even
for possible use, but this implement was found within a few centimeters of HXN
3820 (meat knife) and HXN 3821 (butchering knife).  It is possible, however,
that this piece was used for a similar task but for too brief a period to leave
any unequivocal wear traces.  The edge is straight, and the edge angle is 56°.

### Archeological Layer 1 Main (Lower Industry)

## Hide Scraping

HXN 69:     L62 B46 Th12 B/L .741 Th/B .26; coordinates 694 337, 29.66 above O.D.; fig. 81.

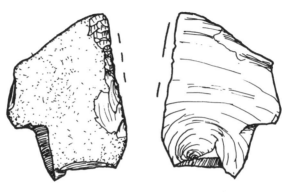

Figure 81.  HXN 69.

A left cortex-backed sidescraper on a primary flake. The microwear polish, which is a fresh hide polish, appears on the very edge of both aspects of the distal portion of the scraper edge. The edge is rounded, but there are no clear indications of the direction of use. This implement could have been used as a scraper, but it is also possible that it was used as a flensing knife to remove fat from a hide, with a planing movement or as a skinning knife. The edge is straight, and the edge angles average about 40°.

## Meat Cutting and Butchering

HXN 64:    L153 B86 Th42 B/L .562 Th/B .488; coordinates 690 341, 29.67 above O.D.; fig. 82. An amygdaloid, pointed hand ax with battering on both lateral edges at the point of maximum breadth. The microwear consists of a meat polish on both aspects of the right lateral edge (looking at side 1). There are no striations or other indications of direction, but it seems likely from the disposition of polish that it was used with a cutting motion. The edge shape is convex, and the edge angles average 54°. It is interesting to note that this implement was found only a few centimeters from HXN 69, so they may be part of the same tool kit if they are in their primary context, which seems likely.

## Archeological Layer 2 Main (Lower Industry)

## Wood Wedging

HXN 39:    L52 B70 Th22 B/L 1.346 Th/B .314; coordinates 617 309, 29.48 above O.D.; fig. 83, pl. 111.
A side-struck, partially cortex-covered flake with battering on the striking platform which has removed the bulb. The microwear appears on both aspects of the canted distal end edge and is a wood polish (p. 111). There are no striations or other indications of the direction of use. The utilization damage on this edge consists of SS and MicroStep scars distributed along both aspects. The striking platform, which is opposite the working edge, shows signs of hard-hammer battering with incipient cones and crushing of the edge, particularly on the left edge of the platform. This implement is surely a wood wedge, but its peculiar working edge, which is canted to the right, must mean it was inserted not into the body of the worked piece of wood, but into one of its ends. The edge shape is complex, and the average edge angle is 40°.

HXN 737:   L100 B103 Th33 B/L 1.03 Th/B .32; coordinates 583 294, 29.70 above O.D.; fig. 84, pl. 112.
A large, disc-shaped bifacial implement, finished by soft-hammer flaking. The only traces of use found on this implement occurred on both aspects of the distal end edge (as it is shown in fig. 87). A faint wood polish occurred on the very edge and along some of the flake scar ridges running up from the edge. There were no striations, but the disposition of the polish indicated a direction of use at roughly right angles to the edge. The utilization damage consisted of L Step, S Step, and ½Moon scars on both aspects, LS and SS scars on Aspect 1, and some MicroStep scars on Aspect 2. On the proximal end, opposite the working edge, was an area of soft-hammer battering that resulted in a slightly concave area of stepped scars on Aspect 2 of this edge. The edge is straight, and the edge angles range between 48° and 64°, with an average of 56°.

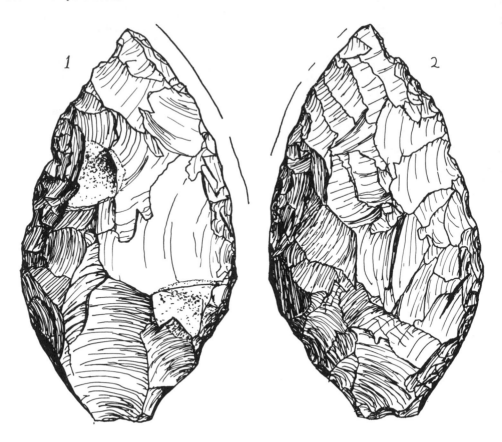

Figure 82.   HXN 64.

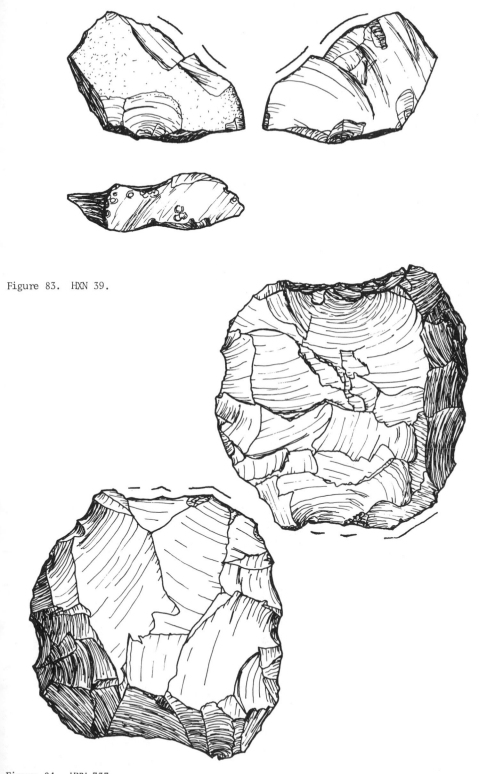

Figure 83.  HXN 39.

Figure 84.  HXN 737.

There can be little doubt that this implement was used as a wood wedge. The only question is Why make such an elaborate implement when the task could have been accomplished with a much less elaborately prepared piece? One possibility is that this implement is a "failed" hand ax which was subsequently used, perhaps after some minor reshaping, as a wedge. Another is that a particularly robust, and perhaps lengthy, wedging task was going on, and a large core or nodule from which the requisite number of large flakes could be struck was not available, so a single, specially prepared implement was constructed instead from a smaller nodule that was handy.

## Meat Cutting and Butchery

HXN 1311:   L121 B92 Th30 B/L .760 Th/B .326; coordinates 568 357, 29.62 above O.D.; fig. 85, pl. 113.

A broad, cordiform hand ax, very finely made. The microwear traces occur along the left lateral edge (as seen on Face 1 in fig. 88) near the tip. The microwear polish seems to be a mixture of meat (pl. 113) and bone polishes and occurs on both aspects of the edge. There are a few striations, running at various angles to the edge. The utilization damage is extremely hard to isolate on a retouched edge like this one, but there are a number of *LS* and *S Step* scars along this edge that may be the result of use. It is likely that this implement was used for some heavy butchering task, like breaking joints, as well as for cutting up hunks of meat. The edge is straight, and the edge angles range between 44° and 49°, the average being 46°.

## Bone Chopping

HXN 637:   L97 B75 Th49 B/L .773 Th/B .653; coordinates 606 319, depth unknown; fig. 86, pl. 114.

A pointed chopper-core with a cortex-covered butt. The microwear traces occur on both aspects of the edges leading to the implement's tip. The microwear polish is bright but rough and sometimes pitted (pl. 114). It is probably a bone polish, although wood polish is a distant possibility. There are a number of striations, generally of the broad, shallow type, running at very low angles to the long axis of the implement. The utilization damage consists of *LS*, *S Step*, and *MicroStep* scars on both edge aspects, *LD* scars on Aspect 1 and *L Step* scars on Aspect 2. On Aspect 2 there is a large (compared to normal utilization damage), shallow flake scar, whose point of percussion is the tip of the implement; this is probably an impact scar created during use. There is little doubt that this tool is a chopper, and it is highly likely that the material chopped was bone. It could have been used to open up bones for marrow extraction, or it might be yet another implement used to break joints. The edge is convex, and the edge angles range between 48° and 65°, the average being 50°.

## Archeological Layer 3 Main (Lower Industry)

## Wood Boring

HXN 352:   L42 B39 Th8 B/L .928 Th/B .205; coordinates 617 341, 29.21 above O.D.

A cortex butted and backed (left) flake with a cusp created by retouch on the right distal edge. This implement was found in the lake sediments and, therefore, must have either been washed or thrown onto the lake bottom. The whole

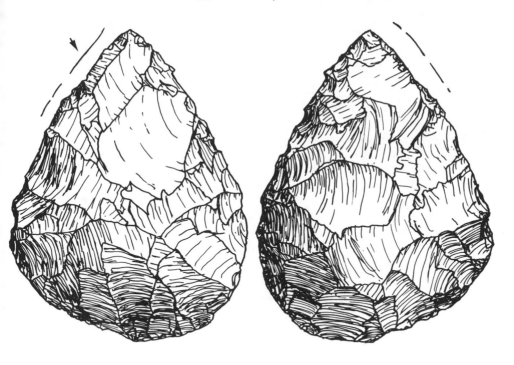

Figure 85.   HXN 1311.

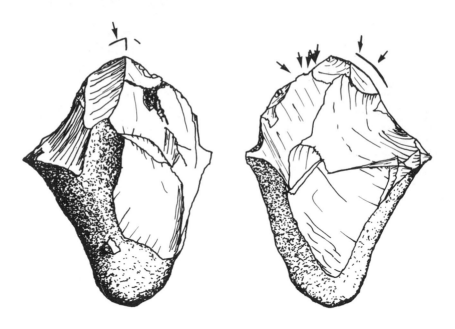

Figure 86.   HXN 637.

flaked surface of the implement is covered with a faint luster, which is probably the result of light abrasion in the lake bottom, but the edges and the
flake ridges are still quite sharp.  Despite this natural wear (if wear is the
right term for it), this piece does retain traces that are recognizable as being
the result of use.  There is a microwear polish, much brighter in appearance
than the natural luster, that is most apparent on the unretouched right lateral
edge of the borer bit.  The original character of this polish has been destroyed
presumably by the same process that caused the overall luster.  This brighter
polish can be seen on all the ridges and edges of the bit.  The utilization
damage, which also is easily seen on the right lateral edge of the bit, consists
of very small ½Moon breakages, *MicroStep* and a few *SS* scars on both aspects of
this edge.  Most of these scars occur on the dorsal aspect of this edge and
probably indicate a use movement turning in a clockwise fashion.  This implement
is probably a wood borer.

### Archeological Layer 6 (Upper Industry)

#### Wood Adzing

HXN 3970:   L54 B69 Th17 B/L 1.277 Th/B .246; coordinates 55 45, depth unknown; fig. 87.
A straight sidescraper formed by a stepped retouch (the "retouche en écaille
scalariform" of Bordes 1961: 8) on a side-struck flake.  The microwear consists
of a wood polish and a few striations (disposed at right angles to the edge)
found on the bulbar aspect of the left lateral edge (the scraper edge).  The
utilization damage is hard to isolate on a retouched edge like this, but the
*MicroStep* and *SS* scars found on the bulbar aspect of this edge are probably the

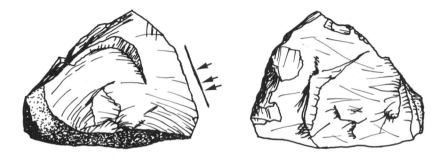

Figure 87.  HXN 3970.

result of use.  This could be a wood-whittling knife, but because the working
edge is at the end of the long axis of the flake and because the prominent bulb
would mean that the angle between the bulbar aspect of the working edge and the
surface of the wood during use would be too high for efficient whittling, it
seems more likely that this tool was used for adzing.  The edge is straight,
and the edge angle is 64°.

## Hide Scraping

HXN 3753:  L68 B109 Th24 B/L 1.602 Th/B .22; coordinates 62 45, depth unknown; fig. 88.

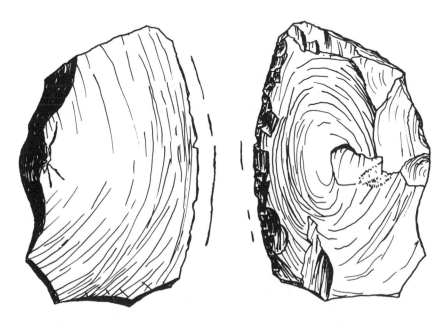

Figure 88.  HXN 3753.

A convex, transverse sidescraper on a side-struck flake. Although the microsurface of this implement has undergone some alteration as the result of weathering, there is still a microwear polish observable on both aspects of the scraping edge. The polish rounds the edge and is most intense on the left side of
the distal edge. There are some diffuse, linear features on the extreme edge
which seem to indicate a movement across and at right angles to the edge. The
material worked was most probably hide, but the weathering changes make it impossible to be certain. The edge is convex, and the edge angle averages 56°.

HXN 3884:   L69 B55 Th15 B/L .797 Th/B .272; coordinates 51 45, depth unknown; fig. 89.

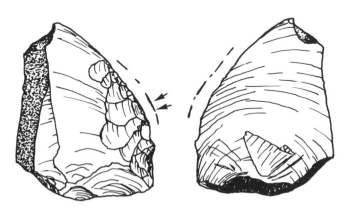

Figure 89.  HXN 3884.

A left cortex-backed, convex sidescraper. The microwear occurs as a hide polish
on both aspects of the medial right lateral edge (the scraper edge). The polish
is more intense on the dorsal aspect, where it occurs particularly on the flake
scar ridges at the edge. There are a few striations of the narrow, deep variety
associated with the polish on the dorsal face, which indicate a use movement at
right angles to the edge. The hide scraped was probably relatively dry, as the
polish is quite rough. And the implement was probably held at nearly a right
angle to the worked material so that the hide could come into contact with the
flake scar ridges on the dorsal aspect of the working edge. The edge is convex,
and the average angle of the edge is 48°.

HXN 4423:   L80 B61 Th18 B/L .762 Th/B .295; coordinates 598 458, depth unknown; fig. 90,
            pl. 115.
            A broad endscraper, with unifacial retouch around the whole of the flake margin.
            On the distal dorsal surface, we should first note an area of gloss which does
            not reach the edge and is most intense on the higher points toward the center of
            the piece. The gloss is very smooth and very bright--in some ways similar to
            corn gloss. There are striations running parallel with the long axis of the
            flake in the polish. It does not seem to be the result of any possible use,
            since it does not affect the bulbar surface or the edge; most natural processes,
            on the other hand, could not affect such a localized area. It is possible that
            before the implement became completely buried in the soil, while only a small
            area of the dorsal surface protruded into the area, wind or water moved very

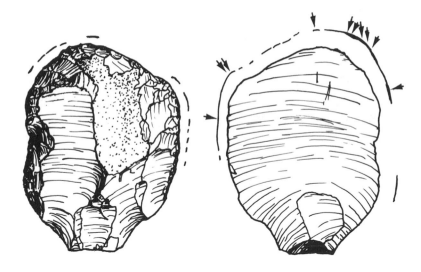

Figure 90.  HXN 4423.

small silica particles across the exposed area, causing a silica gloss and some
slight abrasion.  In any case, this possibly natural gloss is quite different
from the true microwear polish, which occurs mainly on the bulbar aspect of some
parts of the flake edge on this piece.  This polish is rough and matt, with diffuse linear features at the very edge (pl. 115) and is characteristic dry-hide
polish.  There are two principal areas of hide polish--on the distal right lateral edge, and on the left half of the distal end convexity.  There are striations and other linear features associated with these areas of polish, which
generally run at very high angles to their particular part of the continuously
curved edge.  There is little doubt that this implement is a well-used hide
scraper.  The two edges are convex.  The edge angle of the right lateral working
edge is 40°, and the average angle of the left distal working edge is 62°.

HXN 4562:  L79 B58 Th18 B/L .734 Th/B .31; coordinates 62 43, depth unknown; fig. 91.
A convex sidescraper with blunting retouch on the proximal left lateral edge.
The microwear consists of a hide polish rounding the distal right lateral edge
(scraper edge).  The polish is most intense on the bulbar aspect.  There is a
single striation running at about 80° to the working edge on the bulbar aspect.
This implement is clearly a hide scraper.  Since the polish is slightly greasy
in appearance and not very rough, the hide worked may have been fresh.  The edge
is convex, and the edge angle is 55°.

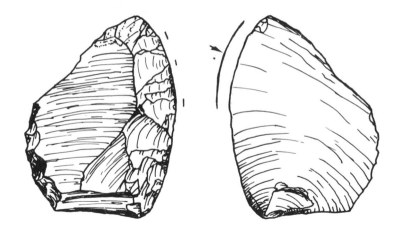

Figure 91. HXN 4562.

## Associations between Wear Traces and Tool Morphology at Hoxne (Lower Industry)

### Use and Edge Angle

Table 27 shows the relationship between the angle of the working edge and the particular use of an implement. There are too few used edges to allow any clear patterns to emerge. One thing is clear--that for most uses, the creators of the Hoxne Lower Industry preferred an edge angle of around 40°. The large number of meat and butchering cutting edges with edge angles between 35° and 49° is probably a direct reflection of their being the most numerous type of used edge.

*Table 27*
*Hoxne (L.I.), Use and Edge Angle (counting edges)*

|  | <35° | 35°-49° | 50°-64° | 65°-79° | >79° | Totals |
|---|---|---|---|---|---|---|
| Wood whittling |  | 1 | 1 |  |  | 2 |
| Wood chopping/adzing |  | 1 |  |  |  | 1 |
| Wood scraping |  | 2 |  |  |  | 2 |
| Wood wedging | 1 | 2 | 2 |  |  | 5 |
| Hide scraping |  | 3 | 1 | 1 |  | 5 |
| Hide cutting |  | 2 |  |  |  | 2 |
| Meat cutting/butchery | 3 | 5 | 2 |  |  | 10 |
| Bone chopping |  |  | 1 | 1 |  | 2 |
| Plant cutting | 1 | 2 |  |  |  | 3 |
| Boring* |  |  |  |  |  |  |
| Totals | 5 | 18 | 7 | 2 |  | 32 |

*boring (*N*=2) not included.

### Use and Edge Shape

The relationship between particular uses and edge shapes is a little clearer, although still uncertain because of the small numbers involved (table 28). The meat-cutting edges

*Table 28*
*Hoxne (L.I.), Use and Edge Shape (counting edges)*

|                       | Convex | Straight | Concave | Complex | Totals |
|-----------------------|--------|----------|---------|---------|--------|
| Wood whittling        | 1      |          | 1       |         | 2      |
| Wood chopping/adzing  |        |          | 1       |         | 1      |
| Wood scraping         |        | 2        |         |         | 2      |
| Wood wedging          | 1      | 3        |         | 1       | 5      |
| Hide scraping         | 1      | 2        |         | 2       | 5      |
| Hide cutting          | 1      |          |         | 1       | 2      |
| Meat cutting/butchery | 6      | 1        | 1       | 2       | 10     |
| Bone chopping         | 2      |          |         |         | 2      |
| Plant cutting         | 3      |          |         |         | 3      |
| Boring                |        |          |         | 2       | 2      |
| Totals                | 15     | 8        | 3       | 8       | 34     |

are usually convex, as are the plant-cutting edges. Surprisingly, the hide-scraping edges are often straight or complex in shape, but this, as we mentioned above, may be the result of use of a "beaming post" or a curved backboard. The wood scrapers are on straight edges, as was the case at Clacton.

## Use and Retouch

As was the case at Clacton, most tasks were accomplished with unretouched edges (table 29). Only those uses which require a blunt or regular edge, like scraping; a steep, strong edge, like bone chopping; or a special edge shape, like boring, were associated with retouched edges. Evidence for other uses, which only require an edge of appropriate sharpness, was found primarily on unretouched edges.

*Table 29*
*Hoxne (L.I.), Use and Retouch (counting edges)*

|                       | Unretouched | Retouched | Totals |
|-----------------------|-------------|-----------|--------|
| Wood whittling        | 2           |           | 2      |
| Wood chopping/adzing  | 1           |           | 1      |
| Wood scraping         | 2           |           | 2      |
| Wood wedging          | 4           | 1         | 5      |
| Hide scraping         | 1           | 4         | 5      |
| Hide cutting          | 1           | 1         | 2      |
| Meat cutting/butchery | 8           | 2         | 10     |
| Bone chopping         |             | 2         | 2      |
| Plant cutting         | 3           |           | 3      |
| Boring                |             | 2         | 2      |
| Totals                | 22          | 12        | 34     |

However, on six of the implements which had unretouched working edges, there were areas of retouch apparently designed to blunt edges or remove projections in order to facilitate holding of the tool in the hand.

## Use and Blank Size

By looking at figs. 92 and 93 we can see that, in general, the used flakes are longer and broader than the unused flakes.  It is interesting to note that the shape of the frequency polygons for the used flakes in both graphs is more approximately "normal" than that for the unused flakes which are of the skewed "log-normal" type so common with flaked stone data.  It is reasonable to suppose that the makers and users of these implements were creating and selecting larger (but not particularly longer) flakes for use.

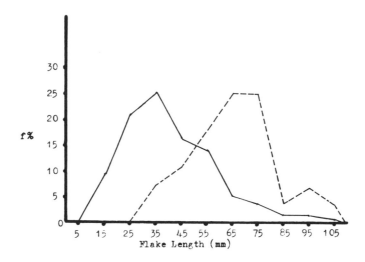

Figure 92.  Hoxne--histograms of used and unused flake lengths.  Solid line=unused flakes; broken line=used flakes.

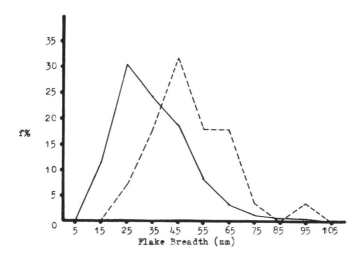

Figure 93.  Hoxne--histograms of used and unused flake breadths.  Solid line=unused flakes; broken line=used flakes.

Table 30 shows the relationship between use and flake length.  It seems that borers were made on short flakes, wood wedges on moderately long blanks, hide scrapers on long flakes, and meat knives on very long flakes.

*Table 30*
*Hoxne (L.I.), Use and Blank Length (counting edges)*

|  | <40 mm | 40-49 mm | 50-59 mm | 60-69 mm | 70-79 mm | >79 mm | Totals |
|---|---|---|---|---|---|---|---|
| Wood whittling |  |  | 1 |  | 1 |  | 2 |
| Wood chopping/adzing |  |  |  | 1 |  |  | 1 |
| Wood scraping | 1 |  |  | 1 |  |  | 2 |
| Wood wedging | 1 |  | 2 | 1 |  | 1 | 5 |
| Hide scraping |  |  | 1 | 2 | 2 |  | 5 |
| Hide cutting |  |  |  | 1 | 1 |  | 2 |
| Meat cutting/butchery |  | 1 |  | 2 | 1 | 6 | 10 |
| Bone chopping |  |  | 1 |  |  | 1 | 2 |
| Plant cutting |  |  | 1 | 1 | 1 |  | 3 |
| Boring |  | 2 |  |  |  |  | 2 |
| Totals | 2 | 3 | 6 | 9 | 6 | 8 | 34 |

The relationship between use and flake breadth is not a particularly strong one (table 31).  It seems that flakes which were small in every dimension were most appropriate for alteration into borers.  Meat knives, while they tend to be long, do not show any tendency to be particularly broad.  Table 32 shows the relationship between the relative breadth (*B/L*) of the flake and use.  Only a few points of interest emerge from this comparison: wood-whittling and butchering knives tend to be on narrower flakes; wood wedges tend to be on broad flakes; and plant-cutting knives tend to be about as broad as they are long.

*Table 31*
*Hoxne (L.I.), Use and Blank Breadth (counting edges)*

|  | <30 mm | 30-39 mm | 40-49 mm | 50-59 mm | 60-69 mm | >69 mm | Totals |
|---|---|---|---|---|---|---|---|
| Wood whittling | 1 | 1 |  |  |  |  | 2 |
| Wood chopping/adzing |  |  | 1 |  |  |  | 1 |
| Wood scraping | 1 | 1 |  |  |  |  | 2 |
| Wood wedging |  | 2 |  |  | 1 | 2 | 5 |
| Hide scraping |  |  | 3 |  | 2 |  | 5 |
| Hide cutting |  |  | 1 |  | 1 |  | 2 |
| Meat cutting/butchery |  |  | 3 | 3 | 1 | 3 | 10 |
| Bone chopping |  |  |  |  | 2 |  | 2 |
| Plant cutting |  |  | 1 | 2 |  |  | 3 |
| Boring |  | 2 |  |  |  |  | 2 |
| Totals | 2 | 6 | 9 | 5 | 5 | 7 | 34 |

*Table 32*
*Hoxne (L.I.), Use and B/L (counting edges)*

|  | <.600 | .600-.799 | .800-.999 | 1.000-1.199 | >1.199 | Totals |
|---|---|---|---|---|---|---|
| Wood whittling | 2 |  |  |  |  | 2 |
| Wood chopping/adzing |  | 1 |  |  |  | 1 |
| Wood scraping | 1 | 1 |  |  |  | 2 |
| Wood wedging | 1 |  |  | 3 | 1 | 5 |
| Hide scraping | 1 | 2 | 2 |  |  | 5 |
| Hide cutting | 1 |  | 1 |  |  | 2 |
| Meat cutting/butchery | 3 | 4 | 2 | 1 |  | 10 |
| Bone chopping |  | 1 |  |  | 1 | 2 |
| Plant cutting |  |  | 3 |  |  | 3 |
| Boring |  | 1 | 1 |  |  | 2 |
| Totals | 9 | 10 | 9 | 4 | 2 | 34 |

The thickness measurements on the used flakes (and the collection as a whole) showed so little variation that comparisons were futile. The same difficulty arose with the relative thickness (*Th/B*) values, but there was variation enough, linked to the *B* values, to produce some patterns. Table 33 shows that the woodworking tools tend to be relatively thick, whereas the other types are on thinner pieces.

*Table 33*
*Hoxne (L.I.), Use and Th/B (counting edges)*

|  | <.176 | .176-.250 | .251-.325 | .326-.400 | >.400 | Totals |
|---|---|---|---|---|---|---|
| Wood whittling |  |  |  | 1 | 1 | 2 |
| Wood chopping/adzing |  |  |  |  | 1 | 1 |
| Wood scraping |  |  | 1 | 1 |  | 2 |
| Wood wedging | 1 |  | 3 | 1 |  | 5 |
| Hide scraping |  | 2 | 2 | 1 |  | 5 |
| Hide cutting |  |  | 2 |  |  | 2 |
| Meat cutting/butchery | 2 | 2 | 5 |  | 1 | 10 |
| Bone chopping |  |  |  |  | 2 | 2 |
| Plant cutting |  | 2 |  | 1 |  | 3 |
| Boring |  | 1 |  |  | 1 | 2 |
| Totals | 3 | 7 | 13 | 5 | 6 | 34 |

## Conclusions

The impressions given by the above cross-tabulations are similar to those obtained from the study of the material from Clacton. At Hoxne too, it seems there is little formalization of functional types, with the majority of tasks being undertaken with flakes selected loosely on the basis of their size and the shape of their edges. There is some formalization to be seen in the use of sidescrapers for scraping hides. One can see in the sidescrapers of A.L. 3 West the morphological and technological precursors of the slightly more elegant sidescrapers of the Upper Industry, with which, it appears from the present study, they share a common function.

Most of the unused flakes are certainly the debitage left by hand ax manufacture, and this raises the question of whether the used flakes were struck from special cores or whether they were simply selected from the larger flakes that are commonly taken off in the initial stages of hand ax manufacture (cf. Newcomer 1971). None of the used flakes can definitely be said to be a hand ax trimmer, although there are a few that may be (4597, 4383, and 4079). There are, however, a few cores from the Lower Industry whose purpose can only have been the production of flakes. There is no reason why the used flakes could not have been both specially struck from cores and occasionally selected from the waste of hand ax manufacture, but my impression is that flake tool blanks were specially struck from "Clactonian" cores with a hard-hammer.

The results of the above cross-classifications of pieces from the Lower Industry can be summarized as follows:

Wood-Whittling Knives: these were made on bladelike (B/L mean .600), relatively thick (Th/B mode .326) flake blanks; no other morphological associations are apparent except the use of unretouched edges.

Wood Adze: with only a single specimen, it is impossible to make any generalizations.

Wood Scrapers: the flakes employed were always narrow, though their absolute length was variable; the edges were unretouched, straight, and of average angle.

Wood Wedges: other than the one large bifacial example (HXN 737), the wedges were made on flakes which were relatively broad (B/L > 1.0) and somewhat thick (Th/B > .251); the edges were slightly steeper than average, unretouched (except for the biface), and usually straight.

Hide Scrapers: these were made on flakes of moderate breadth and thickness but usually long (>60 mm); the edges were retouched, of various shapes and of average angle.

Meat, Skin, and Butchering Knives: the flakes employed were usually long, of variable breadth but with relative thickness (Th/B) values in the region of .251 to .325; the edges were unretouched, convex, and moderately sharp (10 of the 12 edges had edge angles of less than 50°); two typical hand axes were employed as meat knives.

Bone Choppers: both implements were chopper-cores and they had little in common except the convexity of their edges.

Plant Knives: the flakes employed were of varying size, but with B/L values in the .800 - .999 range, and two were relatively thin (Th/B < .25); the edges were unretouched, sharp (all <40°), and convex.

Borers: the flake blanks were relatively small (L < 49 mm, B < 39 mm); the edges were retouched.

## Comparisons with Clacton

### Percentage of Flakes Used

The percentage of used flakes at Hoxne were only slightly more than half that at Clacton. This may be simply explained by the fact that hand axes were being manufactured in the Lower Industry at Hoxne (the presence of finished hand axes and of numerous hand ax finishing flakes confirms this), while they were not being made in the Clacton industry.

The manufacture of a single hand ax can produce an astonishing number of flakes and chips (Newcomer 1971a), and the majority of these are too small for use. The flakes struck off in the secondary shaping and finishing stages of hand ax production, while often having a dimension greater than 20 mm (meaning they can be comfortably held), possess edges almost always too thin and too acutely angled to be suitable for use. One does not need much experience with the use of flint tools to learn that thin edges with edge angles less than 35° are often useless for working even the softest of materials, because these brittle and fragile edges quickly incur severe edge damage that dulls the edge and reduces the amount of work done for the amount of effort expended. The majority of soft-hammer finishing flakes from hand ax manufacture are, therefore, waste in every sense of the word. The initial hard-hammer struck flakes from the "rough-out" stage of hand ax manufacture may be suitable for use because they are usually large, thick, and have more steeply angled edges. But, in fact, not many of these are actually likely to be suitable for use simply because when the knapper removes them, he is intent on shaping and reducing the raw nodule, and is consequently paying scant attention to the edge morphology of the flakes he is removing. Thus, only a few of these flakes will by chance be suitable for use or further modification into a tool. In short, only a handful of the 100 or so flakes over 20 mm long produced in the manufacture of a hand ax from a nodule or cobble will be potentially useful, and in an Acheulean industry, the percentage of utilized flakes among all flakes present will always be low, if the site is one where hand ax manufacture took place.

Where the lithic technology does not involve the production of specialized core tools, as seems to have been the case at Clacton, then the proportion of utilized to waste flakes is likely to be higher. This is because flakes can be struck off with their potential use or uses in mind. With the simple flaking technology of the Clactonian (hard-hammer, and limited knowledge of core preparation), a few flakes might have to be struck off before one suitable for use or further modification was produced. Given that the knapper is reasonably skillful, the number of these flakes should seldom exceed six. The presence of "Clactonian" flake cores at Hoxne, indistinguishable from those found at Clacton (and Swanscombe), indicates that the "Acheuleans" preferred to rely on the "less sophisticated" (that is, more direct) techniques for production of usable flakes rather than to hope to recover suitable ones from the waste of biface manufacture. For these reasons, we should not be very surprised to find that the ratio of utilized to waste flakes is 1:9 at Hoxne and 1:4 at Clacton.

## Activities Represented

In table 34, the frequency of different uses at Clacton and Hoxne (Lower Industry) are compared. One cannot, of course, take these figures at their face value, any more than one would a pollen diagram. Just as in a pollen diagram, the relative frequency of any particular pollen type does not necessarily reflect the relative frequency of the parent plant species in the plant community; neither does the relative frequency of a particular microwear pattern represent exactly the frequency of its associated activity. Some plants, like pine, produce more pollen, which scatters more widely than other plants; in the same way, some activities might produce more used tools than others, for example, wood wedging. Certainly, given the small number of used pieces in each case, one can make no specific generalizations about the frequency of particular uses at Clacton as opposed to Hoxne. It is nevertheless worth noting that, within the respective excavation areas, woodworking was more common at Clacton, and butchery and hide processing more common at Hoxne. Also, the most common method of working wood represented at Clacton was whittling, while wedging was

*Table 34*

*Frequency of Various Uses at Clacton and Hoxne Lower Industry (counting edges)*

| Use | Clacton | | Hoxne | |
|-----|-----|-----|-----|-----|
| | No. | % | No. | % |
| Wood whittling/planing | 10 | 20.0 | 2 | 5.9 |
| Wood chopping/adzing | 4 | 8.0 | 1 | 2.9 |
| Wood sawing | 2 | 4.0 | 0 | |
| Wood scraping | 5 | 10.0 | 2 | 5.9 |
| Wood wedging | 1(?) | 2.0 | 5 | 14.7 |
| Hide scraping | 3 | 6.0 | 5 | 14.7 |
| Hide cutting | 1 | 2.0 | 2 | 5.9 |
| Meat cutting/butchery | 10 | 20.0 | 10 | 29.4 |
| Boring, wood and bone | 4 | 8.0 | 2 | 5.9 |
| Plant cutting | 0 | | 3 | 8.8 |
| Other | 10 | 20.0 | 2 | 5.9 |
| Totals | 50 | 100.0 | 34 | 100.0 |
| Percentage wood working | 50.0 | | 32.3 | |
| Percentage use on meat and hide | 28.0 | | 50.0 | |

the most common method apparent at Hoxne. However, all the differences in the frequencies of various uses between Clacton and Hoxne may simply be the result of "sampling error."

## Associations between Tool Morphology and Function

At Hoxne, unlike Clacton, it seems that the ancient inhabitants did not primarily select flakes for use on the basis of their edge shapes and angles but paid more attention to their size. Nevertheless, there are certain similarities between the two industries: most tasks were accomplished using unretouched edges, and there was little morphological formalization of functional types. Certainly the used flakes from Hoxne are, on the whole, larger and longer than those from Clacton. This is probably the result of differences in the forms of flint available for knapping at both sites. In general, the flint available for flaking at Clacton was in the form of river cobbles, sometimes with frost cracks in them, while the flint used at Hoxne seems to have consisted of fresh nodules from the chalk, with frost-cracking rare. It is likely that had good chalk-flint nodules been available at Clacton, the used flakes would have been accordingly larger and longer.

## Conclusions

The differences between the Hoxne and Clacton tool-kits that were brought into focus by the results of their microwear analysis seem more often differences of degree than of kind. Certainly, the overlapping ranges of activities demonstrable at the two sites lends little support to the idea that the Clactonian and Acheulean are simply functional variants of a single "culture," an hypothesis that suffers also from their chronological and technological differences. The Clactonian, for example, has a notable lack of the soft-hammer technique and an absolute lack of hand axes (see Ohel 1977 for similar conclusions). The results of the microwear analyses lends support to the idea that, while these Clactonian "characteristics" are negative, they are nonetheless probably "cultural," rather than simply the result of the underrepresentation of some function or activity at known Clactonian sites. There remains the possibility that Clactonian sites are functional variants of the Early Acheulean, which may be represented in Britain prior to the Hoxnian (Roe 1975).

## The Uses of Handaxes

The discovery of meat-cutting traces on two of the hand axes from the Hoxne Lower Industry allows, one might almost say requires, us to discuss the possible functions of hand axes in the British Middle Acheulean. Are we to conclude, from the Hoxne evidence, that all hand axes were used as meat knives, or should we mistrust the evidence of these implements as likely to be the result of sampling error? Given that the microwear traces on the Hoxne hand axes provide the first real glimpse, albeit a very brief one, of the true purpose of hand axes, I feel bound to speculate on this subject. Unfortunately, further direct evidence, based on microwear analysis, from hand axes at other British sites was not obtainable because of a technical limitation: most hand axes simply would not fit between the objective and the stage of the M20 microscope; luckily, the two fresh hand axes from Hoxne fit, just barely. Nevertheless, the one significant fact that does emerge from the Hoxne study is that there is an overlap in function between hand axes and flake tools. The two hand axes from the Lower Industry were both used for cutting meat or butchery, but there was also a large number of flakes, from the same industry, that were used for exactly the same purpose. Since meat polish (and bone polish, for that matter) is a slow-forming polish which causes relatively mild alterations to the flint microtopography, it is improbable that these hand axes were previously used for some other purpose, the wear traces of which have been removed by the meat polish. The question is then an old one--why make hand axes if flakes will do the same jobs just as well? The answer may be that hand axes as a class (excluding specialized types like the ficron, the cleaver, and perhaps small twisted ovates) were *not* made for any particular or exclusive function (that is, to accomplish some task that their creators could not or would not undertake using flake tools) but nevertheless were made to fulfill some important but more general purpose.

We may discover some clues to this purpose by examining the nature and context of hand ax finds in Britain. The vast majority of British hand axes have been recovered from secondary or "geological" contexts, usually river gravels. At some of these secondary context sites, like Warren Hill, Furze Platt, and Knowle Farm, hand axes have accumulated in huge numbers (Roe 1968). There are, of course, thousands of finds of one or two isolated hand axes. Roe (1968) was only able to isolate five sites that were likely to be primary context floors: Caddington, Bowman's Lodge, Gaddesden Row, Round Green, and Stoke Newington. (A few more names could perhaps now be added to this list, including Hoxne.) The number of hand axes found on these floors was relatively small: Caddington (from several floors) 35, Bowman's Lodge (from a single floor) 30, Gaddesden Row (from a single floor and scattered finds) 45, Round Green (from a single floor) 14, Stoke Newington (from one or possibly more floors over a large area) 63. While it is clear that the overwhelming majority of hand axes have been found away from living floors (not all the primary context occurrences mentioned above are necessarily "living" floors; Caddington, for example, may be a manufacturing site), we know that hand axes *were* manufactured at the living sites, from the presence of numerous hand ax trimmers among the flakes (see Roe 1968: 9-10). Indeed, Worthington Smith (1894: 151) found flakes at Caddington which, when conjoined, formed a partial "mold" of a hand ax, which was not itself present at the site. In summary then, when we find primary context sites in Britain, we find very few hand axes, and hand axes are most commonly recovered accumulated in alluvial deposits and as stray finds.

A similar finds distribution, this time involving projectile points, occurs in the later prehistory of the American West. Relatively few projectile points are found on actual camp or village sites, although it is clear they were manufactured on such sites; however, they occur in great numbers as isolated finds, at kill sites and in special localities (for example, hundreds of 'bird-points' on the edges of and in marshes). We cannot take this analogy too far, since it is extremely unlikely that hand axes were projectiles of any kind, but it gives us an idea of the kind of finds distribution likely to be obtained when the purpose of an expendable tool is associated with the acquisition of food or essential materials, away from the "home base," rather than with their processing and consumption once they have been brought back to camp.

Considering the facts mentioned above, it seems reasonable to propose as a hypothesis that hand axes, at least in the British Middle Acheulean, were implements made to be taken on hunting and gathering expeditions away from the home base, while in the main, flake tools provided the cutting edges "at home." Why not take, on such expeditions, a collection of flakes, which have sharper cutting edges? The answer may be that the advantage of the hand ax lies not in its suitability for any one particular task, but in its usefulness for any number of tasks. The retouched edge of a hand ax may provide a sturdy, resharpenable cutting edge with a variety of edge angles; its weight and compact form make it usable as a chopper and hammer (signs of heavy battering on one side of the heavy butt is not an uncommon feature of larger hand axes); the point on some types of hand axes renders them useful both for stabbing and for more delicate tasks like boring or prying; while, if the implement is large enough, the hand ax can even serve as a core from which flakes providing additional cutting edges can be struck. To provide for all these tasks with flakes, one would need to carry an inconvenient number of them of various sizes, shapes, and edge angles, plus, perhaps, a core and hammerstone--not a very handy assortment to carry on the chase. And when the hunters (or gatherers) were ready to return home, laden with meat (or other material), the hand axes could be abandoned if necessary, since others could easily be manufactured at the home base. Of course, some hand axes would be used and abandoned before they left the camp, or else brought home from an expedition, as the Hoxne examples may have been.

Given the wide variation in hand ax shapes, it would be silly to suppose that all hand axes were made to serve as Lower Paleolithic "Swiss-army knives." It seems likely that such specialized types as the ficron, the classic twisted ovate, and the cleaver had a narrower range of functions than the more generalized pointed, knife-edged hand axes that epitomize the Middle Acheulean. But until examples of these special types are found in suitable condition and subjected to microwear analysis, their exact place in Lower Paleolithic life will remain a mystery. I would also like to stress that this hypothesis is only meant to apply to Britain and certainly not to all hand axes everywhere.

Through the kindness of the excavator, Mr. T. A. Betts, I was given the opportunity to examine some hand axes from a recent, isolated, probably primary context, find of four hand axes, with a few flakes (which seem to be resharpening flakes), discovered recently in South Woodford in north-east London (Essex). The implements were found at the interface between a silty gravel layer and a silt layer. Four of the hand axes were either very slightly abraded or else too heavily weathered to be useful for microwear analysis. But one small ovate hand ax (fig. 94) was in completely fresh condition and showed microwear traces on both aspects of its right lateral edge (viewed from Aspect 1). This microwear consisted of a meat polish and a single striation indicating movement during use

Figure 94.   South Woodford hand ax, SR2.

roughly parallel with the working edge.  This hand ax, like those from Hoxne, was a butchering knife.  One of the other hand axes had signs of battering on its butt and a broken tip.
One of the flakes found with these hand axes seems to be the tip of a hand ax that had been
removed by a resharpening tranchet blow.  None of these flakes, however, clearly represented
original manufacturing debris.  These artifacts may be all that remains of an Acheulean
butchering site.  The remains of one unidentifiable long bone survived, but, in fact, conditions at the site were highly unfavorable (pH5) for the preservation of bone.

Returning to Hoxne, there is the question of the 111 hand axes (Roe 1968) found there
before the University of Chicago excavations began.  In putting together the data for his
metric study of hand axes from Hoxne, Roe (1968: 16) lumped together all the measurable
hand axes from the site, following the then-current interpretations of its archeology (West
and McBurney 1954), in which the Lower and Upper Industries were not distinguished.  Thus,
it seems quite likely that many of the extant Hoxne hand axes are from strata younger than
those containing the Lower Industry.  Many of these hand axes were collected from the com-
mercial brick-earth excavations, so their stratigraphic and horizontal relationship with
the Lower Industry are very unclear.  Were we able to weed out hand axes that were not related to the Lower Industry, it is likely the number of hand axes remaining would be similar to the numbers found at the other primary context sites (see above).

## Horizontal Distribution

Figure 95 shows the horizontal distribution of the fresh implements in A.L.3 West.
The scatter takes the form of a broad band 5 to 8 m wide and about 18 m long.  There are
no definite signs of "activity areas," but it is notable that in the central area of the
spread (in a circle with a radius of 3 m drawn around point 310-170) the used implements
are *only* meat and butchering knives or hide scrapers.  The two plant knives were found
just 1.7 m apart up (for location, see the upper right corner of fig. 95).

The number of implements from the other archeological layers were too small to make
the drawing of horizontal scatter diagrams worthwhile.

## General Conclusions and Discussion

The study of microwear on implements from the Lower Industry at Hoxne has revealed
that a number of activities took place within or nearby the excavated areas--the butchery

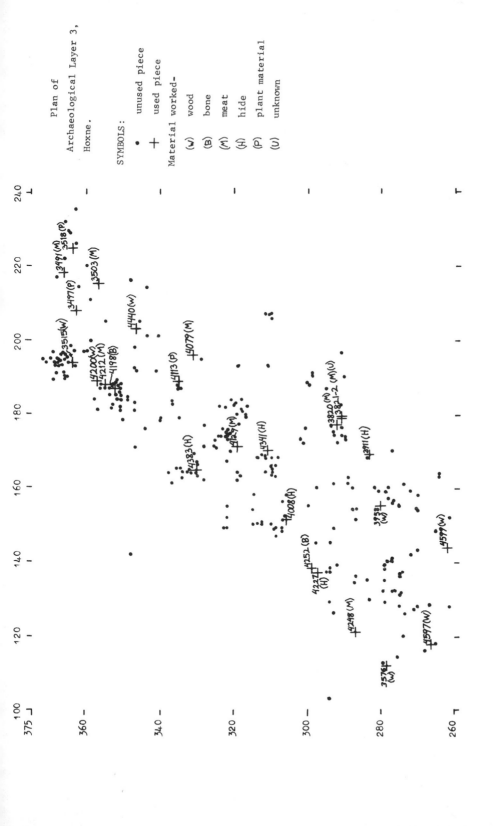

Figure 95.  Plan of Archeological Layer 3, Hoxne.

of animals, hide preparation, woodworking, the boring of bone, and the cutting of plant material. The large numbers of hand ax trimming flakes found indicates that the production of bifaces also occurred in the Lower Industry levels. This wide range of activities makes it quite clear that A.L.s 1 Main, 2 Main, and 3 West are either occupation floors or were quite close to such.

Two of the activities represented in the microwear on the Lower Industry specimens require some further discussion: bone boring and plant cutting. Other than the crude chopping, splitting, and flaking of bone, no traces of fine bone work (comparable to the bored and graved bone objects so common in the Upper Paleolithic) have been found in European Lower Paleolithic. The one exception is an engraved ox rib from Layer 8 at Pech de l'Azé II, but from the Mousterian levels. If the inhabitants of Hoxne were boring bone, it is perhaps hard to see why they were doing it. It could have been part of some rather delicate method of extracting bone marrow, but there is no direct evidence to support this idea. The possibility that it was to make holes for the suspension of pendants or beads is perhaps not as farfetched as it sounds. W. G. Smith (1894: 272-76) found 200 examples of the fossil *Coscinopora globularis* at Bedford which showed "an artificial enlargement of the natural orifice, which seemed to indicate that the fossils had been used for personal ornaments as beads" (W. G. Smith 1894: 272). These were found "with unabraded implements and flakes and carbonized vegetable remains" (W. G. Smith 1894: 273). Some of these "beads" had a black substance in their hole which was found to be "nitrogenous organic matters, of which animal tissues are composed" (W. G. Smith 1894: 273). I have examined a number of such "beads" in the possession of the Pitt-Rivers Museum (Oxford) from this same site (whether they are actually the ones that Smith found cannot be determined), and there is no doubt that some of these fossils show artificial enlargement of their natural orifices. If the people of the Lower Paleolithic were capable of constructing beads out of fossils, it is very likely they were capable of constructing pendants or beads out of bone, which is a softer material. With so few primary context sites for this period, it is perhaps not surprising that such delicate items as bone beads have not been recovered, if they were, in fact, made by "Acheuleans."

Again we turn to Worthington Smith for information pertinent to the use of nonwoody plants in the Lower Paleolithic. At Stoke Newington, he found masses of the compacted fronds of *Osmunda regalis* which he believed may have been "beds," on the Paleolithic floor (W. G. Smith 1894: 292). In one mass of ferns he found "a keen-edged Palaeolithic implement and a leg-bone of a horse." He also found, at Bedford, an implement (from his description probably a ficron or a large lanceolate) "which had the butt-end when first found wrapped round with herbaceous stems, probably rushes, as if for a protection for the hand" (W. G. Smith 1894: 222). In South Africa, at a late Acheulean site, Montagu Cave, Keller (1970: 190) found dark bands rich in plant opal and beetle remains that he believed were the traces of bundles of grass carried into the cave to serve as bedding. There is no way of telling from the microwear polish on the two plant knives from Hoxne exactly what vegetable material was being cut. But my guess, based on the resemblance of the wear to sickle gloss and the likely swampy environment of Hoxne at the time, is that rushes are the most likely possibility.

It seems clear that the sidescrapers of both the Lower and the Upper Industries were hide-working tools. How far one can generalize from this fact to the scrapers from other sites of a similar age is hard to say. But, judging from my brief examination of a few sidescrapers from High Lodge, Suffolk, and the French Mousterian, it would not be very surprising if the great majority of convex sidescrapers of the Lower and Middle Paleolithic were found to have been used for scraping hide.

Finally, some mention should be made of a prior unpublished study of the functions of implements from the Lower Industry at Hoxne. In a study using low-magnification techniques and concentrating on edge damage, Mr. Glenn Cooper found that about 95% (of flakes) were utilized, including small ones less than 2 cm long (Singer and Wymer 1976: 19). This figure differs by a factor of ten from those obtained in my study of the same collection. Until the details of Mr. Cooper's study are published, it is impossible to be sure what accounts for his much higher estimate of used pieces. However, since I examined some, at least, of the same material studied by Cooper, my guess is that he interpreted edge damage that had in fact been caused by soil movements, spontaneous retouch or perhaps trampling as being the result of use. It is worth emphasizing again that almost every Lower Paleolithic artifact is likely to have a few edge-damage scars, particularly on its sharpest edges, as a result of being buried for a couple of hundred thousand years under a considerable weight of overlying deposits. The Hoxne implements are no exception and almost all of them show a few such damage scars, the occurrence of which are completely independent of other evidence of utilization. These breakages create no problem in high-magnification studies of microwear, since edge damage is never used solely as the criterion of use, this role being given instead to the microwear polishes whose appearance and placement cannot, as we have seen, be imitated by natural forms of wear. While use of this latter method is likely to result in a slight underestimate of the percentage of used pieces, the error will be confined to uses like meat cutting and fresh hide scraping, where the microwear polish forms slowly. My experimental study indicates that this error is unlikely to be more than 10-20%, even if implements are used only very briefly. This would imply that the real percentage of used pieces in A.L. 3 West is unlikely to be more than 12% (the actual figure obtained by the writer was 9%). This means, *pace* Cooper, that the majority of the flakes from the Lower Industry can go back to being just what they appear to be--the debitage of hand ax manufacture.

## 8.  AREAS FOR FUTURE RESEARCH AND SOME SPECULATIONS

This chapter is devoted to a discussion of some potentially productive areas for future research and to some speculations (which also have implications for future research) about some aspects of tool use and life in the Paleolithic.

In the course of any research project, a number of intriguing but essentially tangential lines of research are revealed to the researcher, which he must reluctantly put aside if he is to achieve his original research goals. The most common of such "tangents" are those questions or puzzles which, although interesting, do not offer any serious obstacles to the continued progress of the main research program, that is to say, there is no obligation to solve them before proceeding. Because attempting to solve these puzzles may mean a substantial loss of time and momentum with regard to the main research program and because the attempt may require the acquisition of specialized technical expertise, the researcher leaves them aside, perhaps after a brief sortie, in the hope that some future investigator, or perhaps himself, will eventually take them up. For example, in this present research, the precise causes of the microwear polishes are a puzzle of just this type.

There are also questions which create something of an obstacle to progress, but which must be, for various reasons, circumvented rather than directly attacked. Few such problems, fortunately, were encountered in the course of this research, but the necessity of investigating soil movement effects by nonexperimental methods because it proved impossible to replicate natural soil movements experimentally could be considered in this category. Until the appropriate methods and equipment are created which would allow direct investigation, problems of this sort are likely to remain intractable.

Often, the chance discovery of one or two facts during a study can set off a train of thought which can be strengthened into an interesting argument. However, such arguments often involve making an unwieldy number of assumptions and usually rest upon a small empirical base. However, these arguments deserve mention, since they point to new areas for future research.

### Microwear Polishes

Although the present research has demonstrated that use of stone implements on a variety of materials causes microscopically visible polishes to form on the tool's working edge, and that the characteristics of these polishes are directly related to the materials worked, it is still not clear exactly why or how these polishes form, or what causes them

to be distinctive.  Some possible explanations were put forward in the sections of chapter
3, where the individual polishes were described, but these were all hypotheses suggested by
evidence that was gathered without the specific problem of causes in mind.  The fact that
friction plays such an important part in the formation of these polishes leads to the idea
that frictional heat plays a role as well.  To test this hypothesis requires a certain
amount of specialized technical knowledge and perhaps special (and expensive) equipment.
Bearing in mind that, while the phenomenon of friction is (empirically) well understood
and described in the field of industrial wear and engineering, a theoretical understanding
of the cause (or causes) of friction itself is still undeveloped (see Bickerman 1976), one
may wonder whether a real understanding of the cause (or causes) of microwear polish is
attainable.

     Another area for future investigation is the cause of the distinctiveness of the vari-
ous microwear polishes (that is, wood polish, meat polish, and so on).  The possibility
that certain polishes like wood polish, corn gloss, and bone polish owe some of their distinctiveness to an actual incorporation of certain substances from the worked material has
been discussed in chapter 3.  The testing of these hypotheses requires the application of
sophisticated methods of chemical analysis and elaborate equipment which were beyond the
scope and means of the present study.  Recently, for example, Patricia Anderson of the
University of Bordeaux (pers. comm.) has observed, at magnifications in excess of 1000X
with an SEM, small rods of material being "melted" onto the surface of flint edges used to
scrape wood.  This material survives HCl and NaOH, and the strong presumption is that it
is plant opal and is the source of the wood polish, as suggested in chapter 3.  These "melting" rods are not found associated with polishes forming on bone- or hide-working edges.
This splendid work, soon to be published, strongly supports the contention that not only do
the various microwear polishes appear different and show measurable differences but that
they also have different origins (that is, "melting rods" with wood polish--none with bone
or hide polish).

     Since antler working appears to be comparatively rare in the Lower Paleolithic, the
wear traces to which it gives rise were not intensively studied in the present project.
But the experiments that were completed with this material indicated that the character of
the microwear polishes produced by antler working varied according to the method of use--
sawing producing a rough polish, and the other methods of use producing a smoothly pockmarked polish.  For those interested in applying microwear analysis to Upper Paleolithic
materials, more antler-working experiments are obviously in order.  A series of well-
controlled antler-working experiments might also provide a clearer picture of the conditions, and therefore the possible causes, of the two different antler polishes.

     Also, this study will be seen to be weak in knowledge of the wear traces left by the
cutting of plant materials other than wood.  The problem was to decide which experiments
to conduct and which would be most relevant, given that time and funds were strictly
limited.  Our knowledge of the human use of plant resources prior to the introduction of
agriculture is still abysmally poor.  Regarding the Lower Paleolithic in Britain, a major
investigation, involving consultation with paleobotanists, would be necessary even to determine satisfactorily which plant resources might have been available to British inhabitants during the late Middle Pleistocene.  The more vexing question is In what ways would
stone implements have been employed in the acquisition and processing of the available
usable plant materials?  Common sense and a few excursions into the ethnographic literature
certainly indicate that the gathering and preparation of most plant foods--like berries,

nuts, greens, and roots--very rarely require the use of cutting or scraping implements. A pounder, a stick, and the unaided hand are usually the only "implements" needed to acquire and prepare vegetable foods, fibers, or other useful soft plant materials. There is, obviously, room for further inquiries along the paleobotanical and ethnographic lines regarding plant utilization in the Paleolithic.

## Microwear Traces on Rocks Other Than Flint

The experiments done as part of this study were made primarily with tools of chalk flint, but there is now some evidence that the results of these experiments are applicable to similar rock types from around the world. Recently Patricia Anderson in Bordeaux has established that the limestone cherts of southwestern France produce microwear polishes directly comparable with those observed in this study when used on the same worked materials (pers. comm.). I have also observed this to be true of fine-grained cherts from South Africa and Washington State (USA). It therefore seems likely that the microwear traces produced by the same uses on fine-grained cryto-crystalline silicas (chert, flint, jasper, chalcedony, and so on) will be roughly similar. But this similarity should be treated as an open question for the moment, and no one should apply the experimental results reported here to archeological specimens made of, let us say, Texas chert.

The kind of wear traces produced on more disparate rock types--like obsidians, quartzites, lydianites, and fine-grained basalts--is, of course, a wide open question. Obsidian, which is a softer material than flint (by about 1 unit on the Mohs scale), is much more susceptible to scratching than flint. The few archeological obsidian implements I have examined are usually completely covered with randomly oriented microscopic scratches, and the presumed microwear traces consist of abrasion rather than polish. Only a series of experiments designed to investigate the traces observable on these materials will provide the answers.

## Technological Effects

Because pressure flaking, except for pressure against a hammerstone, is not known to have been practiced in the Middle Pleistocene, no experiments were conducted to investigate the microscopic traces left by such technology. Anyone wishing to apply microwear analysis to pressure-flaked implements must obviously make a careful study of the technological effects left by the various pressure-flaking techniques (see Keeley 1974a). There is also room for a study of microwear traces on implements which had been heat-treated prior to their being finished, as such treatment might affect the receptivity of the flint to microwear traces.

## Hand Axes

In chapter 7, a possible function was proposed for lanceolatelike hand axes. The testing of this hypothesis is a research project in itself. As far as Britain is concerned, such a project might involve the microwear analysis of suitable fresh hand axes from existing collections. Such hand axes are likely to be found in the old collections from Hoxne, Caddington, Round Green, Stoke Newington, Bowman's Lodge, and Gaddesden Row (cf. Roe 1968), which are scattered in various museums around England. Greater attention should be paid to the context and associations of isolated finds of fresh hand axes or of the small numbers of completely unworn implements which sometimes occur in secondary contexts. The ideal solution, however, would be the discovery and excavation of more primary context occupation floors.

Some significant information may arise from a classificatory or typological study of British Middle Acheulean hand axes with special attention paid to those morphological characteristics likely to be of functional significance--like edge angles, the outline shape of the tip, the "heaviness" of the butt, the situation of flunting or retained cortex, and so on. Of course, any such study would have to make its comparisons or generalizations based on data recorded only from "finished" hand axes, not "rough-outs" or "failed" implements; such a distinction may not be always easy to make, and where the number of hand axes is small, this might lead to serious problems with the reliability of any statistical generalizations made from such data.

Moving from the realm of the British Lower Paleolithic to the wider world of the Acheulean in general, we might consider the implications of hand axes as multipurpose gathering tools for some of the debates which have occupied Lower Paleolithic archeologists in recent years. While most prehistorians interested in the Acheulean would now accept that many of the differences between assemblages are likely to be functional, that is, that the differences are due to different suites of activities having been conducted at the respective archeological occurrences, the question of precisely what "functions" are involved is still a vexed one (Isaac 1975). These arguments about functional variability have centered around the purpose of the hand ax. Clark and Haynes (1970) have made the suggestion, based upon the flake implements found associated with an elephant kill and butchery site in Malawi, that large bifaces like hand axes and cleavers had functions unrelated to hunting or the initial butchery of large animals. Unfortunately, the site upon which they based their hypothesis is of Middle Stone Age date, not Acheulean. If one wishes to make a case either for or against the use of bifaces as primary butchering tools based on the associations of such tools on Acheulean primary context sites, then there is always a large body of evidence that must be ignored or explained away. Against Clark's and Haynes's case, which Binford (1972) has taken up as well, one must set the butchery sites where the number (not necessarily the proportion) of bifaces is high (see Isaac 1975: table 4). Clark and Haynes use Torralba-Ambrona as a site supporting their case because bifaces are a relatively small proportion of the finished tool classes of the assemblages there, but Freeman (1975) reports that large bifaces at that site show an association, determined by factor analysis, with certain types of bone remains that strongly suggests they were tools used for certain heavy butchering operations. Also Klein (1978) has convincingly argued that one of the bone accumulations at Elandsfontein is a "butchering site" at which bifaces are a very common, in fact, almost the only, tool type recovered.

If one were to maintain the opposite--that bifaces *are* primarily butchering or flensing tools--then one must explain the sites where bifaces are common but bone remains are nonexistent or dispersed and uncommon. There is nevertheless a good, though not totally convincing, case to be made for this latter argument. Stone implements are many times more likely to survive from the Middle Pleistocene than bone. If there are many scavengers about, most of the bone may never get a chance to become incorporated into an archeological deposit (Isaac 1968: 258). Indeed, well-preserved bone is still the exception in archeological deposits rather than the rule. Thus, any comparisons between the number of bifaces and the density or condition of bone remains on a site must be treated with a certain amount of suspicion, since these two materials show such differential rates of preservation. If the hypothesis presented in chapter 7 is correct, then the archeological associations of hand axes are likely to be varied and complex; there can be no simple division of contexts along the lines suggested by Clark and Haynes or by Binford into "bifaces rare = butchery" and "bifaces common = plant gathering."

There is now little doubt that the main axis of variation, with regard to finished tools, in Later Acheulean assemblages in Africa is an inverse correlation between large bifaces (hand axes and cleavers) and small tools, especially scrapers (see Binford 1972; Isaac 1977). Binford (1972) and Clark (1975) regard this negative covariation, as we noted above, as indicating the functional distinctiveness of bifaces and small tools. However, there are some interesting aspects of covariation in Acheulean assemblages that have been overlooked so far. The correlations upon which Binford's factor analysis was based, as well as Isaac and Corrucini's principal components analysis of the same data (Isaac 1977), have only been calculated between the finished tool classes, leaving aside waste and "utilized" material.

But if we work out the correlations between the percentages of hand axes, the percentages of small scrapers, and the percentages of waste on the same data used by Binford and Isaac, we find some very interesting patterns. As expected there is significant negative correlation between %HA and %SScr ($r = -.65$) (Isaac 1977), but there is also a significant negative correlation between % Waste and %HA ($r = .502$). Waste and small scrapers are positively correlated ($r = .469$). The negative correlation between bifaces and waste is quite unexpected, as the production of hand axes creates a large amount of waste.

Our conclusions from these findings are that bifaces tend not to accumulate at sites where tools are manufactured, nor at sites where small tools are abandoned (and presumably used)--but that where there is good evidence of tool manufacture (that is, a high percentage of waste), larger numbers of small tools are abandoned. This evidence conforms very well to the expectations generated by the hypotheses presented in chapter 7, since we would expect that at "home bases" or relatively long-term occupation sites, the remains would reflect tool manufacture, resharpening, and the use of "tools to make tools"--like scrapers (for working wood and hides), borers, and so on. The relative rarity of hand axes on such sites must indicate that they were used and abandoned elsewhere.

In conclusion, it is clear that "the trouble with hand axes" (see Roe 1976) will continue to plague Lower Paleolithic studies until a comprehensive series of research projects is initiated to investigate their function and associations by means of microwear analysis and the critical comparison of carefully selected assemblages.

## Red Ocher, Hides, Endscrapers, and Houses in the Magdalenian

Leaving the realm of the Lower Paleolithic altogether, it is perhaps appropriate that this section should end with a speculative attempt to tie together several strands of archeological evidence from the Magdalenian in a systematic fashion. The evidence is derived from the results of microwear analysis, some recent excavations at Pincevent and Gönnersdorf, and ethnographic analogy. While not strictly relevant under the title of this thesis, it arises entirely out of the work done, as a set of connected ideas, and will serve to bear out some of the points made in the section on methods and techniques.

There have been many investigations of wear traces on Magdalenian endscrapers (Bosinski and Hahn 1973; Leroi-Gourhan and Brezillon 1972; Rosenfeld 1971), none of which came to any firm conclusions about the uses of these implements. These studies all used relatively low magnifications (generally less than 60X); nevertheless, they all distinguished "abrasion" or edge rounding on the scraper edges of this class of tool. Andrée Rosenfeld (1971) found, as well as wear traces, clear traces of red ocher associated with the worn parts of the tool: "On one strongly abraded scraper . . . the flint surface was markedly impregnated with ochre on either side of the abrasion band, clearly indicating its use on an ochreous surface" (p. 182). The scrapers Rosenfeld examined were thirty-four examples from La Madeleine, held in the British Museum's collections.

The author has examined 10 Magdalenian endscrapers, in the Pitt-Rivers Museum collections, from La Madeleine, Abzac and Laugerie-Basse, using high-magnification techniques. All of these implements showed some microwear polish on their scraper edges. In all cases, the polish was clearly a hide polish. The hides worked by these 10 scrapers were not fresh hides but had been dried to some extent. Traces of red coloring matter were found in pits and cracks on the working edges of most (8) of these pieces. However, a couple of these pieces had fragments of breccia still adhering to them which were dark red and could in these two cases have been the source of the coloring matter on the working edges as well. But a conclusion one might reasonably draw from the author's microwear analysis, coupled with the observations of Rosenfeld, is that the Magdalenians were rubbing ocher (probably mixed with fat or grease) into their prepared hides.

The thin patches of red ocher sometimes found associated with the floors of Magdalenian "houses," for example, at Pincevent (Leroi-Gourhan and Brézillon 1972: 89-93) and Gonnersdorf (Bosinski 1975: 261), may be the traces left by the decay of ocher-treated hides which were used as floor coverings and/or to cover the roof and walls. When the inhabitants moved from these sites, some of the hides used on these houses would have suffered enough damage and decay to be left behind to rot away, or the occupants might have left all the coverings on the huts, intending to return after a short absence, but were unable to do so before the hides rotted away. If the house or hut site was reoccupied on successive occasions, perhaps as a station in a "seasonal round," then a layer of ocher-stained earth would gradually build up on its floor. Indeed, Leroi-Gourhan and Brézillon (1972: 89) believe there is a relationship between the intensity (or duration) of the occupation of a particular "habitation" and the intensity of its red ocher staining. They also discount the possibility that the red ocher was spread onto the floor all at once on a single occasion, as one might expect if it was part of some house inauguration rite or custom, and conclude that the impregnation of the soil with ocher took place "progressivement" (Leroi-Gourhan and Brézillon 1972: 92). The association of red ocher patches with house floors, and some of the evidence produced at Pincevent, is compatible with the hypothesis that these patches are caused by the decay of ocher-impregnated hides.

There is an alternative hypothesis which is also compatible with the preceding facts-- that is, that the red ocher patches are the areas where hide preparation, especially the rubbing of ocher and fat into the hides, took place. The wastes from this process would tend to accumulate on the ground surface, forming patches of the sort found at Pincevent. However, at Gönnersdorf, the red ocher color covers the whole floor area of the hut. It is hard to envisage the whole interior of a hut given over to hide preparation; surely, this is an activity that is better conducted outdoors. The smaller isolated patches of red ocher often found on such open-air sites, unassociated with any hut remains, seem more likely to be traces of the original preparation of the hides than do the more extensive patches associated with the hut floors.

If these house-floor patches of red ocher are the remains of rotted, red ocher-impregnated hides, then there is the possibility that the red ocher associated with certain Magdalenian burials like those from Chancelade, Les Hoteaux, and Saint-Andre-de-Cubyoc (Coles and Higgs 1969: 252), are in some cases the traces of ocherous hide clothing or burial wrappings, though the large quantities of ocher present on some occasions might be difficult to account for solely as the remains from ocherous leather clothing or "shrouds."

Finally, we might consider some of the reasons why the Magdalenians rubbed red ocher into hides. The most obvious reason that springs to mind is aesthetic--they simply preferred colored hides. Untanned hide is usually very light in color, so that the brick red or red brown shades created by the application of ocher might have been regarded by the Magdalenians as a distinct improvement over the duller, more monotonous shades of untreated hides. There could, however, be some more practical advantage in impregnating hides with ocher.

Rosenfeld (1971: 182) claims that iron oxide has no known preservative action on hide, but this may not be true. Hide is composed primarily of collagen and decays when attacked by bacteria producing collagenase, an enzyme which destroys collagen. There is good evidence that metal ions, including those of iron, inhibit the action of collagenase (Mandl 1961). This means that the application of iron oxide in the form of ocher to hides may inhibit, or at least slow, the decay of hides.

Many primitive peoples, for example, the Australian and Tasmanian aborigines, or the Maasai, rub mixtures containing iron oxide and grease on their bodies and into their hair. Bonwick (1898: 24) claims that greasing with red ocher by the Tasmanians "was useful as a defence for the naked skin against insects and changes of weather; it certainly was a check to life in the hair." Ling Roth (1890: 137) also mentions ocher and grease as a preventative of vermin, but claims there is no proof that it was used by the Tasmanians for that reason. Sollas (1924: 277), speaking of the use of red ocher by the Australian aborigines, claims that "This served as a protection against vermin and was evidently very efficacious." It may be that the Magdalenians rubbed grease and ocher onto the skin-side of their clothing, sleeping rugs, and house coverings with the purpose of keeping down vermin.

To verify these hypotheses about the use of scrapers, red ocher, and hides, a considerable amount of work would need to be done. One obvious piece of work that might provide crucial information would be the proper microwear analysis of the endscrapers from Pincevent and Gönnersdorf to establish that they were used to rub hides and to see whether there are any traces of red ocher on their working edges. A careful restudy of Magdalenian burials might be useful, though it seems likely that the crucial information about the ocher distribution around the bones of these burials was not usually recorded in sufficient detail. Of course, any future finds of Magdalenian burials must be very carefully excavated and scrutinized for traces of ocher. Unfortunately, it is difficult to envisage any chemical method that would be capable of detecting whether the ocher found on the hut floors had simply been sprinkled onto the ground or had been left by the rotting of an ocherous hide. If research is undertaken into this problem in the future, then, at the very least, we will obtain a clearer idea of the place ocher occupied in Magdalenian life. And it is worth recalling that red ocher was also used by many other Paleolithic peoples and others in the later prehistoric periods. So far as the Paleolithic is concerned, however, the Magdalenian will surely offer the best evidence bearing on all aspects of the problem.

## Conclusion

It is apparent that there is still a great deal of work to be done in the field of microwear analysis--some of it directed toward the improvement of the techniques and methods of microwear analysis in general, but some of it attempting to solve, via microwear analysis, a few of the crucial problems that have vexed prehistorians for over a century. There are, of course, many more topics ripe for future investigation than have been mentioned in this chapter--dozens of questions, both great and small, peculiar to the prehistory of areas and periods outside the purview of this thesis, for which microwear analysis might provide or help to provide the answers.

## 9. SUMMARY AND CONCLUSIONS

In chapter 1, a critical review of the current literature on microwear analysis revealed that most recent microwear studies have not been particularly successful in providing precise and reliable information on the functions of ancient stone implements. This lack of success was found to be the result of inadequate techniques and a lack of methodological rigor. Two fundamental approaches to microwear analysis were described, which were basically different in their technical and methodological strategies. One approach concentrated on the low-magnification study of edge damage, while the other employed a more catholic approach but nevertheless concentrated on the high-magnification study of microwear polishes and striations. The former approach was found unsatisfactory on several counts: (1) the use of low magnifications insures that certain aspects of the microwear pattern are likely to be overlooked because their most important features are beyond the resolution of the microscopes employed; (2) the use of edge damage as the sole criterion of use is likely to lead to the confusion of use traces with those resulting from certain subtle natural processes and technological methods; (3) the results obtained by this approach show a lack of precision in distinguishing between various uses. It was concluded that the best aid for the inference of the functions of ancient implements was an experimental framework specially constructed to provide information relevant to some particular archeological collection or collections.

In chapter 2, the actual techniques employed in the microwear analysis of the experimental and archeological implements were described. The cleaning techniques employed to insure that the traces observed are true alterations of the flint microsurface and not some extraneous deposit were discussed. The microscopes which were used in this study were described, accompanied by a discussion of their respective advantages and disadvantages. In most instances, a Wild M20 lab microscope with an incident-light attachment and a range of magnification from 24X to 400X was used as the principal instrument of investigation, with a wild M5 stereomicroscope employed occasionally to observe edge damage at magnifications ranging from 6X to 25X. All the photomicrographs were taken through these microscopes by means of a camera attachment. Most of these photomicrographs were taken on fine-grained 35 mm roll films (Kodak Panatomic-X; Ilford FP4). All of these techniques were designed to insure that all types of microwear traces could be clearly observed and adequately recorded.

The framework of experiments, which is central to the present research project, was described in chapter 3. The organizing principles, the materials and the methods employed were described and discussed.  The typology and technology of the experimental implements themselves, the materials worked, the activities engaged in, and the independent variables recorded were all designed or decided upon to insure that the results obtained would be as directly applicable as possible to the microwear study of implements from Clacton, Swanscombe, and Hoxne.  The most important result of these experiments was the discovery that the microwear polishes formed by various worked materials have distinctive appearances and are, indeed, distinguishable from one another.  Not only do these polishes appear different, but they are, in some cases, measurably different.  Utilization damage, on the other hand, was found to be of limited utility in distinguishing between different activities and worked materials.  It was also found that variations in the distribution of polish, striations, and utilization damage were associated with different uses, especially different activities. It was also established that true microwear can be distinguished from various natural and technological effects.  A further test of the validity of functional interpretations based on microwear analysis was conducted by means of a blind test.  Dr. Newcomer of the University of London, who is a specialist in lithic technology, made and used 15 implements for completing a variety of tasks on a variety of materials.  These implements, after cleaning, were then passed on for microwear analysis and functional interpretation.  The results revealed generally close and sometimes remarkable agreement between the actual and inferred uses.  The tasks pertinent to the functional interpretation of prehistoric implements could be arranged in order of difficulty with the isolation of the used portion of the tool being quite easy (88% correct), the determination of the method of use being slightly more difficult (75% correct), and the determination of the worked material being more difficult still (approximately 65% correct).

Chapter 4 discussed the criteria applied in the selection of British Lower Paleolithic assemblages for microwear analysis, including evidence of primary context, adequate excavation and provenience, careful post-excavation handling and availability.  Only three assemblages fulfilled all the stated requirements:  Clacton-on-Sea (Golf Course Site), Swanscombe (Lower Loam) and Hoxne (Lower Industry).

At Clacton (chap. 5), once artifacts showing signs of natural abrasion had been eliminated, 22% of the implements from the Gravel and 16% of the implements from the Marl showed traces of use.  Microwear analysis revealed that butchery, woodworking, hide preparation and even some bone working were activities that had taken place within the excavated area of the Golf Course site (or in the very close vicinity), while the nature of the artifacts show that flint knapping also took place close at hand.  The sum of this evidence implies that this site was probably a living floor (or "home base"), rather than some special activity site (like a kill site or flaking floor).  The predominant activities, represented by the microwear traces, were woodworking (especially whittling and planing) and butchery. Used retouched edges represented less than half of all used edges, although "accommodation" retouches to regularize tool contours and facilitate handling were quite common.  It seems that the inhabitants of the Golf Course site chose flake blanks mainly on the basis of their edge angles, edge shapes, and, to a lesser extent, their size, with little attention to other aspects of their morphology.  On the perennial question of whether Clactonian cores were just cores or were made for use as chopping tools, a little evidence was forthcoming.  At the Golf Course site it was found that only 2 of the 22 cores were used at all. The number of pieces involved is too small for firm conclusions to be drawn, but so far as the evidence goes it certainly suggests that the production of suitable flakes was the main aim of Clactonian knapping.

At Swanscombe (chap. 6), the number of flakes in suitable condition for microwear analysis was unfortunately small, and only four of these showed traces of use. The morphological characteristics of these used implements were, in fact, comparable to those of implements with similar functions found at Clacton. This is gratifying, but one ought not to make too much of it, since the sample is so small.

At Hoxne (chap. 7) only 9 percent of the flint artifacts from the Lower Industry levels were found to have been used. The smaller percentage of used pieces at Hoxne, when compared with Clacton, undoubtedly reflects the hand ax manufacture which took place at the site, inevitably leaving prolific quantities of unusable debris to figure in the counts. The large majority of trimming flakes produced by hand ax manufacture usually have edges too acutely angled and fragile to be suitable for use. At any Acheulean site where hand axes were manufactured, the percentage of used flakes is liable to be low, even if the absolute number is not.

The activities, as reflected by the microwear traces, that took place within the excavated area at Hoxne were butchery, hide preparation, woodworking, boring of wood and bone, and, rather interestingly, the slicing or cutting of plant material. The associations between tool morphology and function were less clear at Hoxne than at Clacton. Most tasks seem to have been accomplished with edge angles in the 40-49° range, although this may be a reflection of the small number of pieces used for tasks other than butchering. However, it seems that size and crude shape (as expressed by the $B/L$ and $Th/B$ ratios) played a more important role in the selection of flake blanks for particular uses or tasks than at Clacton.

Two fascinating small details concerning the technology of the Acheulean inhabitants of Hoxne emerged: (1) they draped, or pegged, their hides over a round object (probably a log) when they worked them, and (2) they commonly employed wedges for splitting wood.

The examination of a small sample of the well made side scrapers from the Upper Industry at Hoxne revealed that most of these implements were probably used for scraping hides.

Two of the hand axes recovered from the Lower Industry levels at Hoxne showed traces of use indicating that they had served as butchering implements. However, the majority of meat and butchering knives at Hoxne were flakes, and it may be that hand axes were not implements designed to fulfill only one particular function that could not be fulfilled by any other type of implement.

From a discussion of the differing representation of hand axes at various British Middle Acheulean sites, and a fuller consideration of the functional capabilities of lanceolate hand axes in particular, the speculative hypothesis was put forward that the purpose of such implements was to serve as compact multifunctional tools and that they were made primarily for taking on hunting and gathering expeditions away from the home base. But it was stressed that this and related problems can only be solved by a major project involving the microwear analysis on existing and newly discovered Acheulean artifacts in suitable conditions for study.

An earlier functional analysis of implements from Hoxne, by another worker, using the low-magnification/edge-damage approach, produced a claim that 95 percent of all flakes from the Lower Industry were used. This claim apparently arose through a failure to distinguish true utilization damage from "spontaneous retouch" and from the normal small edge-damage scars that inevitably occur on flake edges when they remain buried in a deposit for 200,000 years.

Chapter 8 ranged more widely over the field of microwear analysis and was devoted to brief discussion of some potentially productive topics for future research, such as the causes of the microwear polishes, the microwear traces produced on rock types other than flint, and the traces left by pressure flaking. There was also a brief outline of the kinds of evidence needed to confirm or deny the hypothesis about hand ax functions introduced in chapter 7. Concluding this chapter was a speculative discussion of the use of red ocher in hide preparation during the Magdalenian, arising out of an examination of some Magdalenian endscrapers.

The research reported here was undertaken with the hope that, by the careful application of a wider range of techniques and a more rigorous methodology than had been hitherto employed in microwear analysis, the precision and reliability of functional interpretations based on this method could be increased. It was also intended that the information gleaned from a framework of experiments be applied to the microwear analysis of selected British Lower Paleolithic assemblages, in order to obtain a clear picture of the activities carried out on such sites and in the hope that information about the functions of Clactonian and Acheulean tools would be useful for answering certain archeological questions about these industries. Despite some inevitable disappointments, these hopes and aims were generally fulfilled.

This research has produced many interesting facts and conclusions, and for the purposes of summary those which I consider most important are as follows.

1. It has demonstrated the advisability of employing a full range of laboratory, photographic, and microscopic techniques. Those which I found effective have been fully described in the text.

2. It has demonstrated the necessity of basing functional inferences on experimental data and the productivity of using a framework of experiments specially constructed for application to the particular period and area under study. No generalized experimental program can ever hope to solve all the microwear problems of prehistory.

3. It has amply demonstrated the folly of relying on only one class of microwear phenomena for functional information.

4. It has uncovered a high correlation between the (detailed) appearance of various microwear polishes, under appropriate magnifications and lighting arrangements, and the various worked materials which caused them.

5. It has established that certain types of microwear (expecially the polishes) can be readily distinguished from traces resulting from processes other than use.

6. It has sought to confirm the distinctiveness of the various microwear polishes (wood polish, meat polish, hide polish, and so on) by the measurement of light reflection under certain conditions and by means of a "blind" test, with some success. As regards the light reflection measurement, this is a pioneering experiment which others, with more sophisticated equipment, will doubtless take further.

7. It has demonstrated the direct applicability of experimental results to archeological assemblages and uncovered many fascinating details about the technology of the Lower Paleolithic, not the least of which are the existence of plant "gathering" knives and information about the methods of hide preparation employed. It is very difficult to see in what other ways information of this character could be reliably obtained.

8.  It has uncovered some interesting relationships between the morphology and function of implements in the assemblages from Clacton and Hoxne.

9.  It has provided a little tantalizing information pertinent to questions concerning the purposes of hand axes in the Middle Acheulean, and clearly there is great potential here for further research.

Further work and development along the lines adopted and evolved during this study can only increase the utility and reliability of microwear analysis. Without a doubt, some of the conclusions and interpretations presented in this study will be successfully challenged by future work. That is only what one would expect, but if those challenges are stimulated by the present study, then the concession of some points would be a trivial price, which I would regard as a privilege to pay, for what can only be considerable gains in the study of implement function and for prehistory in general.

APPENDIX

List of Experimental Implements

| No. | Material | Activity | Edge Angle | Ret. | Edge Shape | Fig. |
|-----|----------|----------|-----------|------|-----------|------|
| 1a | wood (pine)* | whittling | 52 | - | concave | - |
| b | wood (pine)* | sawing | 50 | - | straight | - |
| 2 | wood (pine)* | whittling | 44 | - | concave | 96 |
| 3a | wood (birch) | scraping | 34 | - | concave | - |
| b | wood (birch) | scraping | 30 | - | convex | - |
| 5 | wood (pine)* | sawing | 32 | - | straight | 97 |
| 6 | wood (pine)* | sawing | 20 | - | convex | - |
| 7 | wood (willow)* | whittling | 47 | - | convex | - |
| 8 | wood (walnut)* | chopping | 58 | - | convex | 98 |
| 9a | wood (yew) | whittling | 52 | - | straight | 99 |
| b | wood (yew) | whittling | 38 | - | straight | - |
| 11 | wood (birch) | scraping | 50 | - | straight | - |
| 12a | wood (walnut)* | whittling | 42 | - | concave | 100 |
| b | wood (walnut)* | whittling | 80 | - | concave | - |
| c | wood (walnut)* | scraping | 86 | - | concave | - |
| 15a | wood (birch) | scraping | 30 | - | concave | - |
| b | wood (birch) | scraping | 34 | - | concave | - |
| 23 | wood (yew) | whittling | 25 | - | concave | - |
| 26 | wood (willow) | scraping | 88 | + | convex | 101 |
| 27 | wood (yew) | sawing | 23 | - | straight | - |
| 28 | wood (yew) | sawing | 28 | - | convex | - |
| 29 | wood (walnut)* | whittling | 48 | - | convex | - |
| 33 | wood (birch) | sawing | 28 | - | convex | - |
| 36a | wood (yew) | sawing | 30 | - | straight | - |
| b | wood (yew) | whittling | 50 | - | concave | - |
| 40 | wood (yew) | boring | n.a. | + | cusp | - |
| 43 | wood (yew) | adzing | 45 | - | convex | 102 |
| 49a | wood (pine)* | whittling | 75 | - | straight | - |
| b | wood (pine)* | scraping | 46 | - | straight | - |
| 53 | wood (willow)* | scraping | 48 | - | straight | - |
| 54 | wood (yew) | wedging | 37 | - | convex | - |
| 55 | wood (yew) | whittling | 52 | - | straight | - |
| 62 | wood (birch) | whittling | 20 | - | convex | - |
| 66a | wood (yew) | scraping | 60 | - | concave | 103 |
| b | wood (yew) | scraping | 20 | - | straight | - |
| 68 | wood (birch) | whittling | 34 | - | convex | - |
| 69 | wood (birch) | whittling | 56 | - | concave | 104 |
| 70 | wood (pine)* | whittling | 48 | - | straight | 105 |

*seasoned

| No. | Material | Activity | Edge Angle | Ret. | Edge Shape | Fig. |
|---|---|---|---|---|---|---|
| 71 | wood (maple) | chopping | 48 | - | concave | - |
| 72 | wood (birch) | boring | n.a. | + | cusp | 106 |
| 76a | wood (maple) | whittling | 58 | - | concave | 107 |
| 82 | wood (birch) | wedging | 26 | - | straight | 108 |
| 83 | wood (yew) | whittling | 90 | + | concave | 109 |
| 85 | wood (yew) | boring | n.a. | - | cusp | - |
| 88 | wood (yew) | boring | n.a. | - | cusp | - |
| 91 | wood (maple) | chopping | 45 | - | straight | - |
| 102 | wood (maple) | adzing | 67 | - | straight | - |
| 106a | wood (yew) | chopping | 76 | - | straight | - |
| b | wood (yew) | chopping | 62 | - | concave | - |
| 116a | wood (yew) | whittling | 43 | - | concave | 110 |
| b | wood (yew) | scraping | 49 | - | straight | - |
| 117a | wood (yew) | whittling | 63 | - | concave | - |
| b | wood (yew) | adzing | 82 | + | convex | - |
| c | wood (yew) | scraping | 68 | - | straight | - |
| 125 | wood (pine)* | wedging | 26 | - | convex | 111 |
| 138 | wood (pine)* | graving | 83 bit | + | burin | 112 |
| 158 | wood (pine)* | graving | 73 bit | + | burin | - |
| 159 | wood (pine)* | graving | 57 bit | + | burin | - |
| 160 | wood (charred yew) | scraping | 90 | + | concave | 113 |
| 4a | bone (cooked) | sawing | 35 | - | straight | 114 |
| b | bone (cooked) | scraping | 35 | - | straight | - |
| 10 | bone (cooked) | scraping | 58 | - | concave | 115 |
| 13 | bone (cooked) | scraping | 28 | - | complex | - |
| 14 | bone (cooked) | chopping | 42 | - | straight | 116 |
| 21 | bone (fresh) | scraping | 80 | + | convex | 117 |
| 34 | bone (cooked) | sawing | 46 | - | straight | - |
| 35a | bone (fresh) | wedging | 24 | - | straight | - |
| b | bone (fresh) | wedging | 38 | - | straight | - |
| 47a | bone (fresh) | scraping | 90 | - | straight | - |
| b | bone (fresh) | scraping | 46 | - | straight | - |
| 74 | bone (fresh) | whittling | 45 | - | straight | - |
| 77a | bone (fresh) | scraping | 45 | - | concave | - |
| b | bone (fresh) | scraping | 51 | - | straight | - |
| 80 | bone (fresh) | wedging | 55 | - | straight | - |
| 81 | bone (fresh) | wedging | 36 | - | convex | 118 |
| 84 | bone (fresh) | scraping | 80 | - | straight | - |
| 86 | bone (fresh) | boring | n.a. | + | cusp | - |
| 87 | bone (fresh) | boring | n.a. | + | cusp | - |
| 90 | bone (fresh) | sawing | 39 | - | complex | - |
| 103 | bone (fresh) | chopping | 68 | + | complex | 119 |
| 107 | bone (dry) | chopping | 70 | + | complex | - |
| 123 | bone (fresh) | graving | 40 | - | cusp | 120 |

*seasoned

| No. | Material | Activity | Edge Angle | Ret. | Edge Shape | Fig. |
|-----|----------|----------|------------|------|------------|------|
| 124 | bone (fresh) | graving | 43 | + | convex | - |
| 126 | bone (fresh) | wedging | 40 | - | convex | - |
| 129 | bone (fresh) | sawing | 37 | - | straight | 121 |
| 132a | bone (fresh) | scraping | 45 | - | straight | - |
| b | bone (fresh) | scraping | 94 | - | straight | - |
| 133a | bone (fresh) | sawing | 30 | - | straight | 122 |
| b | bone (fresh) | sawing | 56 | - | straight | - |
| 134 | bone (fresh) | graving | 62 bit | + | burin | 123 |
| 135 | bone (fresh) | sawing | 56 | - | complex | - |
| 136 | bone (fresh) | graving | 28 | - | convex | - |
| 157a | bone (fresh) | sawing | 64 | + | convex (HA) | 25 |
| b | bone (fresh) | 'prying' | 33 | + | hand axe tip | - |
| 161 | bone (fresh) | sawing | 60 | + | convex | - |
| 162 | bone (fresh) | wedging | 38 | - | straight | - |
| 17 | dry hide | slicing | 57 | - | convex | 124 |
| 19 | leather | boring | n.a. | + | cusp | - |
| 37 | leather | boring | n.a. | + | cusp | - |
| 51 | dry hide | scraping | 47 | - | convex | 125 |
| 67 | leather | scraping | 72 | + | convex | 126 |
| 78 | dry hide | scraping | 90 | + | convex | - |
| 99 | fresh hide | scraping | 78 | - | convex | 127 |
| 100 | fresh hide | fleshing | 42 | - | convex | 128 |
| 104 | fresh hide | scraping | 60 | - | convex | 129 |
| 105 | fresh hide | de-hairing | 69 | - | concave | - |
| 113 | dry hide | scraping | 41 | - | convex | - |
| 114 | dry hide | scraping | 40 | + | complex | 130 |
| 118a | greased hide | scraping | 80 | + | convex | 131 |
| b | greased hide | scraping | 70 | + | convex | - |
| 119 | greased hide | scraping | 85 | - | straight | - |
| 156a | fat on hide | scraping | 55 | + | convex (HA) | 19 |
| b | fat on hide | cutting | 42 | + | complex (HA) | - |
| 163 | dry hide | scraping | 70 | + | convex | - |
| 18 | meat (cooked) | cutting | 56 | - | convex | - |
| 42 | meat (cooked) | cutting | 55 | - | convex | - |
| 65 | meat (fresh) | cutting | 32 | - | convex | - |
| 73a | meat, etc. | butchering | 51 | - | convex | 132 |
| b | meat, etc. | butchering | 38 | - | concave | - |
| 75a | meat (fresh) | cutting | 52 | - | straight | - |
| b | meat (fresh) | cutting | 48 | - | complex | - |
| 76b | meat (fresh) | cutting | 55 | - | convex | 107 |
| 89a | meat, etc. | butchering | 58 | - | straight | 133 |
| b | meat, etc. | butchering | 61 | - | convex | - |
| 130 | meat, etc. | butchering | 35 | - | convex | 134 |
| 155 | meat (fresh) | cutting | 55 | + | convex (HA) | 18 |
| 44a | antler (soaked) | whittling | 68 | - | straight | - |
| b | antler (soaked) | whittling | 68 | - | concave | - |

| No. | Material | Activity | Edge Angle | Ret. | Edge Shape | Fig. |
|-----|----------|----------|-----------|------|-----------|------|
| 57a | antler (soaked) | scraping | 58 | - | straight | 135 |
| b | antler (soaked) | whittling | 75 | - | straight | - |
| 120 | antler (soaked) | sawing | 39 | - | convex | - |
| 122 | antler (soaked) | scraping | 93 | - | concave | 136 |
| 127 | antler (soaked) | sawing | 48 | - | convex | 137 |
| 128 | antler (soaked) | graving | 87 bit | + | burin | - |
| 137a | antler (soaked) | graving | 84 bit | + | burin | 138 |
| b | antler (soaked) | whittling | 100 | - | straight | - |
| 101 | bamboo (fresh) | sawing | 35 | - | convex | 139 |
| 154 | grass | cutting | 37 | - | straight | 140 |
| 32 | soil | digging | 42 | + | hand ax tip | 17 |

| No. | | Fig. |
|-----|--|------|
| 31 | Control - retouch by pressure against hammerstone | - |
| 79 | Control - hard-hammer retouch | - |
| 92 | Control - hard-hammer retouch | 141 |
| 93 | Control - hard-hammer retouch | - |
| 108 | Control - hard-hammer retouch and spontaneous retouch | 13 |
| 109 | Control - soft-hammer retouch | 142 |
| 110 | Control - soft-hammer retouch | - |
| 111 | Control - soft-hammer retouch | - |
| 38 | Control - spontaneous retouch | - |
| 112 | Control - spontaneous retouch | - |
| 115 | Control - spontaneous retouch | - |
| 121 | Control - spontaneous retouch | 12 |
| 16 | Control - left in soil for 6 months, undisturbed | - |
| 22 | Control - left in soil for 12 months, walked on | 11 |
| 63 | Control - left in soil for 16 months, undisturbed | - |
| 64 | Control - left in soil for 12 months, walked on | - |
| - | Control - flint flake from Eocene deposit showing edge damage | - |
| - | Control - left in soil 6 months, undisturbed | - |
| - | Control - left in soil 6 months, undisturbed | - |
| - | Control - left in soil 12 months, undistrubed | - |
| - | Control - left in soil 15 months, undisturbed | - |

PHOTOMICROGRAPHS

The width of the photomicrographs depends, of course, on the magnification of the microscope when they were taken. The mean widths of the prints are given below (with their standard deviation) for each level of magnification.

| magnification | width in microns |
|---------------|------------------|
| 100X | 376 ± 6 |
| 200X | 187 ± 10 |
| 400X | 97 ± 2 |

If the photograph caption indicates a magnification greater or smaller than the above then the actual width in microns will be stated.

Plate 1

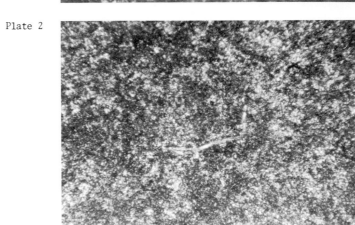

Plate 2

Plate 3

Plate 4

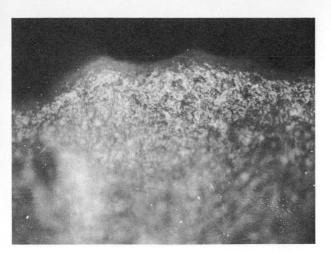

Plate 5

Plate 6

Plate 7

Plate 8

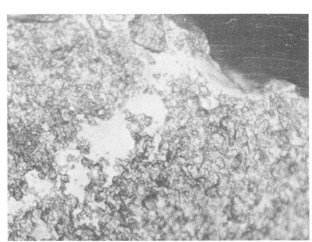

Plate 9

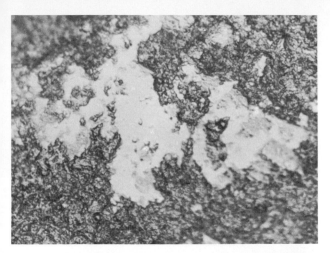

Plate 10

Plate 11

Plate 12

Plate 13

Plate 14

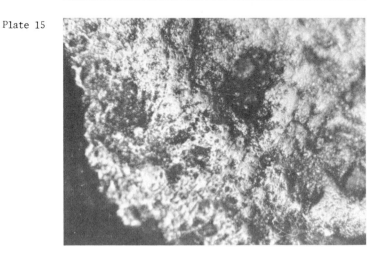

Plate 15

Plate 16

Plate 17

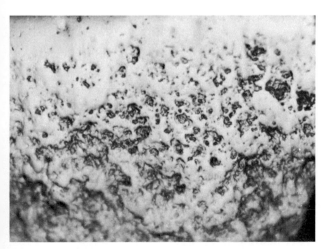

Plate 18

Plate 19

Plate 20

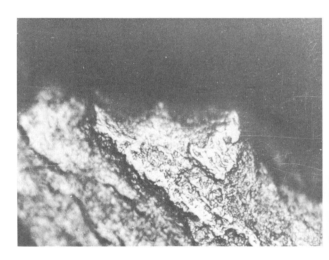

Plate 21

Plate 22

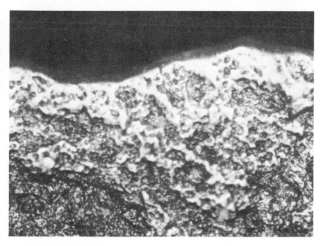

Plate 23

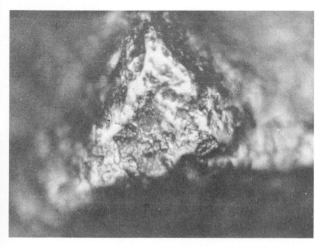

Plate 24

Plate 25

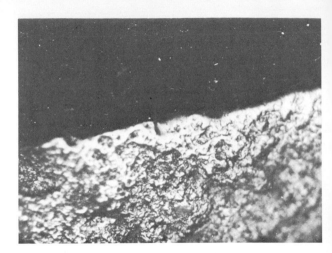

Plate 26

Plate 27

Plate 28

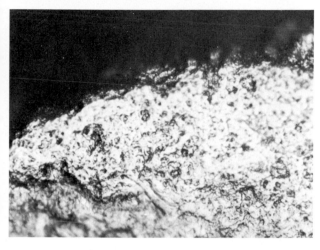

Plate 29

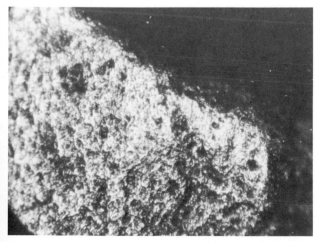

Plate 30

Plate 31

Plate 32

Plate 33

Plate 34

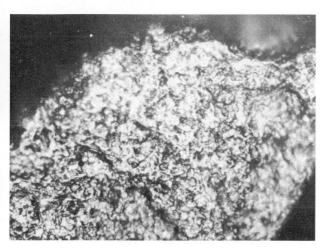

Plate 35

Plate 36

Plate 37

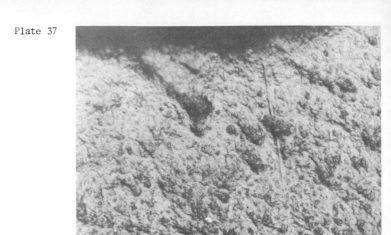

Plate 38

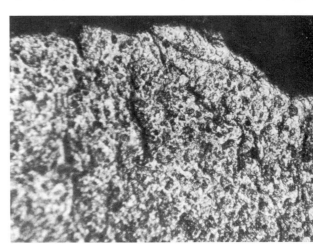

Plate 39

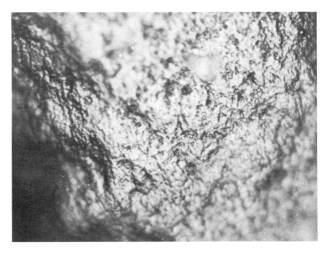

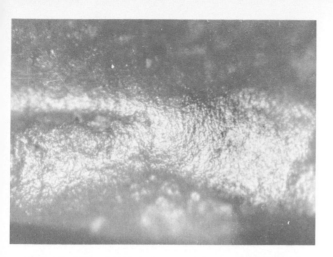

Plate 40

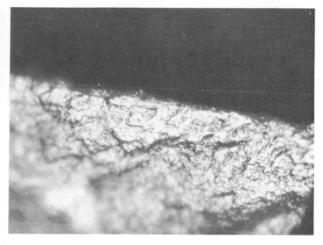

Plate 41

Plate 42

Plate 43

Plate 44

Plate 45

Plate 46

Plate 47

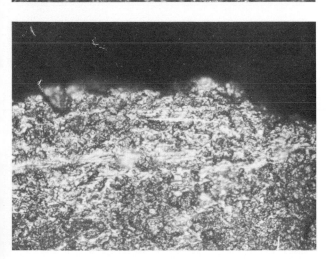

Plate 48

Plate 49

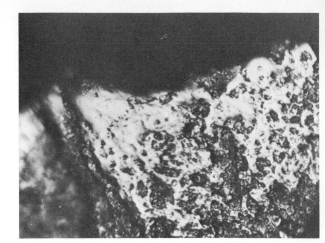

Plate 50

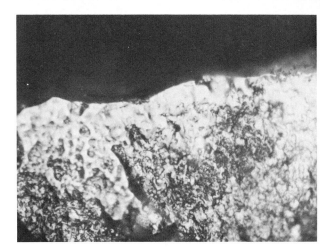

Plate 51

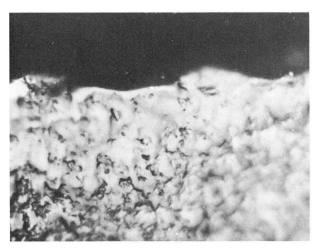

Plate 52

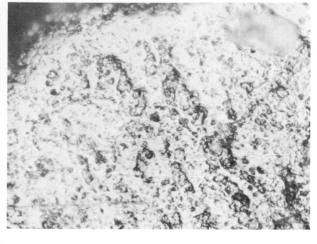

Plate 53

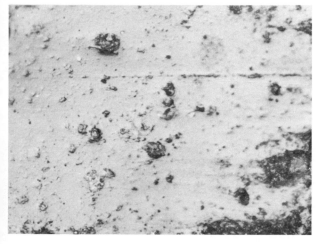

Plate 54

Plate 55

Plate 56

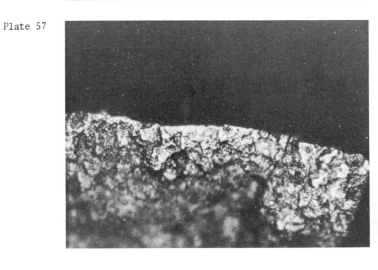

Plate 57

Plate 58

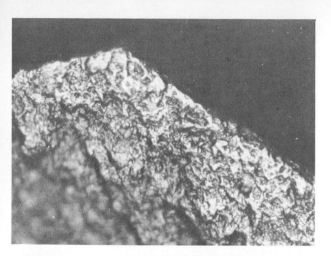

Plate 59

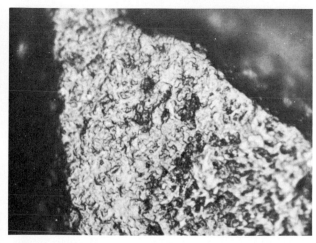

Plate 60

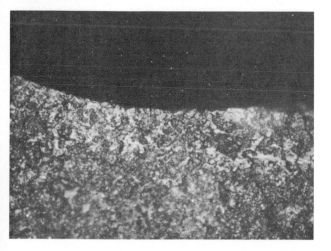

Plate 61

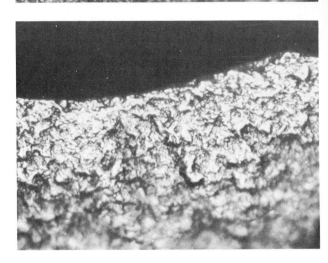

Plate 62

Plate 63

Plate 64

Plate 65

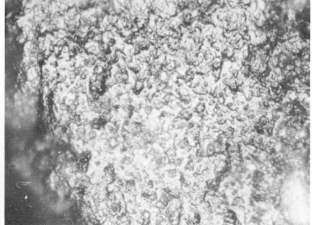

Plate 66

Plate 67

Plate 68

Plate 69

Plate 70

Plate 71

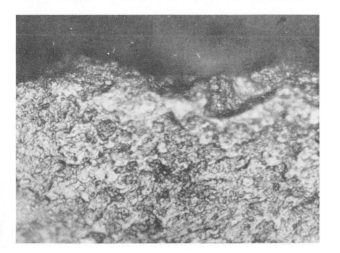

Plate 72

Plate 73

Plate 74

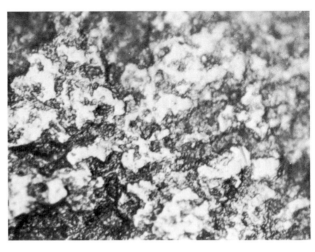

Plate 75

Plate 76

Plate 77

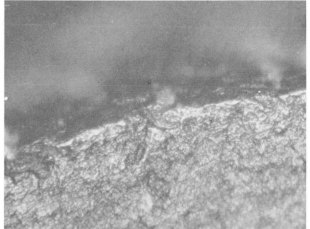

Plate 78

Plate 79

Plate 79

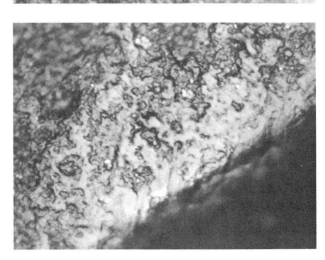

Plate 80

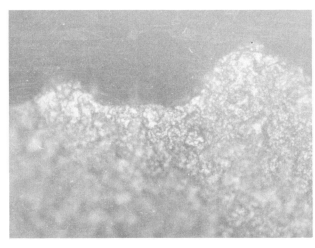

Plate 81

Plate 82

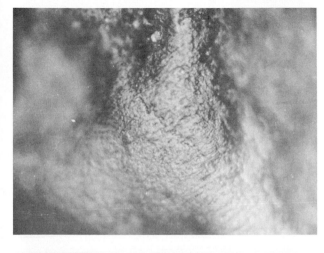

Plate 83

Plate 84

Plate 85

Plate 86

Plate 87

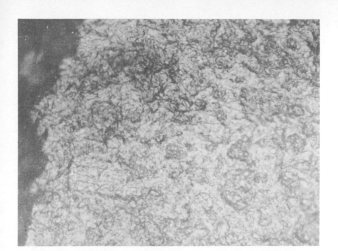

Plate 88

Plate 89

Plate 90

Plate 91

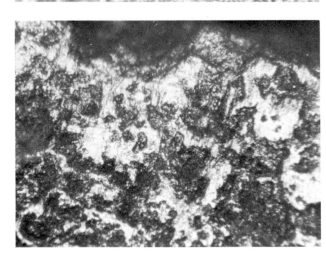

Plate 92

Plate 93

Plate 94

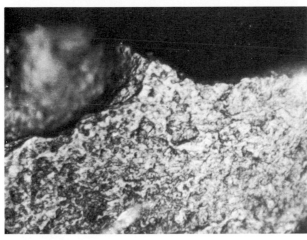

Plate 95

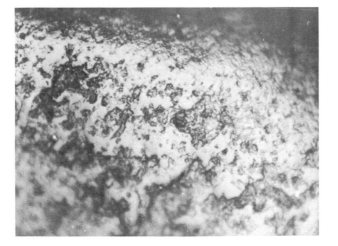

Plate 96

Plate 97

Plate 98

Plate 99

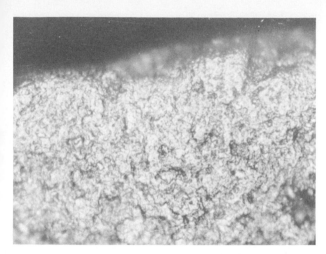

Plate 100

Plate 101

Plate 102

Plate 103

Plate 104

Plate 105

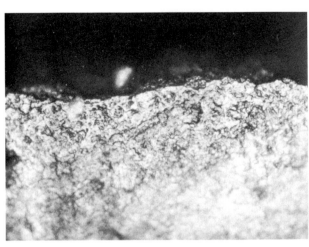

Plate 106

Plate 107

Plate 108

Plate 109

Plate 109

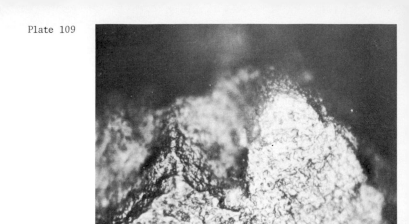

Plate 110

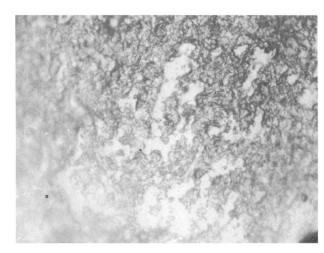

Plate 111

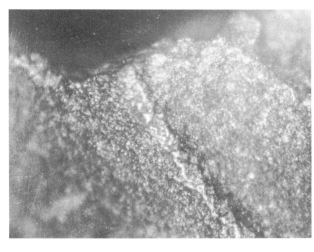

Plate 112

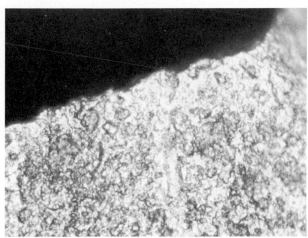

Plate 113

Plate 114

Plate 115

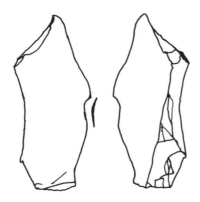

Figure 96.  Exp 2--whittling wood.

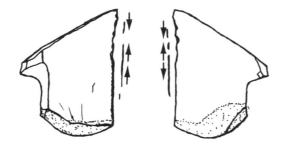

Figure 97.  Exp 5--sawing wood.

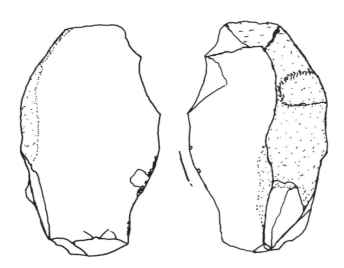

Figure 98.  Exp 8--chopping wood.

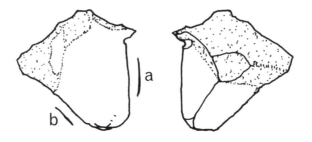

Figure 99, a and b.  Exp 9--whittling wood.

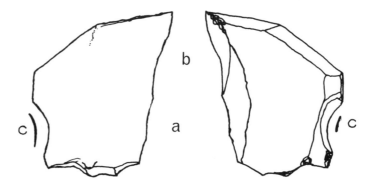

Figure 100.  Exp 12--(a,b) whittling wood; (c) scraping wood.

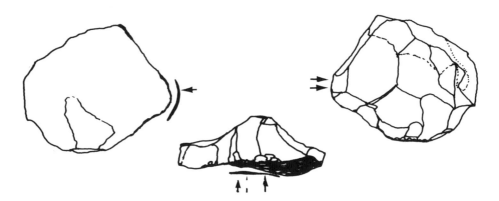

Figure 101.  Exp 26--scraping wood.

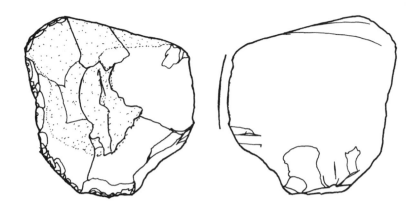

Figure 102.  Exp 43--adzing wood.

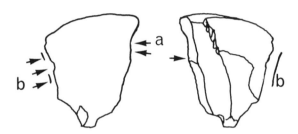

Figure 103.  Exp 66--scraping wood.

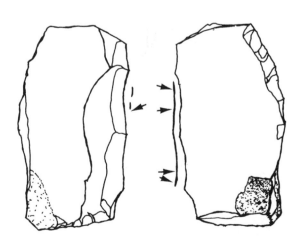

Figure 104.  Exp 69--whittling wood.

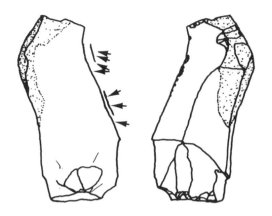

Figure 105.   Exp 70--whittling wood.

Figure 106.   Exp 72--boring wood.

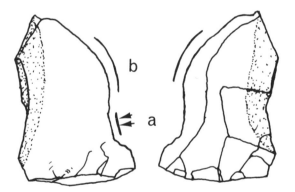

Figure 107.   Exp 76--(a) whittling wood; (b) cutting meat.

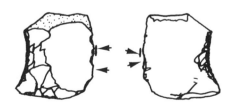

Figure 108.   Exp 82--wedging wood.

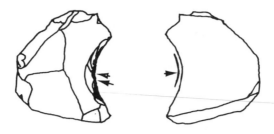

Figure 109.   Exp 83--whittling wood.

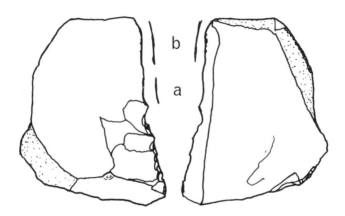

Figure 110.   Exp 116--(a) whittling wood; (b) scraping wood.

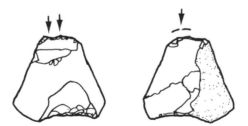

Figure 111.   Exp 125--wedging wood.

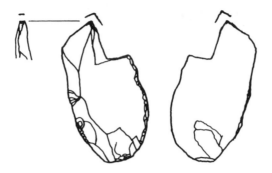

Figure 112.   Exp 138--graving wood.

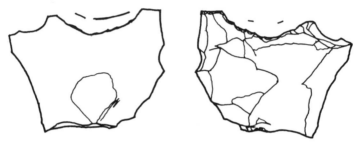

Figure 113.   Exp 160--scraping wood.

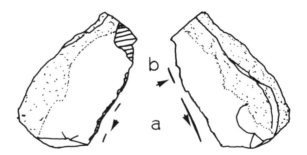

Figure 114.   Exp 4--(a) sawing bone; (b) scraping bone.

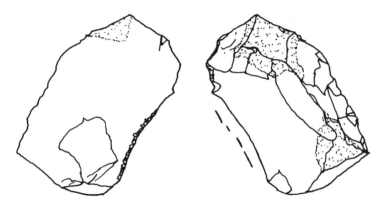

Figure 115.   Exp 10--scraping bone.

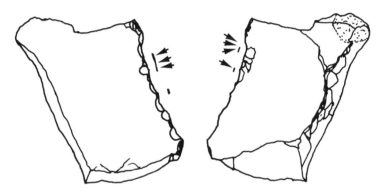

Figure 116.   Exp 14--chopping bone.

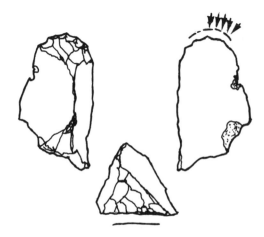

Figure 117.   Exp 21--scraping bone.

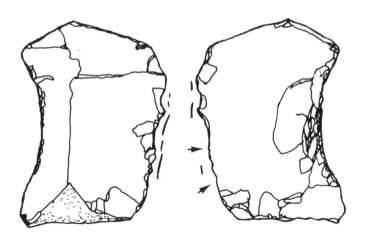

Figure 118. Exp 81--wedging bone.

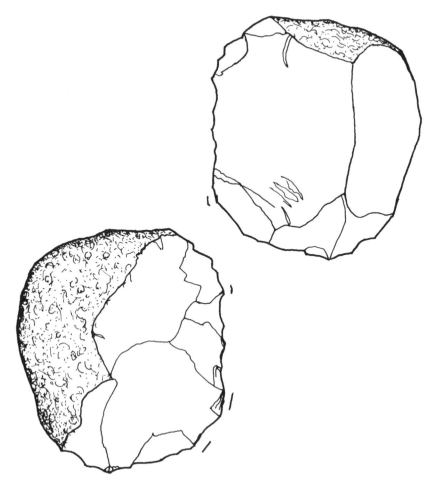

Figure 119. Exp 103--chopping bone.

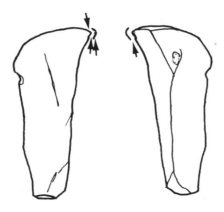

Figure 120.   Exp 123--graving bone.

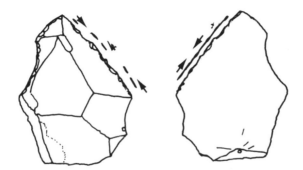

Figure 121.   Exp 129--sawing bone.

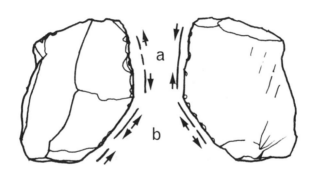

Figure 122.   Exp 133--sawing bone.

Figure 123. Exp 134--graving bone.

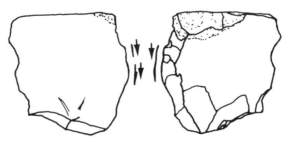

Figure 124. Exp 17--slicing dry hide.

Figure 125. Exp 51--scraping dry hide.

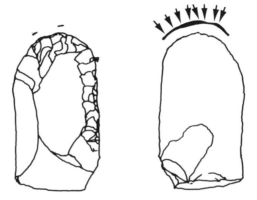

Figure 126. Exp 67--scraping leather.

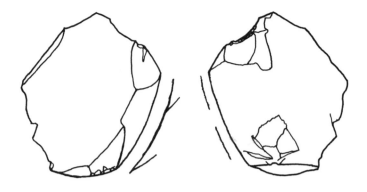

Figure 127. Exp 99--scraping fresh hide.

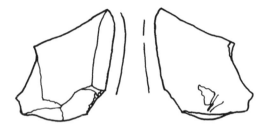

Figure 128. Exp 100--fleshing fresh hide.

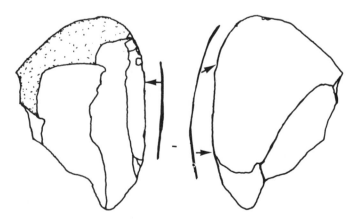

Figure 129. Exp 104--scraping fresh hide.

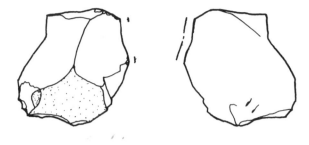

Figure 130.  Exp 114--scraping fresh hide.

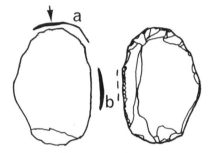

Figure 131, a and b.  Exp 131--scraping greased hide

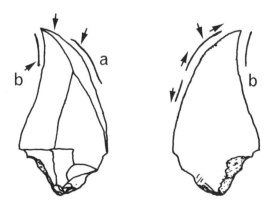

Figure 132, a and b.  Exp 73--butchering.

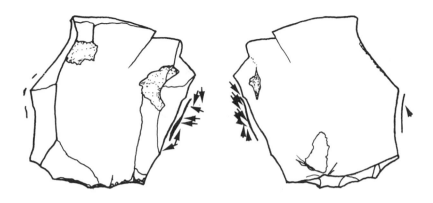

Figure 133.  Exp 89--butchering.

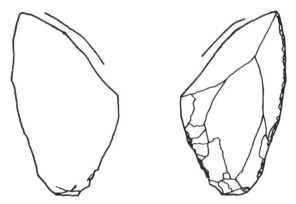

Figure 134.  Exp 130--butchering.

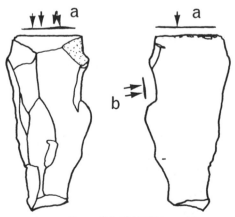

Figure 135.  Exp 57--(a) scraping antler; (b) whittling antler.

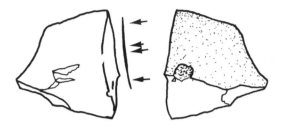

Figure 136. Exp 122--scraping antler.

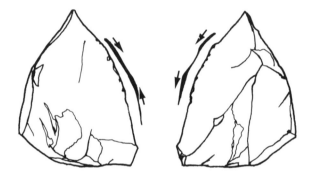

Figure 137. Exp 127--sawing antler.

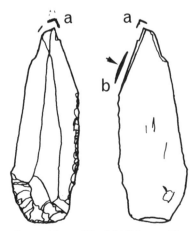

Figure 138. Exp 137--(a) graving antler; (b) whittling antler.

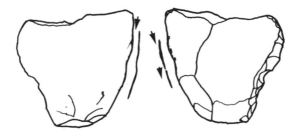

Figure 139.   Exp 101--sawing bamboo.

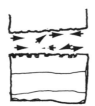

Figure 140.   Exp 154--cutting grass

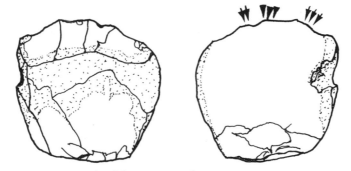

Figure 141.   Exp 92--control, hard-hammer retouch.

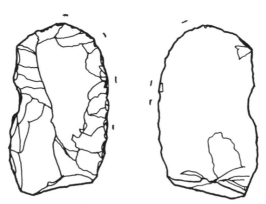

Figure 142.   Exp 109--control, soft-hammer retouch.

BIBLIOGRAPHY

Abbreviations used:

Am. Ant.            *American Antiquity*

Bull. S.P.F.        *Bulletin de Societe Prehistorique Francaise*

PPS                 *Proceedings of the Prehistoric Society*

PPSEA               *Proceedings of the Prehistoric Society of East Anglia*

Proc. R.A.I.        *Proceedings of the Royal Anthropological Institute*

UCPAAE              *University of California Publications in American Archaeology and Ethnology*

Ahler, S. 1971. Projectile point form and function at Rogers Shelter, Missouri, *Missouri Archaeological Society Research Series*, no. 8. Columbia Missouri.

Bickerman, J. J. 1976. Adhesion in friction. *Wear* 39: 1-13.

Binford, L. R. 1972. Contemporary model building: paradigms and the current state of Palaeolithic research. In *Models in Archaeology*, ed. D. L. Clarke, pp. 109-66. London; Methuen.

Bonwick, J. 1898. *Daily life and origin of the Tasmanians*. 2d ed. London: sampson, Low, Marston and Co.

Bordes, F. 1961. *Typologie du Paléolithique*. Bordeaux: Delmas.

_____. 1969a. Reflections on typology and technology in the Palaeolithic. *Arctic Anthropology* 6: 1-29.

_____. 1969b. Os perce moustérien et os gravé acheuleen du Pech de l'Azé II. *Quaternaria* 11: 1-6.

_____. 1970. Observations typologiques et techniques sur le Perigordien superieur de Corbiac (Dordogne). *Bull. S.P.F.* 67: 105-13.

_____. 1971. Essai de préhistoire expérimentale: fabrication d'un épieu de bois. In *Mélanges de préhistoire, d'archéo-civilisation et d'ethnologie Offert à Andre Vavagnac*. Paris: Ecole pratique des hautes études.

_____. 1973. Position des traces d'usure sur les grattoirs simples du Périgordien Superieur Évolué de Corbiac (Dordogne). In *Estudios Dedicados al Professor Dr. Louis Pericot*. Barcelona: Universidad de Barcelona. Pp. 55-60.

_____. 1974. Notes de typologie paléolithique. *Zephyrus* 25: 53-64.

Bosinski, G. 1975. Die Rekonstruktion des Gönnersdorfer Hauses. *Ausgraben in Deutschland* 1: 255-73.

Bosinski, G., and J. Hahn. 1973. *Der Magdalénien - Fundplatz Andernach (Martinsberg)*. Bonn: Rheinland - Verlag.

Brose, D. 1975. Functional analysis of stone tools: a cautionary note on the role of animal fats. *Am. Ant.* 40: 86-94.

Brothwell, D. 1969. The study of archaeological materials by means of the scanning electron microscope. In *Science in archaeology*. 2d ed., Ed. D. Brothwell and E. S. Higgs. London: Thames and Hudson. Pp. 564-66.

Butzer, K., and G. Isaac, eds. 1975. *After the Australopithicines*. The Hague: Mouton.

Cahen, D., and J. Moeyersons. 1977. Subsurface movements of stone artefacts and their implications for the prehistory of Central Africa. *Nature* 266: 812-16.

Campbell, J. B. 1978. *The Upper Palaeolithic of Britain.* Oxford: Oxford University Press.

Clark, J. D., and C. V. Haynes, Jr. 1970. An elephant butchery site at Mwanganda's Village, Karonga, Malawi, and its relevance for Palaeolithic archaeology. *World Archaeology* 1: 390-411.

Coles, J., and E. Higgs. 1969. *The archaeology of early man.* London: Faber and Faber.

Davis, D. D. 1975. Patterns of early formative subsistence in southern Mesoamerica, 1500-1100 B.C. *Man* (n.s.) 10: 41-59.

Evans, J. 1860. On the occurrence of flint implements in undisturbed beds of gravel, sand and clay. *Archaeologia* 38: 280-307.

Freeman, L. G. 1975. Acheulian sites and stratigraphy in Iberia and the Magreb. In *After the Australopithicines,* ed. K. Butzer and G. Isaac. The Hague: Mouton.

Frere, J. 1800. Account of flint weapons discovered at Hoxne in Suffolk. *Archaeologia* 13: 204-5.

Frison, G. 1968. A functional analysis of certain chipped stone tools. *Am. Ant.* 33: 149-55.

Gifford, E. W. 1936. Northeastern and Western Yavapai. *UCPAAE,* vol. 34, no. 4.

Goldschmidt, W. 1951. Nomlaki Ethnography. *UCPAAE,* vol. 42, no. 4.

Gladfelter, B. 1975. Middle Pleistocene sedimentary sequences in East Anglia (United Kingdom). In *After the Australopithecines,* ed. K. Butzer and G. Isaac. The Hague: Mouton. Pp. 225-58.

Gorman, C. 1971. The Hoabinhian and after. *World Archaeology* 2: 300-320.

Gould, R.; Koster, D., and Sontz, A. 1971. The lithic assemblage of the Western Desert Aborigines of Australia. *Am. Ant.* 36: 149-69.

Hamett, H. 1970. A paleo-Indian butchery kit. *Am. Ant.* 35: 141-52.

Hayden, B., and J. Kamminga. 1973. Gould, Koster and Sontz on 'microwear': a critical review. *Newsletter of Lithic Technology* 2: 3-8.

Hester, T. R. and R. Heizer. 1973. Arrow points or knives? Comments on the proposed function of "Stockton Points." *Am. Ant.* 38: 220-21.

Hester, T. R.; Gilbow, D.; and Albee, A. 1973. A functional analysis of "Clear Fork" artifacts from Rio Grande Plain, Texas. *Am. Ant.* 38: 90-96.

Hoffman, W. J. 1896. The Menomini Indians. *Bureau of Ethnology,* 14th Annual Report, 1892-93. Smithsonian Institution. Washington D.C.: Gov. Printing Office.

Isaac, G. Ll. 1968. Traces of Pleistocene hunters: an East African example. In *Man the Hunter,* ed. R. B. Lee and I. De Vore. Chicago: Aldine. Pp. 252-61.

_____. 1975. Stratigraphy and cultural patterns in East Africa during the Middle Ranges of Pleistocene time. In *After the Australopithecines,* ed. K. Butzer and G. Ll. Isaac. The Hague: Mouton. Pp. 495-542.

_____. 1977. *Olorgesailie.* Chicago: University of Chicago Press.

Kantman, S. 1970a. Equisse d'un procédé analytique pour l'etude macrographique des "encoches." *Quaternaria* 13: 269-80.

_____. 1970b. Essai d'une méthode d'etude des "denticulés" moustériens par discrimination des variables morpho-fonctionnelles. *Quaternaria* 13: 281-94.

_____. 1970c. "Raclettes moustériennes": Use étude sue la expérimentale distinction de retouche intentionnelle et les modifications du tranchant par utilisation. *Quaternaria* 13: 295-304.

Kantman, S. 1971.  Essai sue le probléme de la retouche d'utilisation dans l'étude du materiau lithique: premier résultats.  *Bull. S.P.F.* 68: 200-204.

Keeley, L. H. 1974a.  Technique and methodology in microwear studies.  *World Archaeology* 5: 323-36.

_____. 1974b.  The methodology of microwear analysis: a comment on Nance.  *Am. Ant.* 39: 126-28.

_____. 1976.  Microwear on flint: some experimental results.  In *2d International Symposium on Flint, Staringia,* no. 3, pp. 49-51.

_____. 1978.  Note on the edge damage on flakes from the Lower Palaeolithic sites at Caddington.  In *Palaeoecology and archaeology of an Acheulian site at Caddington, England,* ed. C. G. Sampson.  Dallas, Tex.: Southern Methodist University Press.

Keller, C. M. 1966.  The development of edge damage patterns on stone tools.  *Man* (n.s.) 1: 501-11.

_____. 1970.  Montagu Cave: a preliminary report.  *Quaternaria* 13: 187-203.

Kelly, I. T. 1932.  Ethnography of the Surprise Valley Paiute.  *UCPAAE,* no. 31, no. 3.

Klein, R. 1978.  The fauna and overall interpretation of "cutting 10" Acheulian site at Elandsfontein (Hopefield).  *Quaternary Research* 10: 69-83.

Korobkova, G. F. 1969.  Orudiya trud i Khozaistva neoliticheskikh plemen Srednei Azii, *Materiali i Issledovaniya po Arkeologii SSSR,* no. 158.

Lenoir, M. 1970.  Le Paleolithique superieur en surface devant la grotte de Lestrugue, Commune de Soulaleve (Dordogne).  *Bull. S.P.F.* 67: 71-78.

_____. 1971.  Traces d'utilisation observées sur un nucléus à lamelies.  *Bull. S.P.F.* 68: 69-70.

Leroi-Gourhan, A., and M. Brezillon.  1972.  *Fouilles de Pincevent (Gallia Préhistoire,* supp. 7).  Paris: CNRS.

McBurney, C. B. M. 1968.  The cave of Ali Tappeh and the Epi-Palaeolithic in N. E. Iran.  *PPS* 34: 385-413.

MacDonald, G., and D. Sanger. 1968.  Some aspects of microscope analysis and photomicro-graphy of lithic artifacts.  *Am. Ant.* 33: 237-40.

Mandelbaum, D. G. 1941.  The Plains Cree.  *Anthropological Papers of the Amer. Mus. Nat. Hist.* 37: 155-316.

Mandl, I. 1961.  Collagenases and elastases.  *Advances in Enzymology* 23: 164-264.

Marston, A. T. 1936.  Preliminary note on a new fossil human skull from Swanscombe, Kent.  *Nature* 138: 200.

Massaud, J. 1972.  Observations sue l'utilisation des burins multifacettes.  *Bull. S.P.F.* 69: 231-34.

Moir, J. R. 1926.  The silted-up lake of Hoxne and its contained flint implements.  *PPSEA* 5: 137-65.

_____. 1935.  Lower Palaeolithic man at Hoxne, England.  *Bull. of the American School of Prehistoric Research* 11: 43-53.

Nance, J. D. 1971.  Functional interpretations from microscopic analysis.  *Am. Ant.* 36: 361-66.

Newcomer, M. H. 1971a.  Some quantitative experiments in handaxe manufacture.  *World Archaeology* 3: 85-93.

_____. 1971b.  Conjoined flakes from the Lower Loam, Barnfield Pit, Swanscombe (1970).  *Proc. R.A.I.* 1970: 51-59.

Newcomer, M. H. 1976. Spontaneous retouch. *2d International Symposium on Flint.
Staringia,* no. 3, pp. 62-64.

Oakley, K. P. and M. Leakey. 1937. Report on excavations at Jaywick Sands, Essex (1934),
with some observations on the Clactonian Industry, and on the fauna and geological
significance of the Clacton Channel. *PPS* 3: 217-60.

Odell, G. 1975. Micro-wear in perspective: a sympathetic response to Lawrence H. Keeley.
*World Archaeology* 7: 226-40.

Ohel, M. 1977. On the Clactonian: reexamined, redefined and reinterpreted. *Current
Anthropology* 18: 329-331.

Pope, S. 1925. *Hunting with the bow and arrow.* New York: G. P. Putnam's Sons.

Prestwich, J. 1860. On the occurrence of flint implements associated with the remains of
animals of extinct species in beds of a late geological period, in France at Amiens
and Abbeville, and in England at Hoxne. *Philosophical Transactions of the Royal
Society* 150: 277-317.

Purdy, B. A. 1975. Fractures for the archaeologist. In *Lithic Technology,* ed. E. Swanson.
The Hague, Mouton. Pp. 133-41.

Ranere, A. J. 1975. Toolmaking and tool use among the Preceramic peoples of Panama. In
*Lithic Technology,* ed. Swanson. The Hague: Mouton. Pp. 173-209.

Reid, C. 1896. The relation of Palaeolithic man to the Glacial Epoch. *Reports of the
British Association.* Liverpool: 400-416.

Roe, D. A. 1968. British Lower and Middle Palaeolithic handaxe groups. *PPS* 34: 1-82.

_____. 1975. Some Hampshire and Dorset handaxes and the question of 'Early Acheulian'
in Britain. *Proc. Prehistoric Soc.* 41: 1-9.

_____. 1976. Typology and the trouble with hand-axes. In *Problems in Economic and
Social Archaeology,* ed. G. Sieveking, L. Longworth and K. Wilson. London: Duckworth.

Rosenfeld, A. 1971. The examination of use marks on some Magdalenian endscrapers. *British
Museum Quarterly* 35: 176-82.

Roth, H. Ling. 1890. *The Aborigines of Tasmania.* London: Kegan Paul.

Rottländer, R. 1975. The formation of patina on flint. *Archaeometry* 17: 106-10.

_____. 1976. Some of the patination of flint. *2d International Symposium on Flint.
Staringia* 3: 54-6.

Semenov, S. A. 1964. *Prehistoric Technology.* Translated by M. W. Thompson. London: Cory,
Adams and Mackay.

_____. 1968. *Razvitiya Teknike v Kamennon Veke.* Leningrad: Izdatilstva 'Nauka.'

_____. 1970. Forms and functions of the oldest stone tools. *Quartär* 21: 1-20.

Semenov, S. A., and V. E. Shchelinski. 1971. Mikrometricheskoye izucheniye sledov rabori
na palaeolicichekikh orudiyakh, *Sovyetskaya Arkeologiya* 1: 19-30.

Shackley, M. 1974. Stream abrasion of flint implements. *Nature* 248: 501-2.

Sheets, P. 1973. Edge abrasion during biface manufacture. *Am. Ant.* 38: 215-18.

Singer, R.; Wymer, J.; Gladfelter, B.; and Wolff, R. 1973. Excavation of the Clactonian
Industry at the Golf Course, Clacton-on-Sea, Essex. *PPS* 39: 6-74.

Singer, R., and J. Wymer. 1976. The sequence of Acheulian industries at Hoxne, Suffolk.
In *L'Évolution de l'Acheuléen en Europe, Colloque X,* ed. J. Combier. 9th Congress of
International Union of Protohistoric and Prehistoric Sciences, Nice.

Smith, R. A. 1931. *The Sturge collection.* British Museum.

Smith, R. A., and H. Dewey. 1913. Stratification at Swanscombe. *Archaeologia* 64: 177-204.

Smith, R. A. and H. Dewey. 1914. The High Terrace of the Thames: report on excavations made on behalf of the British Museum and H. M. Geological Survey in 1913. *Archaeologia* 65: 187-212.

Smith, W. G. 1894. *Man the primeval savage*. London: Edward Stanford.

Sonnenfeld, J. 1962. Interpreting the function of primitive implements. *Am. Ant.* 28: 56-65.

Sollas, W. 1924. *Ancient hunters*. London: Macmillan.

Stapert, D. 1976. A Pseudo-artefakten. In *2d International Symposium on Flint*. *Staringia* 3: 57-62.

_____. 1976b. Some natural surface modifications on flint in the Netherlands. *Palaehistoria* 18: 7-41.

Swanscombe Committee of the R.A.I. 1938. Report on the Swanscombe Skull. *Journal of the Royal Anthropological Institute*, n.s., 68 (no. 41): 17-98.

Swanton, J. R. 1946. The Indians of the Southeastern United States. *Bureau of American Ethnology, bull.* 137. Smithsonian Institution. Washington D.C.: Gov. Printing Office.

Thomson, D. 1964. Some wood and stone implements of the Bindibu tribe of Central Western Australia. *PPS* 30: 400-422.

Tringham, R.; Cooper, G; Odell, G.; Voytek, B.; and Whitman, A. 1974. Experimentation in the formation of edge damage: a new approach to lithic analysis. *Journal of Field Archaeology* 1: 171-96.

Waechter, J. 1969. Swanscombe 1968. *Proc. R.A.I.* (1968), pp. 53-58.

_____. 1970. Swanscombe 1969. *Proc. R.A.I.* (1969), pp. 83-85.

_____. 1971. Swanscombe 1970. *Proc. R.A.I.* (1970), pp. 43-49.

_____. 1972. Swanscombe 1971. *Proc. R.A.I.* (1971), pp. 73-78.

Warren, S. H. 1914. The experimental investigation of flint fracture and its application to problems of human implements. *Journal of the R.A.I.*, n.s., 44 (no. 17): 412-50.

_____. 1922. The Mesvinian Industry of Clacton-on-Sea, Essex. *PPSEA* 3: 597-602.

_____. 1955. The Clacton (Essex) channel deposits. *Quarterly Journal of the Geological Society* 111: 287-307.

West, R. G. 1956. The Quaternary deposits at Hoxne, Suffolk. *Philosophical Trans. of the Royal Soc. B* 239: 265-356.

West, R. G., and C. B. McBurney. 1954. The Quaternary deposits at Hoxne, Suffolk and their archaeology. *PPS* 20: 131-54.

White, J. P., and D. H. Thomas. 1972. What mean these stones? Ethno-taxonomic models and archaeological interpretations in the New Guinea Highlands. In *Models in Archaeology*, ed. D. L. Clarke. London, Methuen. Pp. 275-308.

Whitney, M. I., and R. V. Dietrich. 1973. Ventifact sculpture by windblown dust. *Geological Society of America Bulletin* 84: 2561-82.

Wilmsen, E. N. 1968. Functional analysis of flaked stone artefacts. *Am. Ant.* 33: 156-61.

Witthoft, J. 1967. Glazed polish on flint tools. *Am. Ant.* 32: 383-88.

Wylie, H. G. 1975. Artifact processing and storage procedures: a note of caution, *Newsletter of Lithic Technology* 4 (no. 1-2); 17-19.

Wymer, J. 1955. A further fragment of the Swanscombe skull. *Nature* 176: 426-27.

_____. 1964. Excavations at Barnfield Pit, 1955-1960. In *The Swanscombe Skull*, ed. C. D. Ovey. London: R.A.I. Pp. 19-61.

Wymer, J. 1968. *Lower Palaeolithic Archaeology in Britain as represented by the Thames Valley*. London: John Baker.

_____. 1974. Clactonian and Acheulian industries in Britain: their chronology and significance. *Proc. Geologists' Association* 85: 391-421.

Wymer, J., and R. Singer. 1970. The first season of excavations at Clacton-on-Sea, Essex, England: a brief report. *World Archaeology* 2: 12-16.

Plate 31.  Bone "polish" before HCl treatment on exp 4b (see pl. 29) (200X).

Plate 32.  Bone "polish" before HCl treatment on exp 134 used for graving (200X).

Plate 33.  Bone polish (after HCl treatment) on exp 134 (200X).

Plate 34.  Bone polish on exp 133 used for sawing (200X).

Plate 35.  Bone polish on exp 14 used for chopping (200X).

Plate 36.  Fresh hide polish on exp 114 used for scraping (200X).

Plate 37.  Dry hide polish on exp 67 used for scraping (200X).  Note the "micro-potlid" just above the center of the photograph and the narrow, deep striation to the right of it.

Plate 38.  Greased hide polish on exp 118a used for scraping (200X).

Plate 39.  Dry hide polish on exp 17 used for cutting (200X).

Plate 40.  Dry hide polish on exp 51 used for scraping (100X).  Note the matt texture and severe erosion of small flake scar edges.

Plate 41.  Fresh hide polish on exp 99 used for scraping (200X).

Plate 42.  Fresh hide/meat polish on exp 100 used for flensing (200X).

Plate 43.  Meat polish on exp 73a used for butchering (200X).

Plate 44.  Meat polish on dorsal aspect exp 76b used for slicing (200X).

Plate 45.  Meat polish on bulbar aspect exp 76b, another portion of the edge (200X).

Plate 46.  Meat polish on exp 73b used for butchering (200X).

Plate 47.  Meat polish and small, narrow, deep striations on exp 89a used for butchering (200X).

Plate 48.  Meat polish and striations on exp 89 used for butchery (200X).

Plate 49.  Smooth antler polish on exp 137a used for graving (200X).

Plate 50.  Smooth antler polish on exp 122 used for scraping (200X).  Note "melting snow" appearance of polish.

Plate 51.  As above (400X).

Plate 52.  Smoother antler polish on exp 57b used for planing (200X).

Plate 53.  Rough antler polish on exp 127 used for sawing (200X).

Plate 54.  "Corn" or "sickle" gloss on sickle from Abu Hureyra, Syria (200X).  Note the "comet-shaped" pits and "filled-in" striation in the top half of the photo.

Plate 55.  "Sickle gloss" on exp 154 used for cutting grain (200X).

Plate 56.  "Plant polish" on exp 101 used for sawing bamboo (200X).

Plate 57.  Wood and meat polish on BT no. 4 (200X).

Plate 58.  Wood polish on BT no. 6 (200X).

Plate 59.  Atypical wood polish on BT no. 7 (200X).

Plate 60.  Meat polish, wood polish and striation on BT no. 8 (200X).

Plate 61.  Wood polish on BT no. 11 (200X).

Plate 62.  "Plant" polish on BT no. 13 (200X).

Plate 63.  Meat polish on BT no. 14, right lateral edge (200X).

9002